ALSO BY DEAN SPEARS:

Where India Goes: Abandoned Toilets,
Stunted Development, and the Costs of Caste

Air: Pollution, Climate Change, and India's Choice
Between Policy and Pretence

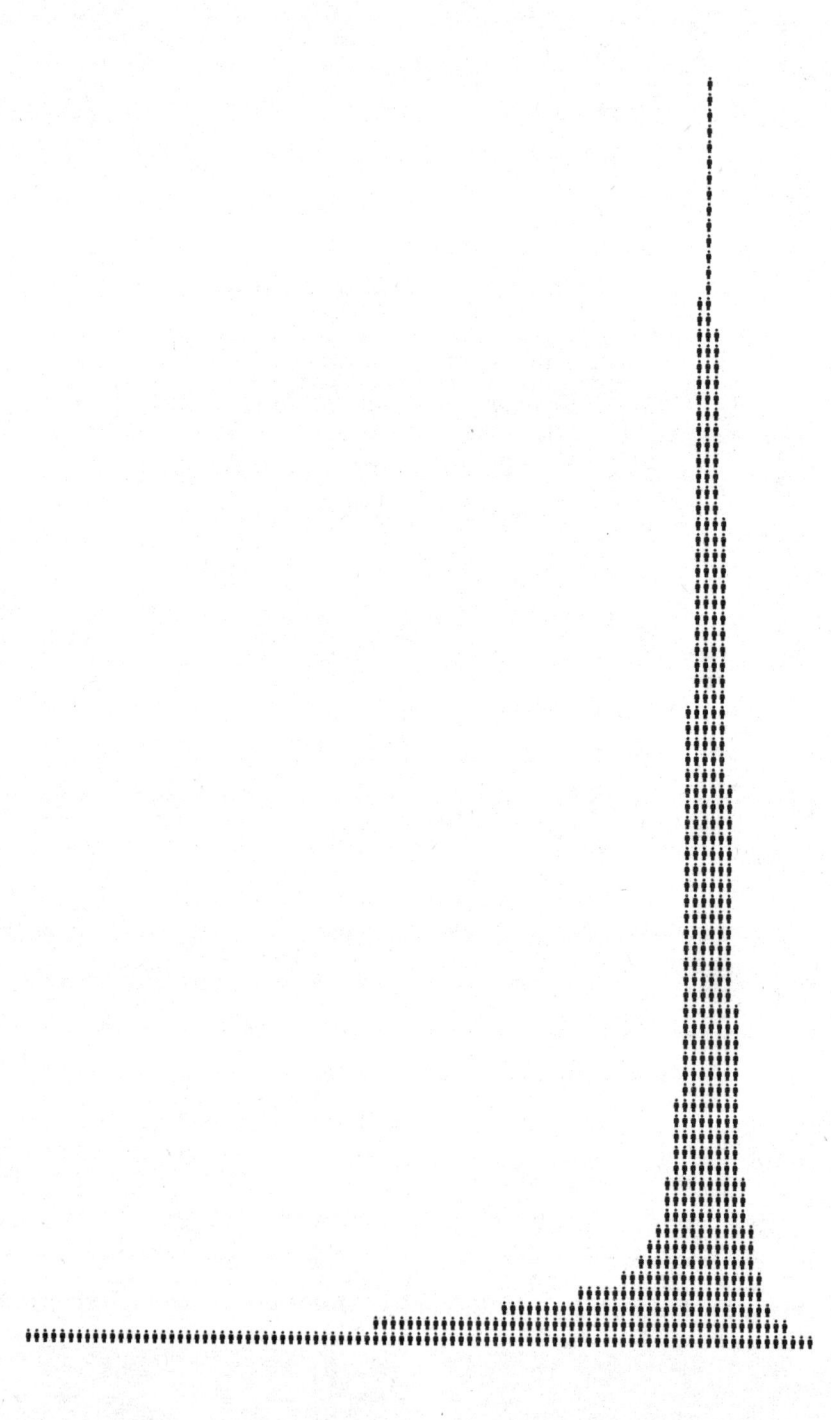

After the Spike

Population, Progress, and the Case for People

Dean Spears and **Michael Geruso**

Simon & Schuster

NEW YORK   AMSTERDAM/ANTWERP   LONDON
TORONTO   SYDNEY/MELBOURNE   NEW DELHI

Simon & Schuster
1230 Avenue of the Americas
New York, NY 10020

First Simon & Schuster hardcover edition July 2025

SIMON & SCHUSTER and colophon are registered trademarks
of Simon & Schuster, LLC

For information about special discounts for bulk purchases,
please contact Simon & Schuster Special Sales at 1-866-506-1949
or business@simonandschuster.com.

The Simon & Schuster Speakers Bureau can bring authors to your
live event. For more information or to book an event, contact
the Simon & Schuster Speakers Bureau at 1-866-248-3049
or visit our website at www.simonspeakers.com.

Manufactured in the United States of America

1   3   5   7   9   10   8   6   4   2

Library of Congress Cataloging-in-Publication Data is available.

ISBN 978-1-6680-5733-9
ISBN 978-1-6680-5734-6 (ebook)

Contents

Contents

After the Spike

Prologue

Humanity is on a path to depopulation.

You, your parents, their parents—any ancestors whose names you know—have been part of a growing population. And now a reversal is on the horizon. Birth rates have been falling everywhere around the world. Soon, the global population will begin to shrink. When it does, it will not spontaneously halt at some smaller, stable size. It will not fall to 6 billion or 4 billion or 2 billion and hold there. Unless birth rates then rise and permanently remain higher, each generation will be smaller than the last. That is depopulation.

This book explains why depopulation is likely, how we can know, and what the consequences would be. The story in this book is not the story of any one country or culture. It is not the story of how demographics will shape international competition and conflict and trade. That will happen, but the stakes of global depopulation are bigger. Depopulation will matter for everyone, everywhere. If the narrow perspectives of one country, one culture, or one generation are all we can muster, then we will miss the biggest story now unfolding. This book is about humanity as a whole.

How will depopulation matter?

It would be easy to think that fewer people would be better—better for the planet, better for the people who remain. This book asks you to think again. No one can know exactly what might be lost in a shrinking world. It would be a mistake of overconfidence to dismiss depopulation—either by shrugging off the consequences or by insisting that it can't happen.

Despite what you may have been told, depopulation is not the solution we urgently need for environmental challenges like climate change. Nor will it raise living standards by dividing what the world can offer across fewer of us. To the contrary, so much of the progress that we now take for granted sprang up in a large and interconnected society. We have flourished beyond the dreams of anyone living in our small-world past. That is no coincidence. Improvements and better lives don't come automatically, simply because time marches forward. *People* have to achieve them.

This book contrasts two possible futures. One possibility is that the population peaks at about 10 billion people within a few decades, then falls and never stops falling. This is where we are headed.

Stabilization is the other possibility. It's a path that looks similar for the next few decades, reaching a similar peak size and beginning a similar fall. But eventually the population stabilizes, roughly balancing the comings and goings of lives beginning and ending. How many people should our stabilized future hold? This book cannot say. It would be beyond the reach of today's social science or climate science or any other science to defend some specific population size as ideal. The stabilization that we argue for is only this: avoiding depopulation without end.

This book shows why stabilization does not look likely—unless societies choose it, invest in it, and work for it. So what would be the consequences of stabilizing instead of depopulating? Which sort of future should we *want* to happen?

Some big claims

This book makes three big claims—with evidence. The first one is this:

> **Part I's big claim:** No future is more likely than that people worldwide choose to have too few children to replace their own generation. Over the long run, this would cause exponential population decline.

But what about the fact that birth rates aren't yet low everywhere? Or that some communities tend to have more children, and their children tend to have more children? Or what if something big changes? We may live at the cusp of a revolution—in AI, or accessible gene editing, or something hard to imagine. Perhaps humanity will unlock secrets that can slow aging and extend lifespans. Perhaps artificial wombs will arrive. Perhaps. And perhaps—even though longer lives and safer, healthier births could be wonderful—these improvements, if they come, would not tilt our path away from depopulation. We'll grapple with these questions and show why a weird future is unlikely to come to the rescue—at least not in any simple or automatic way.

Whether depopulation would be good or bad depends on the facts and depends on our values. We ask about those facts and values, building up to an overall assessment:

> **Part II and Part III's big claim:** A stabilized world population would be better, overall, than a depopulating future.

The middle chapters of this book consider the case against people (Part II) and the case for people (Part III). Sometimes it's complicated, and sometimes we say it's clear. This big claim does not deny that environmental harm, inequality, poverty, and other challenges matter. The question is whether a shrinking population would make things better or worse—in these ways and for everything else that matters. Chapter by chapter, we will see what stabilization and depopulation would mean for the climate, for equity, for gender gaps, for material wellbeing, for progress, for freedom, for the possibility of human extinction, for humanity's general welfare.

These chapters weigh the evidence and reasons and conclude that stabilization would be the better path. How to achieve stabilization is a separate question, so our last big claim is this:

> **Part IV's big claim:** Nobody yet knows how to stabilize a depopulating world. But humanity has made revolutionary improvements to society before—we can do it again if we choose.

It's time to join the conversation

It is time for a compassionate and serious conversation about how to respond to depopulation—how to share and ease the burdens of creating each future generation. This book invites you to join that conversation.

As we go, we might ask you to expand the reach of your values—to consider new questions. But we won't ask you to abandon them. We won't ask you to abandon your concerns about climate change; about reproductive freedom and abortion access; or about ensuring safe, healthy, flourishing lives for everyone everywhere. We won't ask you to consider even an inch of backsliding on humanity's progress toward gender equity. We insist throughout that everyone should have the tools to choose to parent or not to parent.

One place we'll invite you to think hard is on the difficult question of how to value lives lived centuries from now—lives lived by people who may only exist depending on the choices of people living generations before them. Many good lives, like yours or better, might be lived. Or humanity might depopulate and billions upon billions of lives that could have been good may never be . . . anything. One cannot compare such different futures without considering the ethics of population. Does it matter, is it better, if more good lives get to be lived, rather than fewer?

We won't claim to have every answer. And we won't claim to represent the perspectives and experiences of all 8 billion of us alive today—or the many (or few) billions who will follow us next century. No two people born in a rich country in the twentieth century nor any other two people born anywhere, any time, could have the last word on such an important, unprecedented issue that impacts us all. What we do claim to have is facts and evidence for you to evaluate.

Discovering and publishing new facts and evidence is part of our jobs as professors at the University of Texas. The two of us became friends and research partners years ago when we were assigned to share an office as PhD students at Princeton. We studied economics then, and we teach it now, but our corner of economics is not concerned with interest rates or the stock market. We study people: their lives and choices, their health, their births, their deaths. We teamed up when we realized that we saw our vocation as economists in the same way, as a chance to uncover new facts about the wellbeing of people everywhere and to promote the wellbeing of people who need help.

As we wrapped up grad school, Dean and his spouse, Diane, started r.i.c.e., a nonprofit dedicated to research and advocacy for children in India. They moved to Uttar Pradesh, an Indian state where too many babies are born underweight and die early. From his postdoc at Harvard, Mike joined their board and supported their work.

Together over the years since, we wrote about healthcare, nutrition, disease, and sanitation. We wrote about how environmental pollutants affect people, and we wrote about how people affect the environment. We wrote about life expectancy, and we wrote about infant mortality. And all the while, we wondered what all these demographic details amounted to, zoomed out to the whole world and over the long run.

So we started asking broader questions. We asked those questions of the data, and we interrogated the theories. We began to write research papers where the time horizon was generations, not years. Where there were open questions, we looked for answers. Just how much does the lifelong carbon footprint of a child born today differ from a century ago, and how might it differ a century from now? How much could the trajectory of the global population be affected by small, high-fertility enclaves? What would happen if the birth rates that are now normal in India, Europe, or the United States became normal everywhere and stayed that way for a long time?

Mike was tapped to work in the White House, to advise on population trends and health policy as a senior economist at the Council of Economic Advisers. Dean went back and forth to India for his work there. We learned firsthand about parenting, too, becoming fathers in our thirties, and now raising kids in our forties. We kept up the conversation, found new experts to collaborate with, and continued our research. And we began to see the big, global story that this book tells.

In this book, you'll see stories from women in India who are caring for underweight, premature, or fragile infants in a government hospital. Dean and Diane support the hospital's program, called "Kangaroo Mother Care," through their nonprofit. These babies in India and the women who care for them are important—and it's important for a conversation about "population" to understand people and their lives, beyond the numbers and statistics.

In this book, you'll read stories of progress—progress that unfolded as the population expanded. For a long time, India was at the center of fears about "overpopulation." Today, lives in India are richer than ever. They are longer than ever. They are healthier than ever. So "overpopulation" did not bring doom to India—and we have plenty to say in this book about why not.

When we shared our depopulation research in a *New York Times* op-ed article in 2023, thousands of readers wrote back. We were glad that they did, because depopulation deserves not only attention but also serious engagement. Throughout this book, we will keep the conversation going. We will share some of the opinions and objections we've heard, and we will reply. Most claims and comments from readers (and some from our social science colleagues, too) shared a common feature: They were *certain* about something. Yet they pointed with certainty in conflicting directions. The facts that we share with you in this book will be more nuanced than the absolutes that you might hear elsewhere. We all can recognize that change is likely, and we can choose to care, without pretending that the future is certain.

This book does not say we face an immediate crisis. Depopulation is on the horizon. The challenges and risks it presents are vital. But we have a few decades.

Between now and then, humanity has a long list of other problems to solve, too. There are injustices to amend, lives to save, villains to thwart. So why spare any thoughts for depopulation now? Here is one reason: Because some of the people talking about low birth rates are diverting attention from real challenges and solutions. They are talking about depopulation to suit their agendas—of inequality, nationalism, exclusion, or control. If we wait, the less inclusive, less kind, less calm voices in our societies will call depopulation a crisis and exploit it for their purposes. The only way to make sure that more constructive voices are talking about depopulation is to add yours now.

This book is not about whether or how you should parent. It's about whether we all should make parenting easier.

This book asks how we should respond to depopulation, together. That is a question *about* everyone, and it is a question *for* everyone: What should societies, governments, and philanthropies do? The question of *what to do, together* about worldwide depopulation is not the question of choosing *your* family size. Choose your family size as you think best. Make it a big one, or a small one, if you choose.

But speaking for our own families, we might have had more children if caretaking and parenting were more valued. Or if being a parent didn't mean sacrificing so many other goals. Or if education and starting a family didn't often crowd one another out. Or if pregnancy and breastfeeding weren't sometimes so miserable. Or if things were a bit . . . easier for parents. And we know that our own families have it much easier than most!

Where this book differs from what other thoughtful, compassionate people have had to say about low birth rates is this: We cannot agree that whatever each individual chooses, given the world as it is, must be the first and last word on what would make for a better future. No reasonable person would accept that answer to humanity's abuse of the environment. We would not say: However each person chooses to burn, trash, and pollute has no consequence that matters for the rest of us.

And so there is a tension. Whether to parent must be a free, personal choice. Yet whatever is chosen by each for themselves will have consequences for us all. We all matter for one another. We all have a stake in outcomes that affect society as a whole, including the size of the population. Resolving this tension requires seeing a different future—of work, of family, of the social infrastructure that supports parenting and caregiving.

Here's a start at the resolution that we believe in: Over the long run, if we help one another, there's more than one future that could emerge from free choice. The law says that pregnancy is a free choice in France and is a free choice in South Korea. Yet average birth rates in France are over twice those in South Korea. So, yes, to everyone choosing the family that suits them. And, no, that doesn't settle everything, because what people aspire to and choose depends on the world they see around them.

If somebody chooses to have no children or few children, it's not for us to say that they are making a mistake. Probably they're not. But we all are making a mistake, together, when we make it hard for people to choose larger families or to have children. If we want there to be a thriving future, then it's time to start taking better care of one another and of our caretakers.

Humanity needs a big, caring, factful conversation about what is coming and how to respond. This book is an invitation to learn the facts and join the conversation. Each chapter of this book tackles an important piece of humanity's choice between depopulation and stabilization. Each chapter is the single most important piece—according to somebody. Read each chapter, engage with each question and perspective. Then add your voice to humanity's conversation about its future.

PART I

The Path to Here

Chapter 1

The Spike

In 2012, 146 million children were born. That was more than in any prior year. It was also more than in any year since. Millions fewer will be born this year. The year 2012 may well turn out to be the year in which the most humans were ever born—ever as in *ever for as long as humanity exists.*

No demographic forecast expects anything else. Decades of research studying Africa, Asia, Europe, and the Americas tell a clear story of declining birth rates. The fall in global birth rates has lasted centuries. It began before modern contraception and endured through temporary blips like the post–World War II baby boom. For as far back as there are data to document it, the global birth rate has fallen downward—unsteadily, unevenly, but ever downward. So far, falling birth rates have merely slowed the growth in humanity's numbers. So far.

The view from the top of a Spike

There are quite a lot of people in the world. But that hasn't been true for long. Ten thousand years ago, there were only about 5 million of us. That's as many people as today live in the Atlanta metro area, and only a fraction of the number who live in Bangkok, Beijing, or Bogotá. A thousand years ago, our numbers had grown to a quarter billion.

Two centuries ago, we passed 1 billion for the first time. One of every five people who have ever lived was born in the 225 years since 1800. A populous world, on the scale of humanity's hundred-thousand-year history, is new.

Getting big happened fast. And as soon as it has happened, it's about to be over. In the shorter run—soon enough to be seen by people alive today—humanity's global count will peak. There's a gap between the year of peak births and the year of peak population—a gap that we now live within—because the annual number of births, though falling, has not yet fallen far enough to reach the annual number of deaths. That will happen within decades.

Different experts predict slightly different timetables for when. The demographers at the UN believe it is most likely to happen in the 2080s. The experts at the International Institute for Applied Systems Analysis in Austria place the peak a little sooner in the same decade. The Institute for Health Metrics and Evaluation at the University of Washington projects a peak even sooner, in the 2060s.

These dates aren't exactly the same. But on the timeline of humanity, a difference of twenty years is not really a difference. Each group projects that birth rates will keep falling, so each group projects that we peak this century.

What happens after?

Figure 1.1 plots humanity's path. We call this picture—of humanity's past, present, and possible future—the Spike.

We first presented the Spike in a pair of publications in 2023: an opinion article in the *New York Times* and a matching research paper that filled in the scientific details. We asked: What if birth rates stay on their current course? The answer is that if they do, then humanity will depopulate. We do not mean that humanity would stop growing, reach some plateau, and stabilize near our present numbers. Every decade after turning the corner, there would be fewer of us. Within three hundred years, a peak population of 10 billion could fall below 2 billion.

The Spike is not a product of outlandish imagination. The possibility it charts does not assume some shift or reversal in the way people

Figure 1.1. The Spike

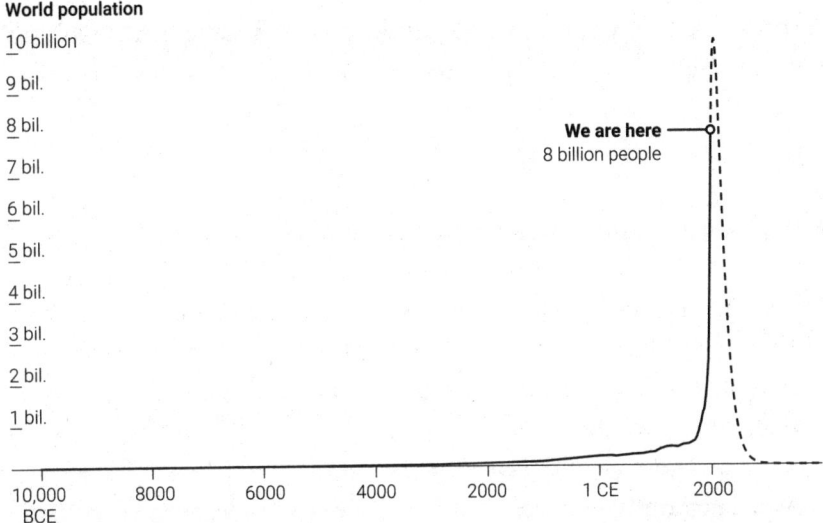

World population

live and behave. The Spike is what would happen if the whole world one day had the sort of birth rates that are already common in many places. In that future, like now, some people would have a few children. Some would have none. And many would have one or two.

We generated the Spike by projecting a future in which, globally, there were 1.6 children per pair of adults, a statistic that matches the current U.S. average. But, as we'll show soon, something like the Spike will happen as long as the worldwide average stays below two children per pair of adults. Below two children is what matters, because it means that one generation isn't replacing itself in the next generation. Is that kind of future likely?

Below-replacement birth rates aren't special anymore.
Already, two-thirds of people live in a country with birth rates too low to sustain their populations over time.

The United States' average of 1.6 kids is not exceptional. The birth rate is below two in Mexico, Canada, Brazil, Russia, Thailand, and many other countries. The European Union as a whole is at 1.5. The two most populous countries, India and China, are both below two. A birth rate below two is found within each U.S. state; when looking only among U.S. Blacks, whites, or Hispanics; and in every Canadian province.

What's normal now, around the world?

You stand now at the top of the Spike with 8 billion others. The story of the future starts with understanding the fact that most of those 8 billion others don't (or didn't, or won't, once they grow up) aspire to parent very many children.

One of those people is Preeti. In 2022, Preeti had a baby in a crowded government hospital in India. Her baby was born very small. So after a nurse rolled up a cart to weigh and assess her baby girl, Preeti was brought to the hospital's new program for underweight newborns, called "Kangaroo Mother Care." Preeti and her baby were assigned one of the program's ten beds in the next room.

Preeti lives in Uttar Pradesh, a populous, poor state in the north of India. She traveled to the hospital from a half-mud, half-brick home in a small village. The nurses down the hall don't have neonatal incubators, which are the standard treatment for underweight babies born in the rich places of the world. But they do have proven, low-cost procedures to keep tiny babies warm, fed, and alive.

The baby was Preeti's first. She expects to have one more. She already loves this girl. But it would be good, Preeti says, if the next one were a boy so she can "get the operation"—meaning sterilization surgery, having done her duty to have a boy.

Preeti's hope for two children is normal now, even in a poor, disadvantaged state in India. This book tells her story and her nurses' stories. Their choices, their lives, are also part of a wider story. A story in which women in rural Uttar Pradesh (where many women are poor, haven't had much schooling, and marry young) choose two children is a story in which many women, everywhere, choose even fewer. Preeti is one eight-billionth of the story that this book tells: Choosing fewer children is becoming normal, everywhere.

Rural India might seem like the middle of nowhere to someone who has never been to Uttar Pradesh. But to an economist or demographer, India is in the middle of the world's statistics: middle in income, middle in life expectancy, and middle in birth rates. And what happens in India is important for the planet as a whole. At some point between when Preeti's baby was born and now, India became the world's most populous country. If there's one thing that many non-Indians know about India, it's that there are a lot of people there: in 2025, 1.4 billion.

What fewer people realize is that India is on a path to a shrinking population, which is a corner that China has recently turned and Japan did in 2010. That's because many women like Preeti plan to have one or two children. In the most recent national data from India, women were having children at an average rate of two per two adults. Because that data point was from 2020, the average has almost certainly fallen to a little bit less than two by 2025. But even back in 2020, those who had been to secondary school (a growing fraction of girls and women in India) averaged 1.8, which matches the average for all U.S. women in 2016. The hospital where Preeti gave birth is in an especially disadvantaged state of India. But young women there said that they want about 1.9 children, on average. Small families are the new normal.

What's so normal about normal?

For many people, a society where women average 1.8 or 1.9 children would feel familiar. But so much familiarity is deceiving.

Normalcy will create something unprecedented. Birth rates that are normal in most countries today will lead to an unfamiliar future of global depopulation.

If today's normal stays normal, then big changes are coming.

And yet, looking around, you might not notice the difference between a society on the track toward depopulation and one headed for a stable future. Figure 1.2 diagrams two (of many) possible futures, with different fractions of people choosing zero, one, two, three, or four children. The taller a bar is, the larger the fraction of adults who have that many children. On the right is a distribution of family sizes that would make for a stabilized population, neither growing nor shrinking. On the left is a depopulating future, with 1.6 births per two adults, on average.

How different are the left and the right? It depends on what we're asking. The bars look only a little different, but their *consequences* are very different. Their implications are as different as a steady, stable global population, on the right, and a decline toward zero, on the left. The next chapter will trace out the arithmetic (painlessly), so you can see why for yourself. But here is our point for now: They don't look *that* different. Both include some families with a few children, plenty with none or one, and a bunch with two. Both look pretty ordinary if you live in a place like Austin, Texas, where we do. Professional statis-

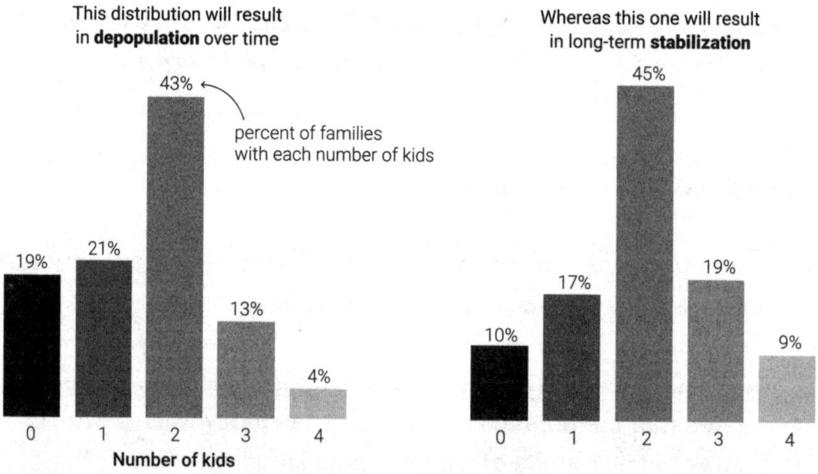

Figure 1.2. Families in two futures: depopulation or stabilization

ticians could tell the difference, if they had all the data. But could you tell the difference on a visit to the park, the grocery store, the pool? Could you see the difference at school drop-off, at the coffee shop, or jogging around the lake? Probably not. And that means the patterns of family life leading to a profoundly different future can slip past our notice.

We may not feel it. We may not see it. But we teeter at the tip of the Spike. Our times, when many people are alive, may prove to be unlike the entire rest of human history, past and future—if what is normal today persists.

Is this story four-fifths over?

Birth rates around the world vary in interesting ways: across countries and provinces, by race and religion, by education and income. In the United States, teen births are most likely to happen in January, but births to married moms are most likely in May. In India, Dalits—the disadvantaged caste group formerly called "untouchable"—tend to have slightly more children than people born into more privileged castes. The varied history is fascinating, too: France's fertility fell fast in the 1700s, long before its neighbors' did and long before hormonal birth control or latex condoms were invented. Experts have written thousands of articles about the details in scholarly journals. But those detailed differences don't help us understand what is likely to happen.

We learn what is likely to happen by seeing what people around the world *have in common*. Every region on Earth today either has low

Figure 1.3. Have four-fifths of humans already been born?

Everyone who has lived in the last 100,000 years

Alive now

Everyone who will ever be born

birth rates, like China, India, or the United States (the three most populous countries), or has falling birth rates, like most African countries.

If humanity stays the course it is now on, then humanity's story would be mostly written. About four-fifths written, in fact. Why four-fifths? Today, 120 billion births have already happened, counting back to the beginning of humanity as a species, and including the births of the 8 billion people alive today. If we follow the path of the Spike, then fewer than 150 billion births would ever happen. That is because each future generation would become smaller than the last until our numbers get very small.

Right about now it would be understandable to think, "But come on! This is all too much confidence about an unsustainable trend! Surely people won't keep having fewer and fewer children forever."

Some trends are indeed unsustainable, and it would be a mistake to extrapolate them indefinitely. We're not making that kind of mistake here. People around the world could continue to have small families. Not smaller *than* today. Small *like* today. They could continue, for a long time, to make individual decisions that add up to 1.4 or 1.6 or 1.8 children on average. A depopulating future would arise from *steady* birth rates at these levels.

How long depopulation could continue depends on what people choose. Our numbers will fall decade by decade, as long as people look around and decide that small families work best for them. That's all it would take. There would never be more than 150 billion humans, if families continue to have a bit less than two children each, on average.

So if—*if*—humanity stays this course, then there would be only 30 billion more of us for the rest of human history. How exactly might we fizzle out in that future? Should anyone literally expect that humanity will depopulate down to the last two people?

No. In a world that sheds 8 billion people, something big would eventually break and knock us off this path, for good or for bad. We would not ride the precise math of the Spike down to the last few million of us.

The off-ramp from the Spike could be sharply down. The end could be some catastrophe that a larger population might have survived but a smaller population couldn't. We have a chapter about this possibility.

Or the off-ramp could be up. Maybe birth rates would rebound, after a disaster or disintegration that staggers us. How? If progress halts or reverses, if life becomes worse, then it would be like we moved toward humanity's poorer past. People had more babies in the poorer past than they do today and tend to have more babies in poorer countries than in richer countries. So perhaps the off-ramp is some disaster that regresses on social, technological, or political progress, knocking backward humanity's millennia-long history of struggle and growth. That might mean higher birth rates, and it might even stabilize the population, but it wouldn't be good.

Might matters reverse automatically, without big changes? The short answer is that that's unlikely. A reversal would break a centuries-old trend of declining birth rates. That trend is founded on social and economic changes that most of us view as progress and that none of us should expect to disappear.

We can learn about the odds of an automatic rebound from the histories of countries where birth rates have fallen low. Since 1950, there have been twenty-six countries, among those with good enough statistics to know, where the number of births has ever fallen below 1.9 births in the average woman's full childbearing lifetime.

Never, in any one of these twenty-six countries, has the lifetime birth rate again risen to a level high enough to stabilize the population. Not in Canada, not in Japan, not in Scotland, not in Taiwan. Not for people born in any year. In some of these countries, governments believe they have policies to promote and support parenting. But all of them continue to have birth rates below two. A 0-for-26 record does not mean that things couldn't change, but it would be reckless to ignore the data. If a reversal happens, it will be because people decided they *wanted* to reverse it and then worked to make it happen, not because automatic stabilizers kicked in.

It takes two (to ever have a stable global population of any size)

Perhaps even at the end of this book you will not agree that a world of 5 billion flourishing people could be better than a world of 500 million equally well-off people. But do you think the size of the population should *ever* stabilize at *any* level—even a level much smaller than today's—rather than dwindling toward zero?

> **Some inescapable math.** For stabilization to ever happen at *any* level—even to maintain a tiny, stable global population— the same math applies: For every two adults, there must be about two children, generation after generation.

Wait, two? Exactly 2.0? Two for *everybody*? No, the next chapter explains. For now, it is enough to see that any population, large or small or tiny, continues to shrink if there aren't at least two children for each two adults. Dwindling toward zero is neither balance nor sustainability.

Notice what this inescapable math implies: Once the global average falls below two, which is a marker that we are likely to pass in a few decades, stabilizing the world population would require the global birth rate to increase and then to stay higher permanently. That has never happened before in recorded demography.

Maybe you feel confident that someday, somebody good and powerful will figure it out. Maybe you are more optimistic than the projections in the Spike that, after some decades or centuries of depopulation, humanity will manage to pull its birth rates back up to two. Even if you think so, read on.

For one, you might be wrong. This book will show that some popular beliefs about the history of how governments and movements have shaped birth rates are wrong.

For another, even if the global population will eventually recover, it makes a big difference *when* the recovery begins. Here are the stakes, even in the optimistic case of an unprecedented recovery: Each decade of delay in starting the rebound causes the final, stabilized population size to be 8 percent smaller, ever after. (Does that sentence leave you motivated, intrigued, or skeptical? You'll reach details in chapter 12.)

It is time to pay attention

Do you remember when you first understood that climate change is a seriously big deal? Most of us born before 1990 went through school without much awareness. Your authors grew up in a time when schoolchildren learned about the problems of an ozone hole, acid rain, and depleted tungsten supplies, not carbon emissions. The first book about climate change for a general audience, Bill McKibben's *The End of Nature*, was not published until 1989. But the basic facts have been known for a lot longer than the social movement has been around. Congress heard scientific testimony in the 1950s. In 1965, President Johnson included in a speech to Congress that: "This generation has altered the composition of the atmosphere on a global scale through radioactive materials and a steady increase in carbon dioxide from the burning of fossil fuels." That year, the White House released a report calling carbon dioxide a pollutant. Progress, such as it is, has only accelerated in recent years. But somebody got started in the 1950s.

Good thing they did, or the climate policy of today would not have the tools, the technologies, and the political awareness to make the progress it is finally making. Scientists in the 1950s and '60s had recognized the threat of climate change. They did not have a complete map to every solution. But they did not believe it was too early to get started, six decades ago.

The tip of the Spike may be six decades from today. (Or a few decades sooner than that.) Like the climate pioneers of the 1950s, all of us alive and working today are decades away from anyone having all the answers we need. But that does not exempt us from facing up to the facts. It's time to start learning. The first step is understanding the population today, where it came from, and where it is heading.

Chapter two-point-zero

The dividing line between growth and decay

Seema is one of the nurses in the Kangaroo Mother Care program in Uttar Pradesh. She is helping Preeti learn to breastfeed and keep her baby warm. As a young woman from a rural village, Seema is remarkable for having a nursing degree and a job in a district capital city. She has already come a long way.

So has Uttar Pradesh. Two decades ago, only 43 percent of homes there had electricity. Over 8 percent of babies died before they were one year old. Now 90 percent of homes have electricity, and less than 5 percent of babies die in infancy. Today, whoever of Seema's three sisters, four brothers, and two parents is available each night uses a smartphone to join the family video call. But Seema remembers when her family first got electric lights and fans at home. These days—increasingly but still infrequently—some women like Seema work as professionals. Her older sister, Reema, a nurse at the same hospital, blazed the trail.

Families are changing, too. Seema's father, a parent of eight children, was one of eight siblings. A generation ago, eight kids was a big family, but not an outrageous one. Seema's parents sacrificed for decades so that all eight children could get an education. Now Seema works in the KMC ward, where she coos to the tiny babies as she weighs them. When her checklists give her a minute, and if Seema is the only nurse in the room, she might sing to one of them. The underweight babies in the ward don't yet make for cute and chubby pictures, but they make Seema smile.

She's a pro in a room with ten tiny newborns. And yet, Seema plans only to have one child. At twenty-two, Seema is already three years older than the new mom Preeti was when she was married. Seema knows that her arranged marriage will come, too. But she hopes her father will find a family that will allow her to continue to work. She loves the big family she grew up in, but that is not what she says she wants for herself. "Now is a different time!" Her big sister Reema says she will have "two. For sure two." Which Seema thinks is a lot.

Reema's 2.0, Seema's 1.0, and the profound difference between them

Thirty years ago, the average woman in Uttar Pradesh had more than four children. Today the average is 2.3. For India as a whole, it's even lower. Seema and Reema are much better educated than the average twentysomething woman in Uttar Pradesh. But their family plans are not so unusual. Young women in Uttar Pradesh tell demographic surveyors that they want about 1.9 children, on average. The difference between 8.0 children and 2.3 children is a big deal. But the difference between 2.3 and 1.9 crosses an important line. It invokes a profound fact:

Profound fact. 1.9 is less than 2.0.

Striking, isn't it? Okay, maybe not yet. But it turns out to be profound because it tells us that Uttar Pradesh is on the path to depopulation. To understand the basics of depopulation, the most important place to start is with two principles.

The first is that population growth and population decay follow the same exponential math. Over the past one hundred years, the size of the world quadrupled. Over the past two hundred years, it grew by a factor of eight. Because the algebra of population decay is the same as the algebra of population growth, over some future period of two centuries it could fall just as quickly. The global birth rate that could cause this isn't unprecedented. It is what is happening today in many places—Bhutan, China, Italy, and Puerto Rico, among others.

The second principle is that whether the population grows or shrinks—whether the world follows a path of exponential growth or exponential decay—depends on whether the average birth rate is above or below *replacement fertility*. The replacement fertility level is the average number of children per woman that would sustain the size of the world's population over the long run: not growing, not shrinking. Because only about half of us are born with eggs and uteruses, replacement fertility implies that women would be having about two children each, on average. This tipping point at two children is what makes the profound fact that 1.9 is less than 2.0 *profound*.

It's not only Seema who wants a small family. Today in most countries, fertility is below replacement. Figure 2.1 captures a world crossing this dividing line. Each dot is a country, and each column is a year. The vertical position of a dot is that country's birth rate in that year. The dots are sliding down, gathering below 2.0. So why exactly is 2.0 so important?

It takes two to make a baby, at least with the science we now have. If two adults together have two kids, that's one per adult. But from here on out, we're going to write statistics about "births per woman," rather than "per adult." When Seema said she wanted one child and Preeti and Reema said they wanted two, they meant they wanted to give birth once and twice, respectively. They were not dividing their desired number of children by two to account for their (real or future) husbands. Seema wasn't thinking that her ideal future family would have 0.5 children per adult. She is one woman who wants one child.

That's a commonsense reason to organize our thoughts as "births per woman." Professional demographers tally births *per woman*, too. Of course, having eggs, having a uterus, being medically able to con-

Figure 2.1. Dropping below two, country by country

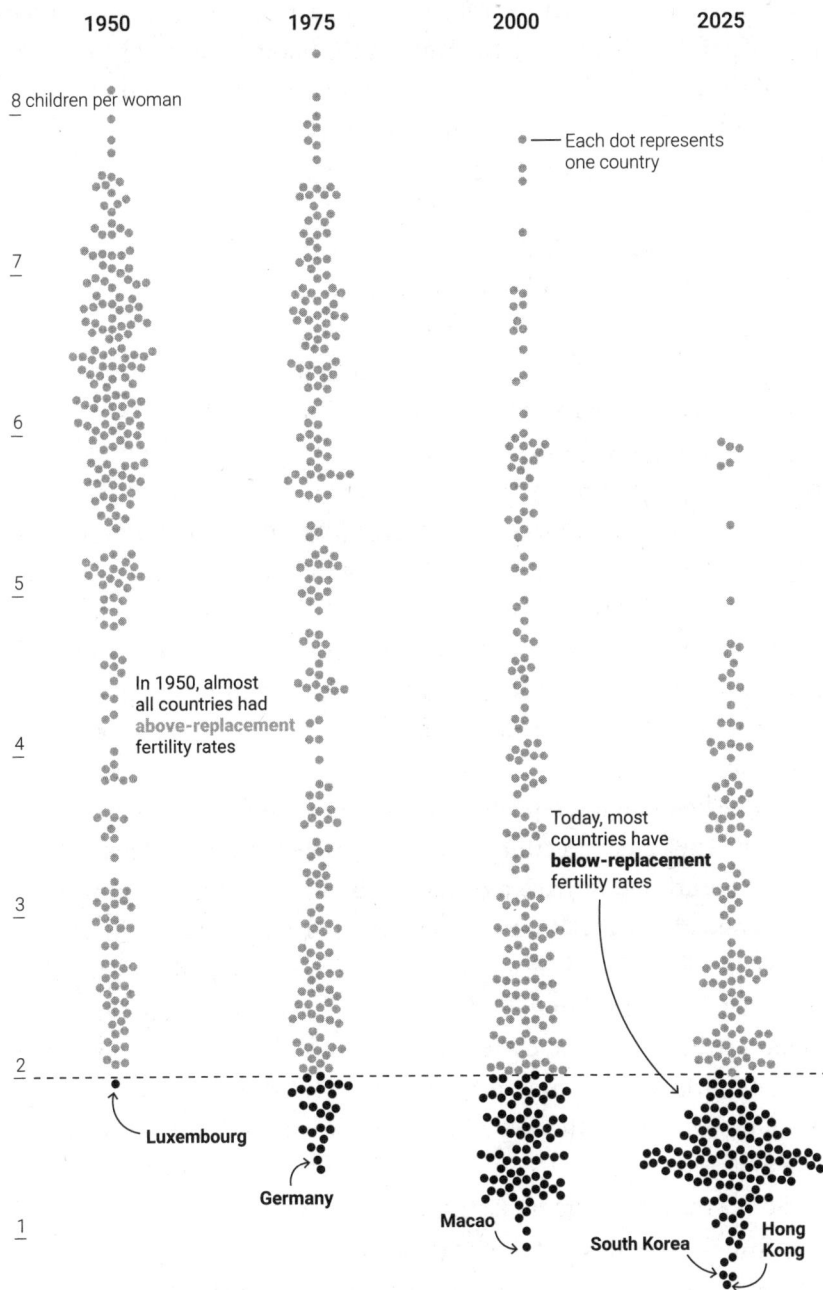

1950   1975   2000   2025

8 children per woman

● — Each dot represents one country

7

6

5

In 1950, almost all countries had above-replacement fertility rates

4

Today, most countries have **below-replacement** fertility rates

3

2

Luxembourg

Germany

Macao

South Korea

Hong Kong

1

ceive, and being a woman are neither synonymous nor fixed throughout a lifetime, but when a surveyor or a statistical agency has collected the sort of data that we use throughout the book, they mostly have not asked the questions that would enable those distinctions. So to understand official UN statistics about birth rates in Africa, or a newspaper article that interviews experts about Europe's demographic prospects, or an academic study documenting what sorts of families women in India now desire, we'll think about birth rates in these per-woman terms. Writing about children "per woman" does not endorse the view that children are only women's responsibility. A refrain of this book is that the future might look brighter if everyone had seen all along that children are everyone's shared responsibility.

There are several ways to measure birth rates, but the most common is the "total fertility rate." (Sometimes, we'll simply write "birth rate" or "fertility" in place of "total fertility rate.") The total fertility rate computes the average number of children that a woman in some population would have in her lifetime, if at each age she had the number of births that is normal in that population. The word "fertility" in population science is not supposed to carry any whiff of medical infertility. In demographic research, "fertility" simply refers to how many babies are born.

We've been saying replacement fertility is about two. Some people say that replacement fertility is 2.1. That is because not all babies survive to adulthood to have a chance to be parents. But if you want to get technical, 2.1 is not quite right, either. That's because the chance that a child dies isn't the same everywhere or stable for all time. In some deadly past when half of babies died before adulthood, replacement fertility would be closer to 4.0: That's four children born, two of them girls, half of those girls surviving to adulthood, leaving only one adult woman in the next generation out of the four babies born to one mother.

So the true replacement fertility rate differs from place to place and over time. Computing it is complicated enough that it's the stuff of scientific journals. The population scientists Stuart Gietel-Basten and

Sergei Scherbov published research calculating replacement rates separately for several states of India. Consider Seema's Uttar Pradesh in the 2010s decade. Infant deaths were even more likely then than they are in Uttar Pradesh now. So, there and then, the replacement rate was 2.39, according to Gietel-Basten and Scherbov's data.

Elsewhere in India, replacement was below 2.1 over the same period. Seema's boss is a professional nonprofit manager. She moved for this job from a richer, healthier Indian state called Kerala. There, the replacement rate was 2.09. In England and Wales at the turn of the twentieth century, where child death was much more common than even in many poor places today, it was 2.6.

And if you *really* want to get technical, you'll need to account for the statistical fact that boys are slightly more likely to be born, due to biological differences. If you imagined a hypothetical healthy population that had no sex-selective abortion or death before age fifty, replacement fertility would be 2.05. That's because for every 205 babies born, human biology, it turns out, would produce about 100 females.

But don't worry about all that. The difference between two children and the true replacement birth rate is small if child death is rare, which it will be in the future. If a total fertility rate is below 2.0, then it is below whatever the replacement rate is. So we will use "two" in this book.

Two is a good enough approximation. It doesn't pretend to be more precise than we need to be. If it all averages out—over the whole world and over long stretches of time—to meaningfully more than two, then that's population growth. Less than two is population decline.

We can use the fertility rate to see how the size of generations will change. Average fertility in Europe today is about 1.5. That means the next generation will be 25 percent smaller than the last. Why? If women are having 1.5 children on average—some of them having several children, some of them having none, and precisely none of them having precisely 1.5—then they are having 0.75 daughters on average. If they are having 0.75 daughters on average, then one hundred women of the last generation will parent seventy-five women in the next.

Now imagine that, counting the whole world together, the fertility rate was 1.5 and stayed that way for generations. How quickly would the planet shrink? Start from 2025, when about 132 million babies will be born worldwide, about 66 million of them girls. Let's assume that they will all survive childhood, because it won't be so many more decades until almost all of them will. If, as adults, these 66 million women have 1.5 children (0.75 girls) on average, then they will have 50 million daughters (and 50 million sons). When that generation of daughters grows up, some to be mothers and some not to be mothers, they will have 37 million daughters of their own, who will in turn grow up to have 28 million.

Now do that exercise again in the next generation, and the next and the next and the next. Pretty soon, that compounding adds up. Or, rather, subtracts. After seven generations, there would be 9 million girls born (and 9 million boys), in total, across the globe: 13 percent of the starting population. In another seven generations, about 1 million. In another seven, it would be 160,000 girls born worldwide each year. That is far fewer than were born this year in Texas. It's a little less than the number of girls estimated to have been born each year ten thousand years ago. The global population would have withered.

The world is headed in that direction. In fact, it has been for a long time.

Birth rates have been falling for as long as anyone has been measuring them

Populations didn't grow because birth rates increased. That's important.

> **Birth rates were falling all along.** For as long as any reliable records exist, and for at least several hundred years while the Spike was ascending, the average number of births per woman has been falling, generation by generation.

The Spike . . . *spiked*. The population soared. And yet birth rates were falling.

In the United States in the early 1800s, married white women (a population for whom some data were recorded) gave birth an average of seven times. Around the same time, the average woman globally gave birth about six times. By the early 1900s, the U.S. number had fallen near four births, for whites and non-whites alike. In France, where birth rates fell fast, sooner than perhaps anywhere else in the world, the average was below three births by the early 1900s. Globally, the average was about 5.5.

But let's focus our comparison of birth rates and global populations on the period when population growth really got going. Since 1950, the size of humanity has more than tripled, from 2.5 billion to over 8 billion of us. And yet, the trend in births over the same period was entirely opposite. Births were falling fast. In the 1950s and '60s, the average woman globally had five children. Since then, the birth rate has halved. The most recent statistic in the UN's database is 2.3, barely enough to replace two parents. But if it wasn't more births, where did so much world population growth come from?

Declining child deaths, not rising births, propelled us up the Spike

There is no migration to or off Earth. The world's population is a closed system, which means:

> **It comes down to births and deaths.** The global population growth rate is the difference between the birth rate and the death rate.

If the rate of world population growth increases, it must be because either deaths declined or births increased. And we've already seen that births were falling, not rising. That means that the revolution that took humanity up the Spike must have been a decline in death rates. Specifically, it was infant death rates: babies became more likely to survive to adulthood.

That's the story that figure 2.2 tells. In these graphs, moving from left to right is moving through history, from earlier centuries to later, including projections for the near future. The top panel plots births and deaths—not the total fertility rate for births, but the "crude" birth rate that simply counts the births per thousand people in the population. The bottom panel plots the percentage growth rate in the size of the population: Positive numbers are a growing population, larger positive numbers imply a population growing more quickly, and negative numbers are a shrinking population.

Long ago, death rates were high and birth rates were high, so population growth was slow, or even near zero. That was in earlier years before the chart starts ❶. When seventeenth- and eighteenth-century women were giving birth six or seven times, not all six or seven children survived to become eighteenth-century adults. Back then, many lives ended in infancy or childhood. So the size of each next generation was not so different from the last. That's the long flat preceding the Spike from chapter 1.

But something changed. Death rates began to fall. More of the children who were born survived to adulthood. That meant more people went on to have children of their own. A gap between birth rates and death rates opened—without birth rates rising—and the rate of population growth increased.

Population growth was fastest when the gap between birth rates and death rates was largest ❷. Population continued growing afterward, but not as quickly. That's because birth rates fell, too. Birth rates stayed high longer than death rates did, but eventually they chased death rates down, with people choosing smaller and smaller families ❸.

Seeing demographic history as a progression from high mortality and high fertility, to low mortality and high fertility, and then to low mortality and low fertility is called Demographic Transition Theory.

Figure 2.2. What got us here: death rates and birth rates

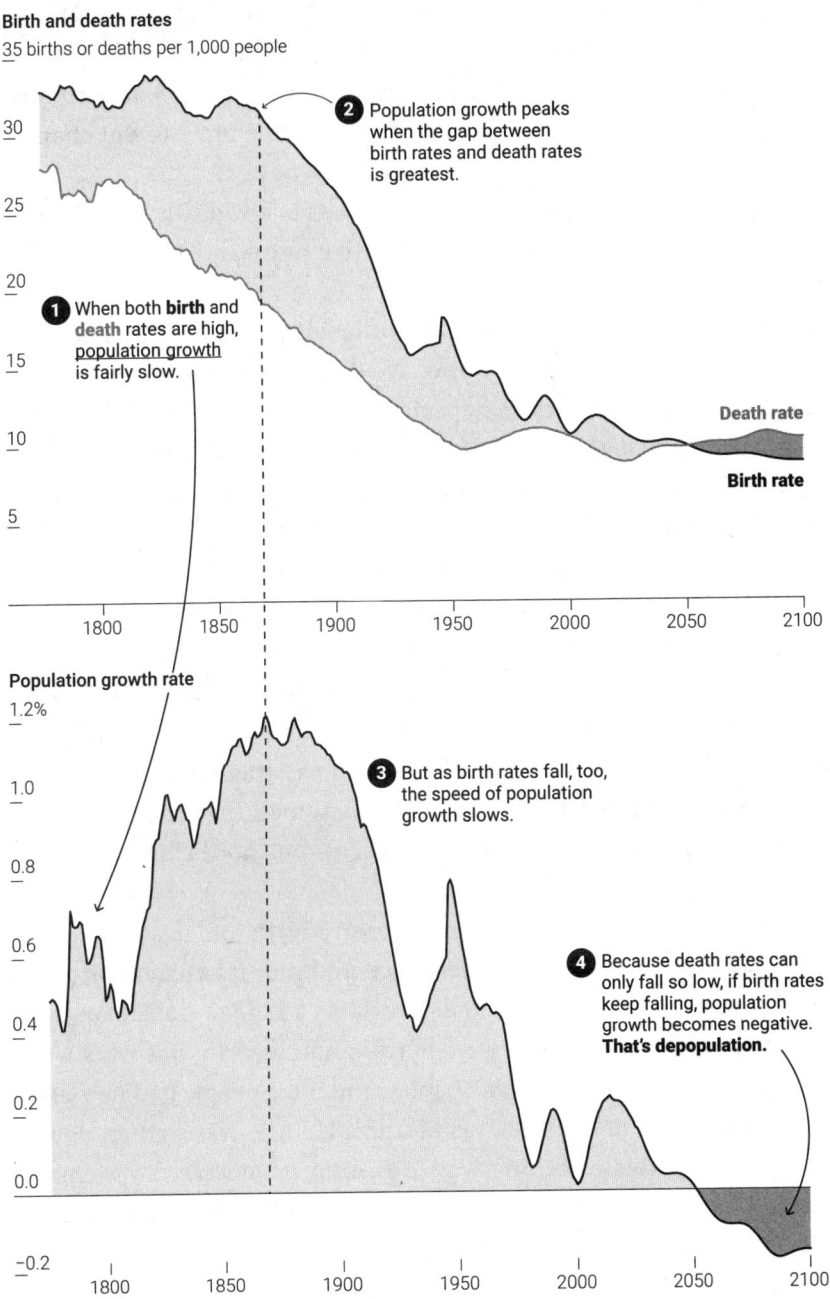

Birth and death rates
35 births or deaths per 1,000 people

2 Population growth peaks when the gap between birth rates and death rates is greatest.

1 When both **birth** and **death** rates are high, population growth is fairly slow.

Death rate

Birth rate

Population growth rate
1.2%

3 But as birth rates fall, too, the speed of population growth slows.

4 Because death rates can only fall so low, if birth rates keep falling, population growth becomes negative. **That's depopulation.**

Demographic Transition Theory is an idea from the mid-twentieth century. Its story ended with equally low birth and death rates. When the demographer Frank Notestein spelled out the steps of the theory in a 1953 essay, he wrote that Europe's "transition . . . was virtually completed." By 1953, Europe's birth rate had fallen to 2.6. But change wasn't over, so this theory didn't say what came next.

If birth rates keep falling, they will cross below death rates. Then, population growth will become a negative number. That is depopulation ❹.

Here's a detail that we haven't mentioned yet: figure 2.2 plots data from Sweden, not the whole world. We don't plot the whole world because we can't. These data do not exist back to 1750 for the whole world.

Sweden happens to be the place that first started collecting and storing enough data on deaths and births to make a graph like this possible. In 1749, Sweden established *Tabellverket* (literally "table work"), a new system for collecting population statistics. The Swedish state enlisted the Church of Sweden to do the table work, because the monarchical Swedish state was already closely tied to the Church of Sweden, and the church already had a large, hierarchical, national organization: clergy. Clergy submitted paperwork about births, deaths, and people in their parishes. These reports were compiled into national statistics. And so, almost three hundred years later, we know something about birth and death rates in eighteenth-century Sweden—but not before then and not elsewhere.

For the world as a whole, comprehensive birth and death registration is relatively new. With inheritance and politics at stake, it mattered a great deal exactly which descendants a king or nobleman had. It mattered what order they were born in and died in. But wars were never fought over most people's babies, and most people had no riches to inherit. So for most of the world's people, little was written down. And in most places, nothing was organized or preserved systematically. That would require something like a modern state bureaucracy to handle the administrative task.

How do historians know anything at all about the demographic past beyond the last couple hundred years, if most lives were never recorded and organized in ledgers? By doing what historians do: interpreting and reasoning about the information that survives. There are cemeteries, with carved birth and death dates; tattered family Bibles, inscribed with baptisms; records of the elite, back when a king's son could die of the same infection that killed a slave; and archaeological footprints of ruined ancient cities. These support only rough estimates: "about a third of babies died before age one," rather than "23 deaths under age 1 per 1,000 live births." And they aren't available for every year or in every place. They might depend on rulers in power or the vagaries of which records caught fire.

The scraps of information that exist in the longer world history, combined with more recent, high-quality data, tell us that the same general shape seen for Sweden shows up globally, but shifted later in history. For Sweden, the moment of fastest population growth came in the late 1800s. But for the world as a whole it was 1968. We can observe *that* because the UN's modern population data start in 1950. Sweden is projected to begin shrinking in 2051 (ignoring future migration, and instead considering only birth and death rates). The world—a population without migration into or out of it—is projected to reach this point in the 2080s or perhaps sooner. But the pattern is the same. First death rates fall and create population growth. Then birth rates fall and create population decline.

The work of keeping babies alive is not quite over (but the era when child death rates shaped population growth is)

Angus Deaton, an economics Nobel laureate and one of our PhD advisers, called the rapid decline in death rates humanity's Great Escape. Deaton built on the account by Robert Fogel, another economics Nobel laureate, who called it an escape from hunger and premature death. "Premature" was key. Mortality improvements didn't come from treating adult ailments like heart disease and cancer. The escape was mostly about improving survival prospects for children. There are many ways in which childhood is different today than it used to be, but the most important way that childhood is different today is that people are more likely to survive it.

The way mortality is reported in the summary measure of "life expectancy" can obscure this fact. Even when and where death rates were high, people didn't tend to die in their thirties. Instead, people died in late adulthood and—if conditions were poor—at the very start of life. So when estimates of life expectancy around 1800 place it at less than thirty years, it does not mean that the average death came to a thirty-year-old adult.

Here's a cartoonishly simplified example. If half of people die just after birth and the rest die at age sixty, but no one dies in between, then life expectancy is thirty. That's an evenly weighted average of the two possible outcomes, zero and sixty. If the world improves and the chance of dying just after birth falls to zero, but nothing else changes, then life expectancy would shoot up to sixty. And that change would happen without any changes to what happens in anyone's thirties, forties, or fifties.

The fact is, that simplification is not so different from reality. Benjamin Franklin wrote in his *Almanack*: "Wish not so much to live long as to live well." And yet he did manage to live long, dying in 1790 at eighty-four. Franklin came from a family of seventeen siblings. Six lived to their sixtieth birthday, four to their seventieth, and three to their eightieth. But four died in childhood.

When global life expectancy more than doubled from below thirty to above seventy, that meant that many lives of nearly zero length were replaced with lives of ordinary, adult length. An "old person" in our times would not be radically older than an "old person" in 1750. But child mortality in our times is altogether different than before.

Figure 2.3 shows how child mortality rates—the fraction of births that end in death before age five—have changed. For Benjamin Franklin and his siblings, it was 24 percent. Facing a one-in-four chance of

Figure 2.3. The Great Escape from childhood mortality

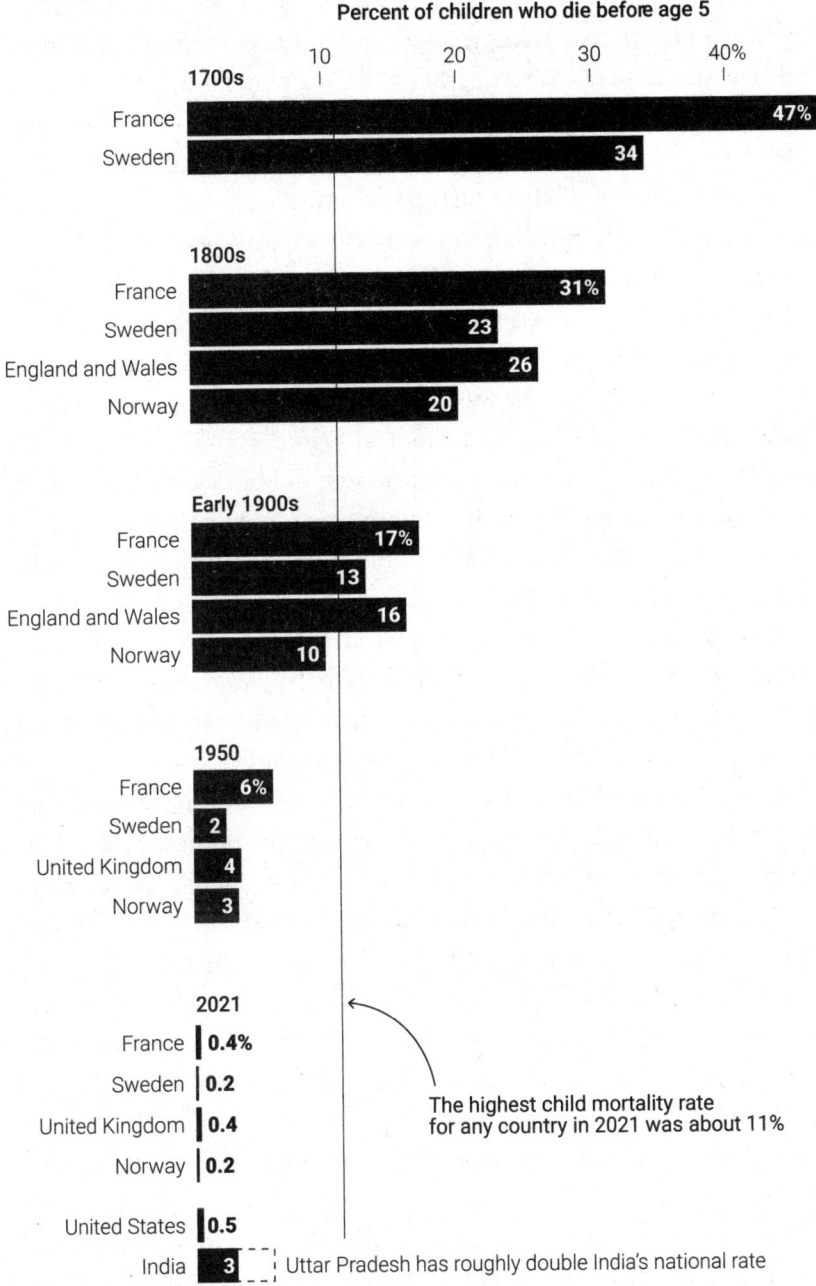

Percent of children who die before age 5

| | 10 | 20 | 30 | 40% |

1700s
France — 47%
Sweden — 34

1800s
France — 31%
Sweden — 23
England and Wales — 26
Norway — 20

Early 1900s
France — 17%
Sweden — 13
England and Wales — 16
Norway — 10

1950
France — 6%
Sweden — 2
United Kingdom — 4
Norway — 3

2021
France — 0.4%
Sweden — 0.2
United Kingdom — 0.4
Norway — 0.2

United States — 0.5
India — 3

The highest child mortality rate for any country in 2021 was about 11%

Uttar Pradesh has roughly double India's national rate

dying in childhood meant that these seventeen were relatively lucky. In the 1700s, between a third and half of lives ended before a fifth birthday in the places we can know about. Franklin went on to have three children, of whom one died in childhood, matching the statistics of his era. Today, in Australia, Germany, and South Korea, the child mortality rate is so low that, of 250 births, 249 survive childhood. That's a pretty good chance of a fifth birthday party. For the world as a whole, the chance of death in childhood now is less than 4 percent.

The era in which declining childhood mortality determined global population growth is over. When child mortality fell from 2-in-10 to 2-in-100, as it did in Sweden between the nineteenth and twentieth centuries, it mattered a lot for Sweden's trajectory. Falling further from modern Sweden's 2-in-1,000 child mortality rate (even all the way down to zero) will matter to the families who will not have to face the death of a child. But stamping out the remaining, infrequent cases of infant and child mortality in privileged communities won't move the needle on population growth rates. The number of lives at stake is too small.

What about elsewhere? In Uttar Pradesh today, the risk of infant death is still much higher than in places like the United States, Europe, or Japan, because of differences in healthcare, maternal nutrition, and disease. And yet "high" child death rates today are a small fraction of what were "normal" child death rates, back when the average woman had six or seven children. Already, children in the poorest parts of the world face better survival odds than the richest nobility of centuries past. A baby in 2020s Uttar Pradesh faces much better chances than in the rich countries of 1800: a quarter of the risk of dying.

This global decline has been one of humanity's greatest moral achievements. In a few more decades, the poor places of the world like Uttar Pradesh will achieve infant mortality rates like that of the United States today. Once that has happened, and child mortality presses down against a lower bound of zero everywhere, there will be no space further to fall.

Past population growth, which was driven by declining child mortality, gives no reason to expect population growth will continue into the future—because in the future, child mortality can no longer decline. That means that the rapid fall in childhood death that pushed humanity up the Spike will not be available to grow humanity's numbers again, or to maintain them against a falling global birth rate. From our moment in history, all the forward motion and all the uncertainty is in birth rates. Depopulation will start when the number of births per year, already falling, crosses below the number of deaths per year.

The number 2.0 is not protected by any unseen magic

The world total fertility rate fell from 3.5 in the 1980s to 3.0 in the 1990s to 2.5 in the 2010s. But all the while, the public conversation about population asked only if the population would grow forever. In 1970, a *Life* magazine cover story celebrated a Yale college student movement for "zero population growth," whose "supporters propose that the U.S. do exactly that: stop growing."

What about the possibility of depopulation? Most governments didn't entertain it. Nor did most activists, nor did the broader public debate about population change. Instead, the two possibilities that anyone imagined were either "grow larger" or "stand still at a constant size." That was true for a long time. By the 2000s, those Yale students had become the parents of high school students taking AP exams. Study guides for the AP Environmental Science and AP Human Geography exams taught students to explain Demographic Transition Theory. That theory tells a story that ends in zero population growth, incorrectly assuming that birth rates and death rates would end up equally low.

Sometimes people make the mistake of assuming balance implicitly. They say that, after a long history of population growth, the size of the population is going to *stabilize* later in the twenty-first century, rather than *peak and fall*. In 1998, economist W. W. Rostow published a demography book about what he called "the great population spike." But Rostow's spike was not our Spike, because Rostow didn't plot a picture of population *size*: He plotted a concept sketch of what population *growth* may look like. His diagram spiked up in the twentieth century to high rates of annual population growth and then fell down to zero growth, but never *below* zero—never into the range where population would begin to shrink. So in Rostow's illustration, the world would hit its peak population and sail on at that high population level forever.

We find examples of this assumption wherever people are writing in public about population trends. J. Bradford DeLong, a leading economic historian, recently wrote this in his book *Slouching Towards Utopia: An Economic History of the Twentieth Century*: "The population explosion turned out to be a relatively short-run thing. Humanity appears to be rapidly moving toward zero long-run population growth." Nope. Humanity is rapidly moving toward *negative* population growth. Zero population growth is the radical, unlikely future that our book hopes might just be possible, if we try. ("Zero population growth" is a more dramatic term for "stabilization.")

The unspoken assumption that population growth could never turn negative is an assumption that birth rates could never fall below replacement, below two. But two has never been the end point where birth rates stop. We have data that speak to this because below-replacement birth rates aren't new. Already by 1980, more than one in five people worldwide lived in a country with a birth rate below two. Europe as a whole—along with Japan, Australia, and Cuba—had already crossed the dividing line between growth and decay in the mid-1970s. Canada did it in 1972 and the United States in 1973. All of those countries are below two now.

History has had plenty of opportunities to show us a case of two births per woman being special, to show us a country where falling birth rates got to two and stopped there for keeps. But that has never happened. A plot of each country's birth rate over time is a squiggle that wiggles down, paying no more heed to the number 2.0 than it did to the numbers 2.71828 or 3.14159. All three are special numbers, but they possess no magic that constrains what people choose for their lives, nor for how those individual choices aggregate up to a global average. So when global fertility falls to two, there is no reason to expect it to stop there.

It's easier to be right about the past than about the future. So we're not saying that everyone should have known exactly what today's birth rates would be. But many people overlooked even the possibility that birth rates in many countries could go below two and stay there, implying negative population growth.

When somebody throws a ball to a kid, it arcs up, reaches some apex, and then arcs back down. It does not hang at its high point or coast, ever parallel to the ground. The same force that slows its ascent tugs it back down to earth after it passes its peak.

The fixation on an exploding global population—and the seeming impossibility that global birth rates could be falling fast over the same decades that population size was rocketing upward—meant that many people were wrong about what the future would look like. Even smart researchers dropped the ball on population.

Once we see that 2.0 is just a number, it makes sense to expect depopulation. It's time to shake any residual belief in the magic, magnetic power of two.

But what about Finland between 2000 and 2010?

Here's an objection that we hear when we say that birth rates have long been falling. It starts with a statistic like this: In 2000, the total fertility rate of Finland was 1.73. In 2010, it was 1.87. The rate went up over that decade, so how can we say that birth rates have always been going down?

We answer like this: Zoom out on those Finland statistics, please. By 2020 in Finland, fertility had fallen down to 1.4. Back in 1960, it was 2.7. In 1900, Finland's total fertility rate was closer to 5.0 than to 4.0. So, over the long run, despite the tick upward in the 2000s, the trend in Finland's birth rate has been clearly down.

Less than one-tenth of 1 percent of the world's population lives in

Finland, so little hinges on this example for the world overall. In fact, if the future of the world averages out to *either* 1.73 (Finland in 2000) or 1.87 (Finland in 2010), then depopulation is coming. Finland in the 2000s is only one instance of the question: "But what about *this* example?" The answer to any such question is the same: The Spike is about the long-term trajectory of the world as a whole.

The Spike is about the signal, not the noise. The top part of figure 2.4 plots the signal, the information that we need to know. The bottom part includes all the detail. Each line in that mess is a country, each point is a year. It's noise.

What is signal and what is noise depends on what somebody is interested in measuring. A data point that is a signal for one question can be noise for another. Knowing that your favorite basketball team scored five points in the last few seconds is a useful data point if your goal is to understand, say, why a bunch of people in the arena wearing the same colors are suddenly out of their seats and shouting with joy. But those few seconds are not a great data point to understand whether the home team is heading to the playoffs. To understand that, you would need to understand what the rest of the season looked like. You need to see the whole.

Knowing that birth rates rose or fell in a single country in a single year is a useful data point if your goal is to understand the details of that time and place. Maybe you need to know because it is your job to staff kindergarten classrooms with teachers. But one data point in one year will not help us understand whether the home team of Earth is heading for depopulation. To understand that, we need to ask what is happening in other countries and years. We need to see the whole.

We made the top part in figure 2.4, the signal, by taking the UN's annual records of the global average total fertility rate and computing a moving average to capture what is true of twenty-year generations. We made the bottom part by simply plotting every country in every year. Both plots contain information. But for our purpose in this book—understanding the long-term path of the population—the bottom graph contains too much information. Lines cross. Lines reverse.

Figure 2.4. The long-run signal in a noisy world

Total fertility rate
9 children per woman

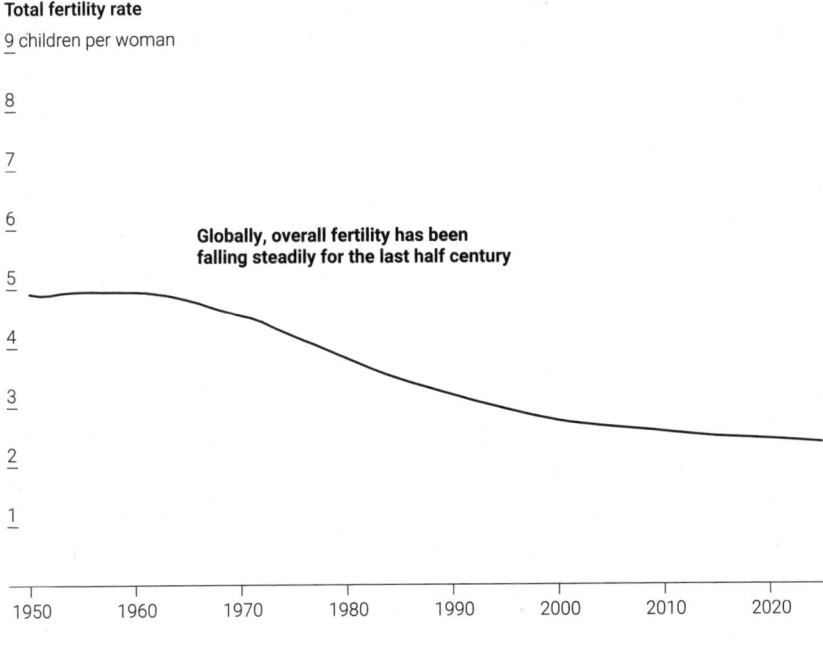

Globally, overall fertility has been
falling steadily for the last half century

1950 1960 1970 1980 1990 2000 2010 2020

9 children per woman

. . . even though individual countries'
fertility rates have varied year to year

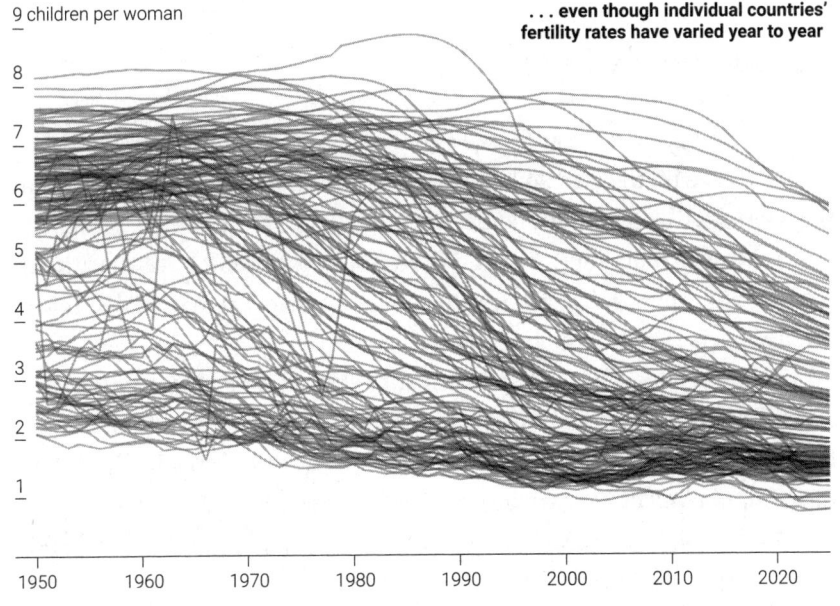

1950 1960 1970 1980 1990 2000 2010 2020

Somebody might memorize all of those facts (What happened in Finland after 2020? And what about Norway?), but they may not have accumulated any more wisdom about humanity's trajectory.

When we say that birth rates have been falling all along, we mean the signal, the top of figure 2.4 that shows a clear, overall decline. Don't be distracted by the noise.

But what about the places still (far) above two? When we write that two-thirds of people live in a place where birth rates are below replacement, that means that one-third don't. Many places still have above-replacement birth rates, especially in sub-Saharan Africa. But "high fertility" in Africa isn't what it used to be. Forty years ago, sub-Saharan Africa's total fertility rate was 6.8. Since then, it's been declining by about 1 percent per year, so that in 2025 it is 4.2. All of the leading teams of population scientists project that birth rates in Africa will continue to fall. As long as lives in Africa continue to improve—at work, at home, at school, and elsewhere—birth rates in Africa will probably continue to fall, and the world is probably on the Spike's path.

But how can we be so sure?

The logical path from low birth rates to depopulation is short. If worldwide average birth rates go below two, and if they stay below two, then the world will depopulate exponentially. That is an *if-then* sentence, and we are sure its logic holds. We're not 100 percent sure that the *if* part is true, that global birth rates will stay below two, but declining birth rates is the clear global pattern.

How much less than 100 percent sure should we be? Not much less, according to Adrian Raftery and Hana Ševčíková, two statisticians at the University of Washington. They published estimates in the *International Journal of Forecasting* in 2023 that there is a 90 percent chance that global birth rates will be below replacement until at least 2300, which is the latest year that they considered.

The pattern of facts that we have seen throughout this chapter—enduring declines in birth rates everywhere we look, and fertility staying low after becoming low—are part of why forecasters aren't predicting that a rebound is likely. Anybody is free to draw their own conclusions from these facts. But these facts justify believing in some high chance of a low-fertility future. And so does the fact from chapter 1 that in none of the twenty-six countries where lifelong birth rates have fallen below 1.9 has there ever been a return above replacement.

And so do other facts. It's easier for younger people to get pregnant than older people, but the trend is to start having families later. No country in any year has ever had a birth rate as high as 2.0 if the average first-time mom gave birth after turning thirty. No U.S. state or Indian state has, either. So on top of the trend toward wanting fewer children, there's the reinforcing trend toward starting childbearing later, and perhaps ending up with fewer children than parents hope for.

Maybe it's a 90 percent chance, or maybe 95 percent or 75 percent. No one can yet know the exact chances, but they are high enough to deserve our attention.

There are many details we are skipping here. These details fill scholarly careers. But sometimes grappling with the coarser facts is more important than sifting through the fine details. If the world continues to release a lot of carbon dioxide into the atmosphere, energy from the Sun will heat the Earth above its preindustrial temperatures. Knowing that is enough to be concerned about global warming, even though other details matter and people rightly devote careers to figuring them out. If fertility rates stay well below two, then generations will shrink one after the other. For the world as a whole, for a timeline measured in centuries, the if-then *is* that simple.

We've talked about child mortality, but what about adult mortality, someone might ask. If life expectancy doubles to 150 years, or quadruples to 300 years, couldn't that prevent the depopulating edge of the Spike? The surprising answer is no. Even if each baby born lived twice as long as today, or even four times as long, if the *number of babies born* is nevertheless decaying exponentially because the birth rate is below two, then the size of the population will continue decaying exponentially, too.

If, on average, two adults in the future have 1.5 babies in their thirties and then live another 270 years before dying, then they will add their life years to the population size, but they won't stop depopulation. So the story of the Spike would stay the same, even if life expectancy quadrupled to three hundred years. In contrast, if adults' *reproductive* spans also changed, so people had, say, one or two babies on average over their twenties, thirties, and forties and then another one on average over their fifties, sixties, and seventies, then that would stop depopulation—but it would be because births changed, not because later-adulthood deaths changed.

And what if we don't know exactly how far below two the world's total fertility rate will fall? To see the biggest-picture fact that depopulation is coming soon and will happen fast, we do not need to resolve this detail. Figure 2.5 shows this by trying out a few plausible futures for global fertility. It is a more detailed version of the Spike from chapter 1. There, we plotted only one possible future. Figure 2.5 shows several.

The world might converge to 1.75, like in El Salvador or Malaysia today. Or to 1.5, like in Europe and Costa Rica today. Or to 1.25, like in China, Puerto Rico, and Spain today. Each of these paths already reflects somebody's normal in today's world. A quarter of people alive now live in countries around 1.25 or below.

Figure 2.5 shows all these possible futures. Do the differences between them really matter, if the concern is a depopulating world, and if we zoom out to the timescale of the whole human era? The answer is no. Projections into the future can be off by half a child per woman—as wrong as the difference between El Salvador and China—and still be right about the big picture.

If you are the finance minister responsible for a country's budget, then it makes a big difference to you whether your country's fertility rate goes toward 1.8 or 1.2, but it does not matter much to the question

Figure 2.5. The Spike: some possibilities

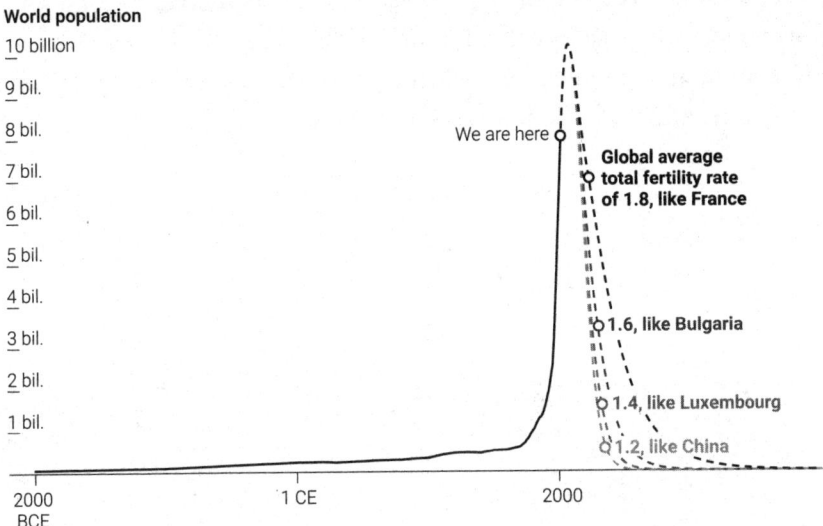

of whether humanity will depopulate. If the world as a whole stays at either, then humanity would be about four-fifths over: 120 billion births in the past, fewer than 30 billion left to come.

.

Nobody should claim to know the exact year when population growth will turn negative, nor when only 4, 2, or 1 billion of us will remain. But we can be confident in this *if-then*: If fertility rates keep falling where they are falling and stay low where they are low, then this future is coming. And we won't be wrong about timing by more than a few decades.

Knowing this, you are ready for the question at the core of our book: *Would depopulation be good or bad?* Should anyone want—and be willing to work for—a different future, where humanity has stabilized its numbers, instead?

Asking that question means asking questions of fact and questions of value, because whether avoiding depopulation would be good depends both on what the consequences will be (How many tons of CO_2

are at stake? What will depopulation mean for living standards and material progress?) and on how to value them (Is there anything important lost when a good life that could be lived isn't?). To compare depopulation and stabilization, we will need to assess the consequences one by one and arrive at an overall judgment.

PART II

The Case Against People

Chapter 3

What people do to the planet

People create and enjoy. People pollute and destroy. More people means more creation and more destruction. So if environmental harms are always bigger in a bigger population, then maybe we should welcome depopulation.

But are the harms always bigger?

In 2013, China faced a smog crisis. Newspapers around the world called it the airpocalypse. The *New York Times* reported that the "United States Embassy rated the air in central Beijing an astounding 755 on an air quality scale of 0 to 500." In the decade that followed, China grew by 50 million people. That addition is about equal to the entire population of Spain or Argentina or Uganda. It's about 1.5 Texases. But over the same decade, particulate air pollution in China declined by half. The harm of particulate air pollution (the haze in the sky from fires, coal plants, and vehicle exhaust) got smaller as China got bigger.

Understanding complications like this one is important. That's because the relationship between population size and the environment is nuanced. Any answer to the question of whether a more populous future would worsen particle air pollution—or would worsen habitat loss, or climate change from greenhouse gas emissions, or any other environmental challenge—needs to make sense of such facts.

Most environmental scientists no longer promote population reduction as a solution. But the old ideas still reverberate, even after environmental leaders have moved on. So this chapter takes stock of where we are and what we know. And it grapples with nuance:

> **Yes, people caused today's environmental problems.** And no, reducing birth rates would not solve them now.

Let us be very clear: Humanity faces profound and urgent environmental challenges. These challenges threaten our future and imperil the most vulnerable people around the world. To treat these challenges with the seriousness they deserve, we must be serious about solving them. Is embracing population decline part of that serious response? Could population change make enough of a difference to be a priority for the environment? And if not, why not?

A crooked path away from our intuitions and through the woods

There is no question that adding more people and changing nothing else about today's world would mean more waste, more pollution, more environmental disruption. So it's understandable to expect that stabilization must be more polluting than depopulation. But we shouldn't skip so quickly past the idea of *changing nothing else about our world*. The link between pollution and population size has not been constant in our past. What about in our future? Can the world decouple population and prosperity from air and water pollution? (It has.) From greenhouse gases? (It can.)

Some answers to these questions are subtle and surprising. They may clash with our feelings and first impressions. So let's take a moment to reset those feelings and impressions.

Breathe. Imagine a modest, traditional cabin in the woods. It's on a pretty site—surrounded by pines and on a gentle, south-facing slope.

The porch looks out to a mountain range on protected state lands. The view is marvelous, and the nearby hikes are pristine. Water bubbles up from a spring on the land. It's winter. There's a wood-burning fireplace, backed up with a buried propane tank for more practical and efficient heating tasks. Stepping out the front door with your coffee, you smell the pine. You might hear the rustling of a snowy weasel or catch a glimpse of a barred owl.

Now imagine a different place to live: a fourth-floor apartment in a mid-rise building, with shared walls on two sides, plus a floor that is someone else's ceiling and a ceiling that is someone else's floor. The view from the window is the cracked facade of another building. Water is piped in from a reservoir far away. Like the cabin, a gas furnace heats the building. Unlike the cabin, there's air-conditioning for the summers. Passing the alley beside the building, you may smell the runoff from a dumpster. Stepping down into the subway station, you might hear the rustling of a brown rat or catch a glimpse of a rock pigeon on an awning overhead. A little Christmas tree air freshener dangling from the rearview mirror of a passing taxi might be as close as you'll get this week to the sight of pine.

Life in the cabin is more natural. Right? Closer to nature, sure. But also worse for nature. The cabin is, compared with the apartment, an environmental disaster. The heat lost through the walls of the apartment mostly goes to productively heat the apartments left, right, above, and below it (using less energy per resident). But the heat lost through the walls of the cabin vents wastefully to the open air. To say nothing of the particulate-matter air pollution and higher carbon intensity of burning solid fuels in that lovely fireplace. The seclusion of the cabin means that electricity comes from far away, with significant waste in transmission losses. And of course, the beans for that cup of coffee or marshmallow for that hot cocoa would have a less carbon-intensive path to the big city than out to any remote mountain. You might enjoy glimpsing the local wildlife, but it has no interest in you settling its home. Go take a hike elsewhere, if you please.

Human life is polluting. That one human settlement in the cabin is polluting, disruptive, and dislocating, so intuition might tell us that the impact would scale with population. In particular, it may seem like it should scale *in a straight line*. If one family on one acre is bad, aren't ten families together on one acre ten times as bad, and a hundred families on one acre—the density of a downtown city—a hundred times as bad?

No, because the consequences of people do not scale in straight lines. It turns out that living together in a dense urban environment generates fewer emissions per person than spreading that same number of people out to far-flung places.

None of this settles what a larger or smaller global population might mean for the environment. The cabin in the woods is merely an example of how an option that in fact emits more carbon could *feel* like the more environmentally responsible choice. Similarly, for many questions of population growth and decline, what *feels* right can often run afoul of what the science tells us.

More people do not bring more lead pollution, ozone depletion, or acid rain

What does one more child born mean for the environment? The answer is more complicated than "it makes everything worse." A few decades ago, some of the most pressing environmental concerns in the United States were lead in the air, a depleting ozone layer in the stratosphere, and acid rain. Now, with the benefit of hindsight, we can ask what a larger population has meant for each of these challenges in the decades since.

Mike's son, Emmet, was born in 2013. Emmet's life didn't cause lead concentrations in the air to increase. Emmet has never ridden in a leaded-gasoline vehicle. That's because people in the United States decided that breathing car exhaust with lead in it was unacceptable. In the 1970s, the U.S. Environmental Protection Agency began phasing out leaded fuel.

Emmet's life hasn't contributed to the release of chlorofluorocarbons to tear apart the protective stratospheric ozone layer, either. That's because the advanced economies of the world essentially ended the use of a long list of CFCs by an international agreement in 1987 (the Montreal Protocol).

Acid rain was a big environmental problem that schoolchildren of the 1990s learned about in their science classes. But when Emmet was born, it didn't lead to more acid rain. That's because the U.S. government took regulatory actions to address the sulfur dioxide emissions that were causing it.

More people need not bring more greenhouse gas emissions

Some of the environmental challenges we face today, including climate change, are bigger than those we faced with lead pollution, stratospheric ozone depletion, and sulfur dioxide emissions, where humanity has already turned the corner. And yet, if Emmet someday has a child—Mike's grandchild—that child could live well past 2100. It could be that they live most of their life after greenhouse gas emissions have turned the corner, too. Maybe even after net emissions have been brought down to zero.

If so, it would be because people in the interim decided to end net greenhouse gas emissions—and developed the policy and infrastructure to do so. That future is available to us to choose, and it has little to do with the number of people on the planet. After all, the technologies, regulations, and treaties that addressed lead pollution, ozone depletion, and acid rain improved the environment while the population was growing.

The implications of one more person for greenhouse gas emissions, for biodiversity, for land use, for particulate-matter air pollution, and for every other urgent priority will depend on what we choose.

Let's clear the air

The cabin in the woods is a story. The life Mike's grandchild might live is speculation. Let's get back to facts, things we can measure and know today. Is more air pollution the straight-line consequence of more people? Here is what the data can tell us. Earlier we noted China's air pollution reductions. But it's not only China. Global average exposure to particulate air pollution has fallen sharply since 2015. All the while, the world added over 750 million people.

"More people, more problems" isn't what shows up if we compare the past with the present. What about comparing across places instead of over time? Figure 3.1 shows the relationship between air pollution and population density. Each dot is a country. For each country, we show the annual exposure to particulate pollution, using a standard measure: the concentration of tiny particles called $PM_{2.5}$, named for their diameter, 2.5 micrometers. Higher in the plot means worse pollution. Farther to the right means more people per square mile.

Air pollution is not completely contained within tidy political boundaries. Wind blows it around—sometimes a long way. And yet most of its harms happen close to its source. So the figure is informative of what countries choose in their environmental and industrial policies.

The United States shows up at the bottom and toward the left. It is not very dense. Nor is it very polluted. Its spacious skies and purple mountain majesties are mostly undistorted by particulate haze, although seasonal wildfires temporarily change the air quality. India's air, the air that Preeti's baby breathes, suffers smoke from coal-fired power plants, crop burning, industry, construction, and more. India appears among the topmost polluted countries, which would surprise nobody who knows India.

If we had only those two data points, India and the United States, then we'd end up at the wrong conclusion: more people, more pollution. But we are here for data, not for anecdotes or to be misled by incomplete comparisons. Looking over the wider world, the shape of

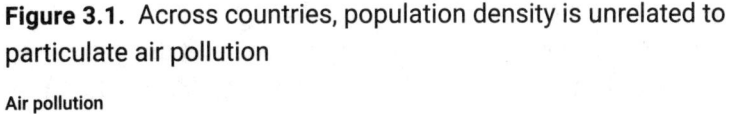

Figure 3.1. Across countries, population density is unrelated to particulate air pollution

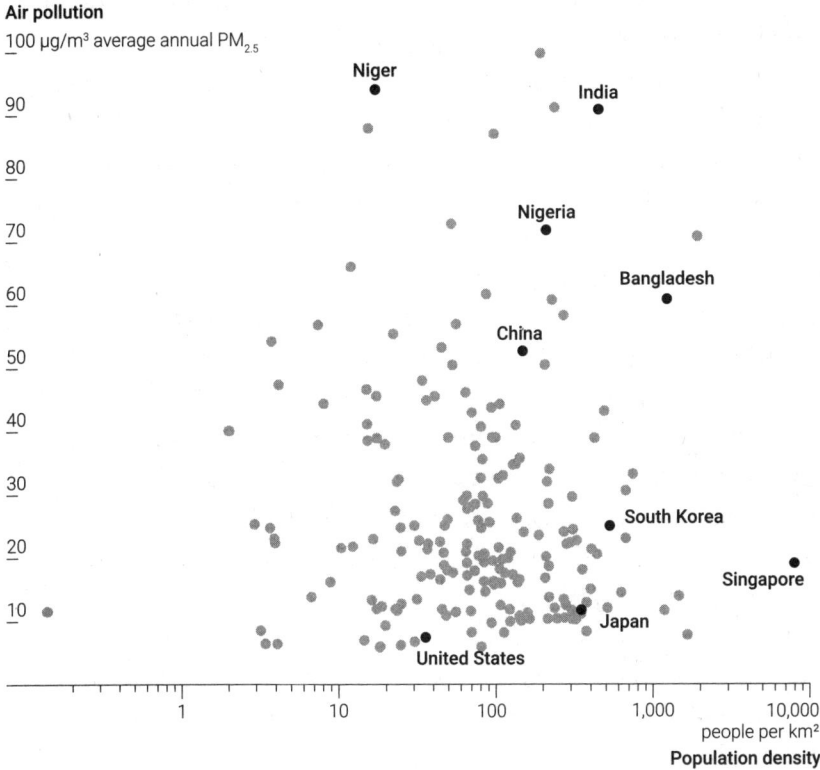

the plot is a disorganized scatter. The relationship between $PM_{2.5}$ and population density is no relationship at all. If we were searching for an example to help our students visualize what a scatter plot looks like when there is no statistical correlation, this figure would do the trick. Japan and South Korea are about as densely populated as India, but breathe much cleaner air. Niger is less dense than the United States, but has terrible air pollution.

Some low-density places, especially middle-income countries, have high $PM_{2.5}$ because they burn coal for power. Lowest-income countries with agricultural economies like Niger suffer high concentrations of air pollution because of burning agricultural waste (there's no cheaper way for poor farmers to clear their fields ahead of the next planting) and because of burning traditional fuel like wood and dung for cooking and heat. Coal-fired power plants and the practice of burning crops and solid fuels are two of the biggest contributors to $PM_{2.5}$ globally.

People in Japan and South Korea manage to live densely and prosperously without polluting their air. That's not because Japan and South Korea are somehow offshoring their particulate air pollution—displacing their coal use and crop burning to a poorer country. Japan and South Korea and Europe and plenty of other rich countries have agriculture (a lot of agriculture, in fact). They also use plenty of energy (much more than in the poorer places of the world where coal is burned). They have less air pollution because of the coal and the crops that they do not burn.

Whether more people cause more air pollution depends on what the people and their governments do. A society can have economic prosperity and a large, dense, thriving population and clean air, all without any contradiction. That can happen if the society makes investments and implements rules to keep the air clean, which often starts with public awareness.

The skies over Mexico City used to look awful. They are blue today. The environmental writer David Wallace-Wells has documented the progress:

> In the 1990s, when Mexico City was more polluted than Delhi, 80 percent of 10 and 11-year-olds asked the color of the sky responded "gray," . . . only 10 percent said "blue." Today the city only just ranks in the list of the world's thousand most polluted cities, with air as clean as the Northern French town of Roubaix, terminus of the famous cycle race.

It's not all sunshine and clear skies, of course. India's air, unfortunately, is trending in the wrong direction. Unlike in Mexico, Indians' average exposure to particulate matter has worsened in the past decade. Dean wrote a 2019 book *Air*, trying to call more attention to

Indian air pollution and to agitate for action. Our question in *this* book is whether depopulation would make anything better. And the flip of that: Would a more populous future necessarily make air pollution worse? The data give no reason to think so. Population is pushing on the wrong lever.

There is no necessary relationship, in theory, between population size and particulate air pollution. There is no actual relationship, in historical fact, either. That is not a fluke. When people and populations touch the environment, what happens next depends on what they do.

Fallout from *The Population Bomb*

In his hugely influential 1968 book *The Population Bomb*, Paul Ehrlich identified the problem standing in the way of environmental progress: "Too many people." Ehrlich warned that we faced a choice: "Population control or race to oblivion."

Ehrlich said that it was the planet or us. And really, there wasn't any actual choice. Because if we chose *us*, we'd destroy the planet, which would in turn destroy us very quickly. Ehrlich proposed that if we didn't embark on a crash program of population control, then "famine, of course, could be one way to reach a death rate solution to the population problem." There was, in Ehrlich's view of the facts, no plausible path to a future with a lot of humans in it.

Ehrlich's book, we are keenly aware, set a high bar for the popularity and influence of books about demography. It sold over 2 million copies. Ehrlich was invited to preach the prophecy of overpopulation on Johnny Carson's *Tonight Show*, a national institution. "Ehrlich's appearance prompted more calls and letters than any other guest during the preceding months," writes historian Matthew Connelly. Ehrlich, a professor of biology at Stanford, had provided apparent scientific backing for what so many knew in their gut.

Almost sixty years have passed since *The Population Bomb* dropped.

The global population has more than doubled. The future that Ehrlich ruled out as impossible—a population of, say, 8 billion—is the present we live in. His big bomb fizzled.

We'll have a lot to say about Ehrlich's ideas in chapter 5, and none of it agreeable. (Ehrlich used his massive public platform to ponder the possibility of mass involuntary sterilizations, including by poisoning public water supplies with "temporary sterilants.") For now, we'll focus on one of the enduring legacies of *The Population Bomb*: Many people today now take for granted that policies that reduce birth rates might offer a potent tool to fight climate change and other environmental harms.

Ehrlich's message is seductive. It has enough truth woven into it that it sounds right. Carbon pollution comes from human activity. So fewer humans should mean lower carbon emissions. Disruptive and destructive land use comes from human activity. So fewer humans should mean less habitat loss, less degradation, fewer species lost to human encroachment. Cut the population to save our planet. It seems simple. But let's really examine it.

What would stabilization mean for climate?

Let's focus in on the most urgent environmental challenge of our time: climate change. To examine what stabilization would mean for climate change and global temperatures, it's time to get specific about what we mean by *stabilization* and *depopulation*. Depopulation means a peak around 10 billion and then an ever-falling population. Depopulation is the Spike that you saw in chapter 1. It is humanity's business-as-usual future.

This book argues for leveling out, maintaining an approximately stable population size. Why *stabilization* (at some population size or another) and not more? Why not an ever-growing population? There are no data about what a world of 100 billion people would be like. Advocating anything like that, based on the science and knowledge of our times, would be wildly irresponsible. But all of us do know what a world with a few billion people is like. It's like the world we live in now. Beyond that, where exactly should humanity stabilize? Six billion? Eight? Ten? Some other number? This book makes the case to stabilize *somewhere*. Exactly where will have to be a question for public and scientific debate.

So figure 3.2 plots many ways that stabilization could happen. It fans out to a range of possible futures. The most realistic stabilized future—if any stabilized future is realistic—is some middle scenario. In any middle scenario, the global population peaks, then shrinks, and then manages to hold steady at some number below the top. When we say stabilization would be better than depopulation, these are the kinds of possibilities we have in mind. (If this isn't a library book, feel free to add another flat line to figure 3.2 that suits you.)

But we don't want to cheat. So when we count the climate costs of stabilization, we use the biggest possibility—the worst possibility according to Ehrlich, and the one with the greatest potential for climate damage. That's the dark line at the top, where "stabilization begins tomorrow," and the world grows to 12 billion people and holds there.

Figure 3.2. Some possible futures: depopulation or stabilization

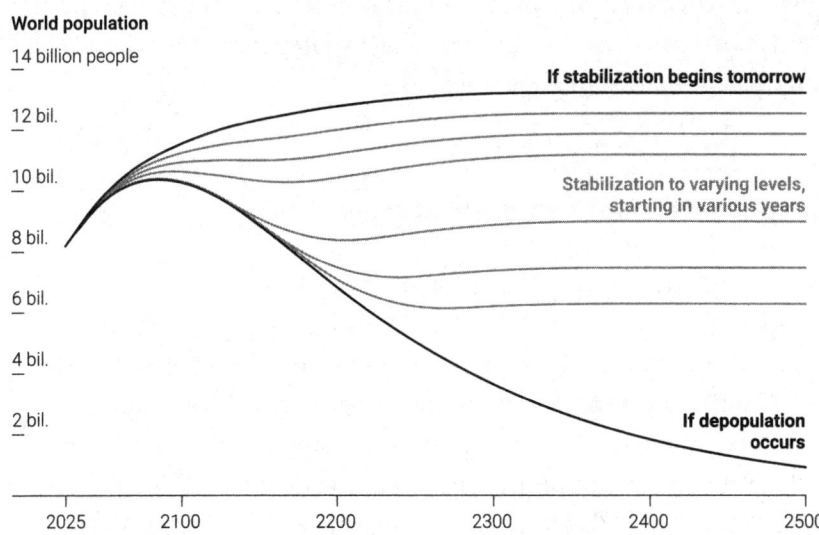

"Stabilization begins tomorrow" represents an illustrative fiction in which low-fertility societies transition to replacement birth rates now (today, this very instant!), and above-replacement places follow UN projections as their fertility drops to replacement levels. Even if stabilization begins tomorrow, it takes more than a century for stable replacement-level birth rates to work out to a stable population size.

If the world population someday stabilizes, it will matter which stabilization scenario occurs. But for the rest of this chapter, when we write *stabilization*, we mean the extreme, instantaneous scenario, where the plateau is close to the peak. Stabilizing at such a large size is not realistic. Between when we wrote this book and when you are reading it, fertility rates, we're betting, did not jump back up to two in the United States, Europe, Latin America, Southeast Asia, and elsewhere, which is the assumption needed to support such an extreme scenario. It's a good test, though, because if stabilizing at the biggest population in the figure wouldn't cause a big increase in global warming, then stabilizing in the middle wouldn't, either.

So how would stabilization and depopulation differ? Both population paths start from where humanity is. And despite how completely these eventually diverge, the two paths are similar for a few decades. That's not because the birth rates in the near term are the same. They're not. It's because even big changes to birth rates today take decades to become big changes in population size.

Conservation and momentum

In the short run of one generation or less, the global population is a very big ship, slow to turn. Here's a simplified example. Perhaps today there are 8,231,613,070 people alive. Let's round that to 8.2 billion. Imagine the greatest possible improvement in survival rates for the coming year: no deaths at all. Then how many people would be alive one year from now, assuming births (now about 132 million per year) don't change? 8.3 billion. Now, imagine instead the greatest possible reduction in fertility for the coming year: no births, but deaths proceed as usual. A year from now, there would be 8.1 billion people. Neither of these enormous, obviously impossible, 100 percent declines in death or birth rates would change the size of the population by much immediately.

That simplified example makes an important point. Changes in birth and death *rates*—even setting these to zero—cannot change the size of the population instantly. It takes time.

> **Irrelevant fact:** If the size of the human population were magically cut by half tomorrow, then we would emit much, much less greenhouse gas next month than last month.

> **Relevant fact:** Population growth operates at the timescale of generations. Cutting the population in half tomorrow is not an option, even if no more babies were ever born.

Understanding this lets us see through the flaws in some common tropes. A 2022 NPR story about schools in developing countries proposed: "Why keeping girls in school is a good strategy to cope with climate change." The idea was that more schooling will cause the next generation to choose smaller families. Education means lower birth rates, the argument goes, and lower birth rates mean fewer people. Fewer people mean less carbon pollution. It's a solution that feels good. An easy win-win.

Here's what that easy win-win story is misunderstanding: timing. In 2025 some children were born. These children will not be in first grade by the 2030 milestones laid out by climate-focused institutions like the UN's Intergovernmental Panel on Climate Change (IPCC). By 2040, they'll be teens. By the 2050 milestones set by the IPCC, humanity ought to be achieving net-zero emissions. The cohort born in 2025 will still be younger than the average age at which people today first get married in most countries in Europe and many countries in the Americas. So even if the children born today grow up in a new world in which their generation and everyone after them experienced wonderful education, and even if that caused them to have fewer children (or even zero!), it will be 2060 or later before we have any opportunity to look around and notice the missing children.

Investing more in education is a great idea for many reasons. But would it address climate change? The Paris Agreement calls for net-zero emissions by 2050. Measured at the speed of demography, 2050 may as well be tomorrow. Population decline would come fast at the level of generations, and yet far too slowly to be more than a sideshow for these challenges. If you have $2 billion, you will still be a billionaire (because of the *size* of your bank account) long after your portfolio switches from growing at 1 percent a year to shrinking at 1 percent a year. Reducing birth rates would have *some* near-term consequences. But neither accelerating nor decelerating population change could have enough effect on climate outcomes for population size to rank among the important, powerful levers to push.

If humanity peaks in the 2080s at around 10 billion, as the UN projects, and then begins a decline that continues indefinitely, there will still be more people on the planet than today's 8 billion in 2100. Decarbonizing our economies, reforming our land use and food systems, and preserving existing habitats and species all require urgent action in this decade and the next. It would be too late to start seventy-five years from now, when we would be passing our present size on the downslope of the Spike. If we wait on population decline to rescue us from environmental disaster, we will have waited too long.

Over the next few decades, while the world urgently needs to address many environmental challenges, the size of the global population is a thing we cannot change—no matter what happens to birth rates today. Hoping that the status-quo future of a shrinking population will rescue humanity from environmental responsibility today is a false hope. Climate progress, in particular, is too important to be distracted by it.

Decarbonization via depopulation?

If you understand how little the population size could deviate from its most likely path over the next few decades, then you already see that population change could not arrive in time to substitute for better climate stewardship. That is the most important realization, and it doesn't require an advanced computational model of climate change. But a few years ago, we realized that other scientists would want to see the evidence using the tools and procedures they were already accustomed to, including the precise temperature changes predicted by the computational models. (As they should!) So we set out to do so, marrying population projections from the population projectors with climate models from the climate modelers.

We assembled a multidisciplinary team to answer the question. We had worked with some of them before on research we published in *Nature Climate Change*, the *Proceedings of the National Academy of Sciences*, and other journals. But this was the biggest question this team had ever set out to answer together. Our task was to compare long-run temperatures in a stabilized future against a depopulating future.

Climate is an area where scientists have developed high-quality, quantitative models to translate from human activity to long-run global temperatures. Scientists use these models to answer questions like: "What would be the effect on long-run global temperatures if the U.S. energy grid reached 90 percent renewables by 2045?" That's not our question. But we can ask the same models: "What would be the effect on long-run global temperatures if the population stabilized rather than shrank down the path of the Spike?"

No researcher could get started evaluating such questions in these models until they specified something important: the projected pace of decarbonization. If we decarbonize slowly, then having a larger population in the future would cause more harm than if we decarbonize fast. So how fast should the model assume that humanity, through its innovation and policy and other changes, will reduce emissions per person?

To test our argument that population change is too slow to meaningfully move the needle on climate, we set up a strong challenge by assuming a pessimistic scenario. We assumed that climate progress would be slower than the world's climate experts now predict. We assumed that net-zero emissions won't happen for another one hundred years and that progress will be slow in the coming decades. In this pessimistic scenario, emissions keep increasing between now and mid-century, reaching their highest level in 2050 (which is the year when the IPCC targets net-zero emissions). That would be awful and doesn't look likely. But if we want to play it safe, evaluating the consequences of population in the bad-case climate scenario is more important than evaluating any good-case scenario. So let's work through the model in this bad-case scenario, step-by-step.

Figure 3.3 gets the model started, assuming the pessimistic future for climate policy. It shows that eventually depopulation and stabilization will lead to very different population sizes ❶. But the key word there is *eventually*. Notice the timing. Even assuming pessimistic climate policy, net decarbonization will happen in the early twenty-second century before the two population scenarios really diverge ❷. The path of stabilization instead of depopulation would eventually be the difference of many billions of lives, but in 2050 the population sizes in the two scenarios would differ by less than 2 percent. That means that, during the near-term future, when emissions per person will still be high and so the climate harms of an additional person are highest, the population difference between depopulation and stabilization will be small ❸.

Global temperature change depends on how much greenhouse gas eventually accumulates in the atmosphere. So before we trace the model all the way to *temperature change*, it makes sense to track how annual emissions add up over time to *cumulative emissions*. In figure 3.4, we tally up the cumulative emissions. It turns out that even big differences in the long-run path of the future population generate only small differences in the eventual accumulation of greenhouse gases in the atmosphere ❹.

So the extra greenhouse gas emissions contributed by the larger population would be small, even under the assumption here that the future is bleak and we go on emitting for another century. If that is surprising, remember *when* the big differences in population size kick in. Fertility rates are different from day one. But almost all of the extra lives in the stabilization path happen many decades in the future, after 2100. It takes that long for the difference in birth rates to accumulate into a meaningful difference in the population size. But by then, policies and technologies and the hard work of organizers, researchers, regulators, and entrepreneurs will have reduced emissions per person—even in the bleaker policy scenario.

And what about what really matters, temperature change? That's the conclusion: Future temperatures are *almost unchanged* across the two population paths under pessimistic policy assumptions ❺. The long-run temperature rise is 4.22°C if depopulation happens. And the long-run temperature rise is 4.28°C if stabilization happens instead. Billions of lives lived would make a small difference to this big problem.

Once we learn that cumulative emissions are only a little different between stabilization and depopulation, it makes sense that global temperatures are only a little different, too. To be clear: If humanity follows either path, depopulation or stabilization, climate change is likely to be *very bad* according to this model. (We are going to keep saying this, so nobody misunderstands us.) In the model, the global temperature increase is a whopping 4 degrees, whether the planet depopulates or not.

That's the answer for the pessimistic climate policy case. What if decarbonization happens quickly enough for a 2-degree future, on a path like the Paris Agreement? That's what is shown in the dashed lines at the bottom of figure 3.4 ❻. (Yes, there are two dashed lines printed there! It's just that the difference between them is thinner than the lines themselves.) If climate policy is close to a 2° outcome, then this huge difference in the population paths makes *zero* difference to temperature change to the third digit: The long-run temperature rise

Figure 3.3. Stabilization versus depopulation, assuming pessimistic climate policy, part 1

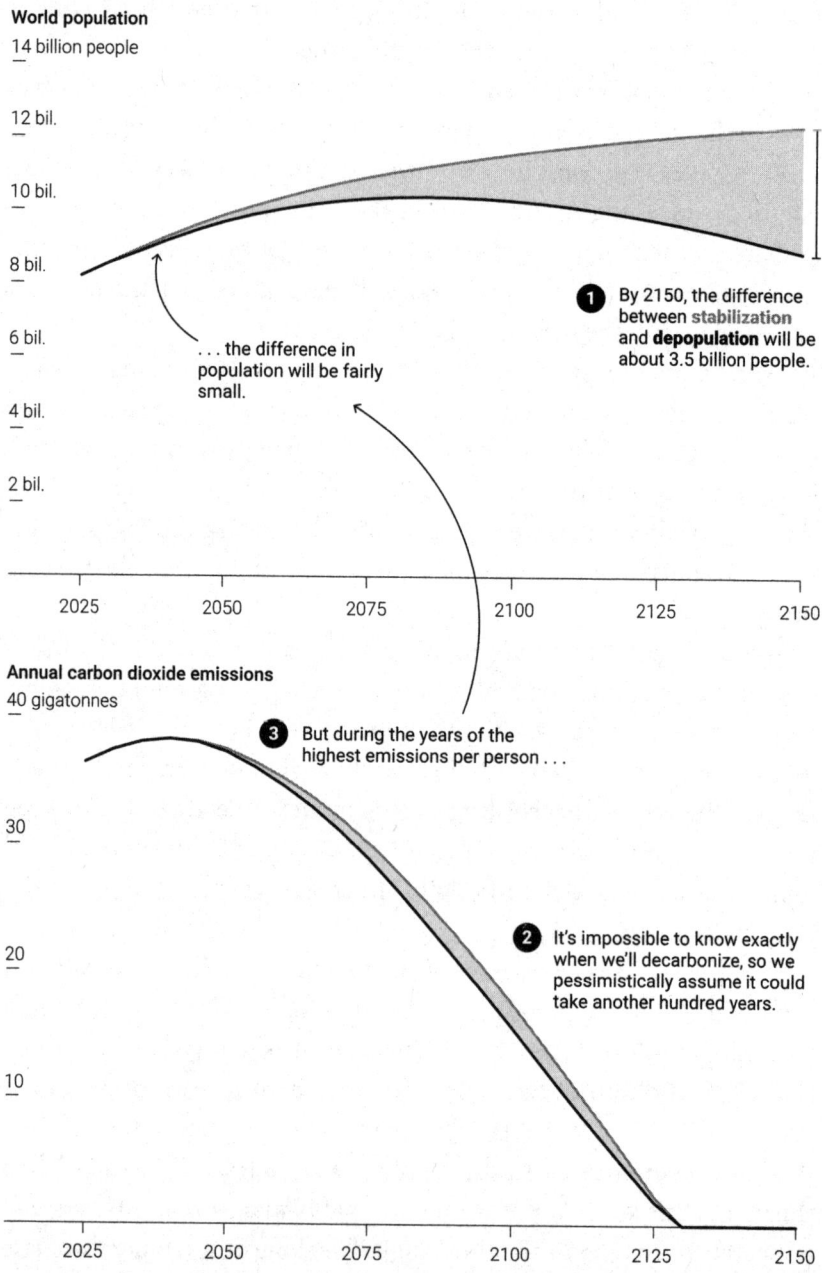

World population
14 billion people

12 bil.

10 bil.

8 bil.

6 bil.

. . . the difference in population will be fairly small.

1 By 2150, the difference between stabilization and **depopulation** will be about 3.5 billion people.

4 bil.

2 bil.

2025 2050 2075 2100 2125 2150

Annual carbon dioxide emissions
40 gigatonnes

3 But during the years of the highest emissions per person . . .

30

20

2 It's impossible to know exactly when we'll decarbonize, so we pessimistically assume it could take another hundred years.

10

2025 2050 2075 2100 2125 2150

Figure 3.4. Stabilization versus depopulation, assuming pessimistic climate policy, part 2

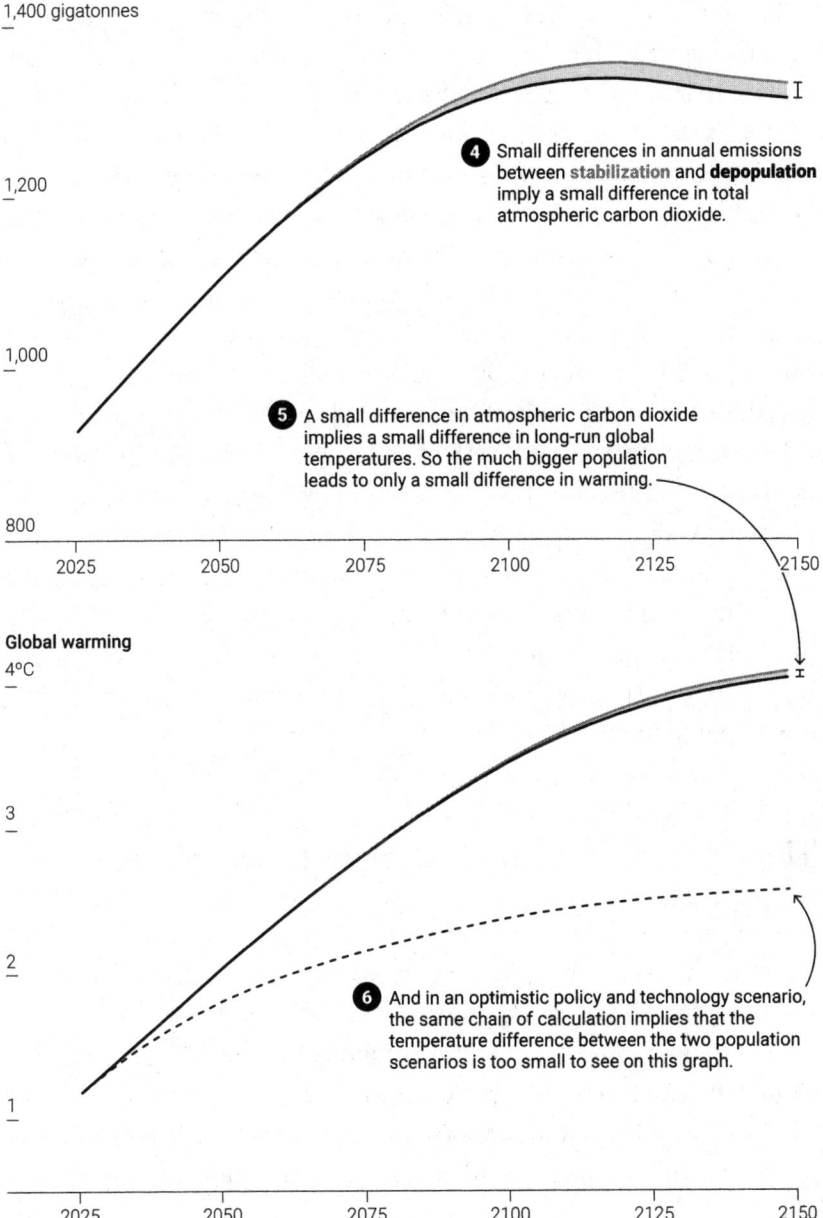

Carbon in the atmosphere
1,400 gigatonnes

4 Small differences in annual emissions between **stabilization** and **depopulation** imply a small difference in total atmospheric carbon dioxide.

1,200

1,000

5 A small difference in atmospheric carbon dioxide implies a small difference in long-run global temperatures. So the much bigger population leads to only a small difference in warming.

800

2025   2050   2075   2100   2125   2150

Global warming
4°C

3

2

6 And in an optimistic policy and technology scenario, the same chain of calculation implies that the temperature difference between the two population scenarios is too small to see on this graph.

1

2025   2050   2075   2100   2125   2150

is 2.06°C if depopulation happens. And the long-run temperature rise is 2.06°C if stabilization happens instead.

The difference between two-point-something degrees and four-point-something degrees is huge. But that's the difference that depends on decarbonization policy and technology, not on population. The difference that population can make is tiny.

And what about what we don't know, because nobody yet knows: Exactly how ambitious and successful will future decarbonization be? No model can say. It depends on choices not yet made and actions not yet taken. So far, the pace of climate action has been slower than the pledges and promises and grand speeches of world leaders to international assemblies. And it has been faster than some serious, sober-minded scientists, regulators, and observers had predicted a mere decade ago. The climate picture looked bleaker yesterday than today.

The only way to confront climate change is to reach net-zero emissions—and soon. If we do that, we will have averted the worst disaster. And if we do that, then an additional person, or an additional billion, born afterward doesn't matter for emissions. At all. Zero times 9 billion is the same number as zero times 8 billion. Climate progress may turn better or worse in the coming decades. But that will be determined by technology, social awareness, and policy, not by population size.

The kids are increasingly all right for the planet

One of our *New York Times* readers confronted us with a worrying idea: "Nothing has a bigger carbon footprint than children." And, well, yes, something like this was probably true when we were kids. We grew up in the suburban U.S. car culture of the 1980s and '90s. But not every child will be or has been as polluting as the two of us were. The people who lived over the hundred thousand years that preceded our carbon-intensive world economy were not. What about the ones who will live after it?

Hannah Ritchie is a leading fact-keeper of our times. She was head of research at Our World in Data. In her 2024 book *Not the End of the World*, Ritchie wrote, "When my grandparents were in their twenties, the average person in the UK emitted 11 tonnes of CO_2 per year. We now emit less than 5 tonnes." She goes on: "This seems hard to believe. How can my lifestyle today be more sustainable than in the 1950s? I won't pretend that I am as frugal as my grandparents. I'm more wasteful. I turn the heating on more readily. I spend many more hours powering gadgets from the electricity grid. Still, I use much less energy and emit much less carbon. Technology has made that possible." It has, and social awareness leading to policy change has made it possible, too.

How big is a child's footprint? In the United States, the average annual emissions that each person generates has been falling for over twenty years.

If annual emissions per person have been falling, what does that mean for emissions over an entire lifetime? And what if we ask this question globally, not just within the UK or the United States? Figure 3.5 plots the baby bump in carbon emissions for the global average citizen. It shows how one person's lifetime effect on emissions, added up over an assumed eighty-year lifespan, depends on when that person was or will be born. We start before 1900, using historical emissions data to see the rise and fall of our carbon-intensive lifestyles. The future is the same pessimistic projection for decarbonization that we used in our model—the 4-degree future. That means we are assuming that decarbonization would take another one hundred years, which we hope and expect will not be the case.

The plot traces the legacy of our polluting past, as a global average. Of course, no one's child is the global average child. Models like this one are the imperfect tools used by climate scientists to learn about our climate future and to inform policymaking. They are useful for seeing the big picture, even though rich babies (not babies in top hats and

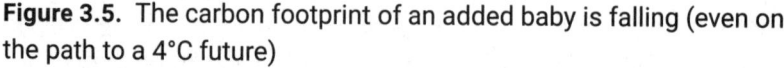

Figure 3.5. The carbon footprint of an added baby is falling (even on the path to a 4°C future)

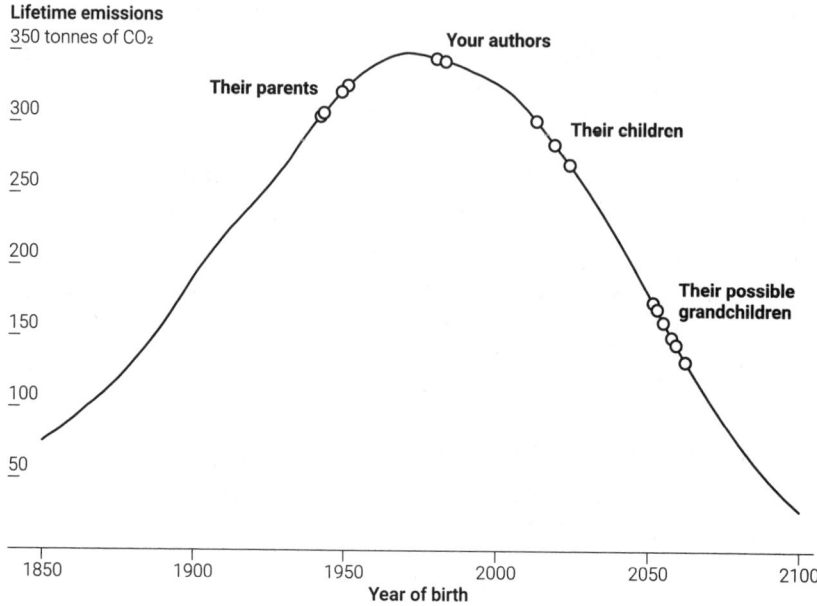

monocles; just babies born to parents in rich countries like the United States) are likely to do more harm in terms of carbon. Babies born in Uttar Pradesh or Africa or many other poorer parts of the world are likely to generate less carbon pollution—even if they might generate more particulate-matter air pollution.

Whatever the lifetime carbon footprint of a new person may be, that footprint is now falling, having peaked with people born in the 1970s. After climbing during a century of industrialization, the plot shows that we're over the hump. A globally average baby born today will accelerate global warming over their lifetime by less than an average baby born ten years ago. An average baby born ten years from now will accelerate global warming by less than one born today. The environmental costs of a new child are not zero. Not by a long shot. Not yet. But they are falling. Each new person who joins the ranks of humanity will add less CO_2 than, well, *you* over *your* lifetime. You, like us, were born in the recent past, participating in humanity's pillage of the atmosphere at or near the peak. Taking the world together as a whole, the lifetime climate footprint of an extra baby has been declining. Babies born in 2025 will live their midlives in 2075, in a world of greater climate progress.

In the fight for the environment, timing is everything

> The next fifty years are a special time. They will decide how strong and healthy the planet will be for centuries to come. Between now and 2050 we'll see the zenith, or very nearly, of the human population; with luck we'll see the maximum production of carbon dioxide, of toxic chemicals. . . . So it's the task of those of us alive right now to deal with this special phase, to squeeze us through these next fifty years.

In his 1998 book *Maybe One: A Case for Smaller Families*, environmentalist and author Bill McKibben wrote those words, arguing that choosing smaller families could make a difference for our environmental problems. This is not his most famous book. McKibben is better known for *The End of Nature*, for his organization 350.org, and for his global environmental leadership. In *Maybe One*, McKibben asked people to consider smaller families for the sake of the planet. He wrote with compassion and without telling anyone what to do with their lives.

We don't agree with everything in *Maybe One*. The book omits the population ethics that we think matters, as we say in chapter 8. And McKibben understands economic growth differently than do our friends like Seema in Uttar Pradesh, where economic growth means the sort of material progress that keeps babies alive and creates opportunities to work in a job to be proud of. But it is a humane book. We agree with a lot of what McKibben writes on the environment, and there is even an important place where we and McKibben agree on the role of population: *Timing* is everything in the fight against climate change. As McKibben explained:

> I'm not saying—crucially—that single-child families are a permanent solution. Clearly, they're not; eventually they would yield populations smaller than almost anyone would want. If I could write this book on paper that erased itself in fifty years, I would; by the middle of the next century our populations, our technologies, our desires, our predicaments may be fundamentally different. Perhaps we will want to unleash another baby boom; perhaps not. There is no way to predict. But should you happen across a yellowing copy of this book in that future time, regard it as merely a historical curiosity.

In 1998, McKibben saw a fifty-year horizon for when family size might matter for the climate. McKibben was wise to see in advance that children would not have a large environmental footprint forever, that eventually the story would change. His fifty-year future is becoming our present. By the time you are reading this book, you are closer to the end of those fifty years than to their beginning. And from where we all stand today, there is no longer any time *within those fifty years* when we can change the population size by any meaningful amount.

For the rest of McKibben's fifty years, let's act on the changing climate and against the other ways that humans put pressure on the environment. This will improve many lives in the near term and in the long term—human lives and lives of other animals, too. In the meanwhile, don't get distracted by population. Climate change is a big problem that deserves thoughtful, factful action. Make the decision for your life and your family that you think best. But influencing population trends is not on the priority list for solving the twenty-first century's climate challenges.

Chapter 4

Population starts in other people's bodies

"But who is going to *have* the babies, if birth rates ever rise?"

That's what a population science colleague asked us at a conference, after we presented the evidence for the Spike. The answer is: women. That was her point—that there is something unavoidably unequal about reproduction. The biology of human life is unequal. The culture and economics of parenting are unequal, too. Throughout history, societies have asked more of women and given more to men, even when parenting isn't involved. These are huge problems.

A stabilized population would mean more children—more childbirth and more child-rearing. For this reason and more, it is important to ask what stabilization, instead of depopulation, would mean for women. Would achieving stabilization mean rolling back hard-won gains, regressing to how things were when birth rates were higher? Any answer to that question depends on *how* the population stabilizes.

To understand the consequences for women, we must be clear on the path to stabilization that we have in mind. A path through coercion—through fewer freedoms, opportunities, and protections for women, in which people are forced or pressured to have a larger family than they want—would be a disaster. This book proposes a different path: a future in which people in free and fair societies weigh their options and, on average, decide that the best life for them would be parenting two kids. That could only happen if parenting changes for the better—more support, more flexibility, more funding, more fairness.

> **We can make a fair, stabilized future.** Humanity could choose a future that's good, free, and fair for women and men and that also has an average birth rate of two. There is no inescapable dilemma.

In that kind of future, people who want to parent would get the support that they need (from nonparents, from taxpayers, from everyone) to choose parenting. In fact, we suspect it's the only approach that could work. The evidence shows that any other approach—coercion, repression, or any form of government control—is unlikely to stabilize the global population. To make that case, we'll begin with a story.

A mess in Texas

In June 2022 in Texas, April learned that she was pregnant. For about two years, she and her husband had been trying for a second child. That happened to be the same month that the Supreme Court released a decision that overturned five decades of precedent, ending the right to abortion, if your state government says so. A draft of that Supreme Court decision had been leaked weeks before her first visit to the obstetrician. So April and her husband were worried. The chances of a miscarriage are pretty high for a forty-year-old woman like April. Would the new law mean that if there was a problem with the pregnancy, she wouldn't be able to get the care she needed?

In the examination room, April asked the doctor question after question, each begging, in different ways, to hear her say: *You will be safe.* But April and her husband were asking for assurances that no doctor could give them. So as they asked their questions, April cried. In a chair in the corner of the exam room, her husband shoved his hands between his knees to try to keep his whole body from shaking with his anxiety.

Later, alone, they talked about moving to another state. In those early months, it was impossible to know exactly how the State of Texas would cause harm to pregnant women. But they knew enough to worry. In the months that followed, women were indeed forced to carry nonviable pregnancies at significant risk to their health and lives. The law has endangered both women who wanted their pregnancies and women who wanted abortions.

April miscarried a few weeks after that initial obstetrician visit, though during a trip outside of Texas, where a small consolation was that she had less, but not zero, fear around getting the healthcare that she needed. (How much blood loss was too much? How long should the bleeding last? Why did the hospital staff seem to be holding back on confirming the pregnancy was miscarried and over?)

April and her husband decided to stop trying after that.

Over forty, the chances that the next pregnancy would lead to the next miscarriage were pretty high. They were particularly afraid of facing that possibility in Texas. State law wasn't the only reason they decided to stop trying. These decisions are always complicated. But the mess in Texas was a big consideration.

No doubt there are more women like April who have decided it's not worth the risk. Other women and other families have had and will have different experiences. We get to choose the stories that we put in our book. But we didn't select this one to tell because it fit some point we wanted to make. We didn't sift through hundreds of interviews, discarding story after story until we found the unique case where banning abortion contributed to a couple giving up on trying for a baby.

The fact is, April is married to one of your authors. Mike was the husband shaking in the exam room's corner chair. The story of April's pregnancy, miscarriage, and difficult decision isn't one we went looking for. That trouble found us.

Restricting reproductive healthcare in Texas made it harder for Mike and April to have the second child they were hoping for. In 2024, when a judge temporarily banned IVF in Alabama by declaring frozen embryos children, it made it harder for people there to have a child that they were hoping for. And yet there are people who suggest that rolling freedom backward would be a constructive response to depopulation.

Understanding why restricting reproductive freedom wouldn't be a constructive response requires answering questions of ethics and questions of fact. We address them both—ethics in chapter 8, where we discuss the moral abhorrence of forced births, and facts in chapter 10, where we discuss what nearly everyone misunderstands about the consequences of abortion bans for birth rates (and in the other direction, the consequences of China's One Child Policy). These are big questions that deserve their own separate treatments. But we can summarize as a starting point for this chapter: *What people, especially women, choose and aspire to for their families is what will matter for the future of fertility.*

Is a birth rate of two compatible with some people not wanting children?

The most plausible way humanity might stabilize—and the only way this book endorses—is if societies everywhere work to make parenting better. Yet even if they do, parenting still won't be for everybody. The stabilization birth rate is about two. Two means two *on average*, not two for everyone.

> **What average doesn't mean:** "Average" is not "for everyone." There are infinitely many family combinations that work out to an average of two.

Different countries and different communities and different generations and different people could find different paths that average out to the same fertility rate. Consider Canada and Czechia. In both countries, women born in 1973 (when today's Czechia was still part of

Czechoslovakia) grew up to have an average of 1.8 children. More than half of women in Czechia had exactly two children, but less than two-fifths in Canada did. Instead, women in Canada were more likely than women in Czechia to have three or more children. Women in Canada were also almost twice as likely as in Czechia to have zero children. Family sizes were more uniform in Czechia and more varied in Canada, but both places averaged out to the same birth rate.

Figure 4.1 samples from the many, many possibilities that could, in principle, stabilize the population. In one example possibility, two is the most common number of children. But it could be that zero, one, two, or three is the most common number and still the average is two. How could this work out? Because *most common* does not mean the same thing as *average*.

Average—in the sense of the statistical mean—is what matters for population growth. In the second example of the figure, the most common number of children is one. But there are lots of threes and plenty of twos, so the birth rate averages out to two. In the last example of the

Figure 4.1. There are many possible ways for a population's birth rates to average out to stabilization: each of these hypothetical examples averages to 2.0

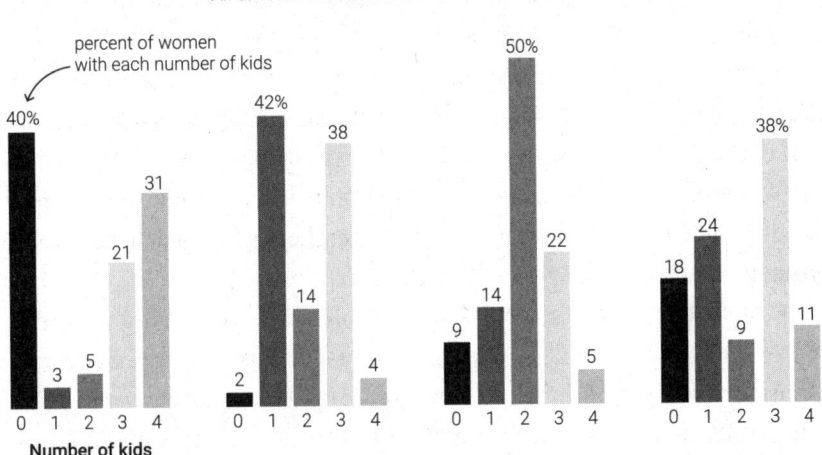

figure, three is most common, but there are lots of zeros. Even zero children, in the leftmost example, could be the most common choice in a replacement-fertility population, if there are enough large families to average together with the zeros.

None of these four examples will ever be exactly what any country or the world as a whole does. The point is that there are ways of getting to an average of two that accommodate plenty of diversity in what people want. Getting to stabilization leaves room to choose, room to be different, and room for many people to have one child or none.

Stabilization doesn't mean stagnation

In 1893, New Zealand became the first country where women could vote in national elections. In the thirteen decades since, the global birth rate has halved (at least). Humanity has made huge but incomplete progress toward better, freer, fairer lives for women and girls.

These big trends—lower birth rates over time, better lives for women over time—threaten a big dilemma. Would stabilizing the population with an average birth rate of two require progress toward gender equity to halt or reverse? Do fairer societies only emerge as birth rates fall from 2.0 to 1.8 and from 1.5 to 1.3? Must stabilization come at the cost of never achieving equity—in the workplace, in the home, in politics, in cultural power?

No. If humanity chooses, then there could be a future when half of the political leaders are women, half of the shift managers are women, half of the people talking are women, half of the people reading quietly are women, half of the grown-ups sitting around at kids' swimming lessons are women, half of the people remembering to pack lunches are women—and the average birth rate is two.

A birth rate of about two is compatible with continuing progress for women. We know it is possible because it has already happened. Consider the United States in the thirty-five-year span between 1975 and 2010. Life in America changed a lot over these years, especially for women. So what happened to American birth rates over this decades-long stretch? The answer is: not very much. In 1975, the U.S. total fertility rate was 1.77. It hovered around this level for decades, rising and falling slightly. Between 1979 and 2016, the U.S. birth rate stayed above 1.80. In 2010, it was at 1.93.

The fact that U.S. birth rates were so flat, even rising a little, over these decades is a minor anomaly in population science. We ourselves aren't quite sure why. Nor do we think anyone else has a satisfying explanation. Dean recently asked one of his PhD students about it—during the defense of her dissertation about how American women choose how many children to have. Her defense succeeded and she graduated splendidly, but she wasn't sure, either.

Europe's total fertility rate fell from 2.07 in 1975 to 1.61 in 2010. Japan's from 1.94 to 1.39. And Canada's fell from 1.85 to 1.63. So the birth rate in the United States was unusually stable over a stretch of history when it was falling in these places and many others. This anomaly isn't a big deal for the big story of the Spike. U.S. birth rates fell before this flat period, and they have been falling after it. But it is an opportunity to learn about what's possible from a special case.

If it were an iron law of social science that women's opportunities move up only when birth rates move down, then we might expect economic, social, and political progress for U.S. women also to have stagnated over these thirty-five years of flat birth rates. But the opposite is true. These years were a period of remarkable improvement.

The gender pay gap fell. Full-time, female U.S. workers in 1970 earned less than 60 percent, as an annual average, of what males did. By 2010 this ratio was over 75 percent. That's not equality, but the trend pointed in the right direction, even as birth rates weren't moving in any direction. Year after year, the General Social Survey has asked Americans: "Do you approve or disapprove of a married woman earning money in business or industry if she has a husband capable of supporting her?" In 1972, when the birth rate was 2.01, 65 percent of Americans approved of women working. By 1998, when the birth rate was an almost-identical 1.99, 81 percent approved. In her book *When*

Everything Changed, writer Gail Collins explains: "In the 1970s the nation came to grips with the fact that most women were going to work outside the home. But it was in the 1980s that the country got used to the idea that women would not only make money to help support the family but also have serious careers." The General Social Survey stopped asking this question after 1998—itself a sign of progress because researchers want to ask questions where there are disagreements, not near unanimity. When CNN asked a similar survey question in a 2012 poll, only 2 percent disapproved.

Girls today see a bigger, better set of options and possibilities for what their lives might include. In 1960, no woman had yet been on the U.S. Supreme Court, or on the Indian Supreme Court, or among the British Law Lords, or in the Boston Marathon. No woman had become CEO of a Fortune 500 company. No woman had yet been a president of an Ivy League university. That wouldn't happen until the 1990s. At Princeton, where the two of us got our PhDs, even the first class of female *undergraduates* didn't graduate until 1973. In 1960, no women had raced in the Indianapolis 500, had been ordained a priest of the Church of England, or had been recognized by FIFA as a referee. All of these have happened since. It was in 1981 that the first woman joined the U.S. Supreme Court. Collins marvels to remember that an American generation "born into a world where women were decreed to have too many household chores to permit them to serve on juries, and where a spokesman for NASA would say that 'any talk of an American spacewoman makes me sick to my stomach,' would come of age in a society where female astronauts and judges were routine."

By the late 1970s in the United States, more women than men earned associate's degrees. They have every year since. By the early 1980s, more women than men earned bachelor's degrees. They have every year since. By the late 1980s, more women than men earned master's degrees. They have every year since. By the early 2000s, more women than men earned doctoral degrees. They have every year since.

In 1974, the Equal Credit Opportunity Act made it illegal to discriminate by gender in making loans. Before then, a woman might not be able to get a credit card without a husband and his signature. California became the first U.S. state to permit no-fault divorce in 1970, making it much easier for women there to leave bad marriages. In 2010, New York became the last state to permit it. Marriage changed again in 2015, when the Supreme Court recognized a constitutional right to same-sex marriage. Today a woman can have a marriage, a divorce, and a credit card, all without ever having had a husband.

Don't misinterpret the story of these thirty-five years in the United States. Just like any other thirty-five-year stretch, progress wasn't inevitable. But the fact that these improvements happened during the decades when birth rates were flat does tell us that combining birth rates of about two with continuing progress toward equity is an achievable goal. It is a proof of concept. It is only one example, but it is one decades-long example that refutes the too-simple claim that improvements cannot happen without birth rates falling.

Is a birth rate of two compatible with fairness in the workplace?

Let's look beyond a few decades and beyond the borders of the United States, comparing statistics across countries today. A key economic indicator of gender inequality is the gender pay gap: How much less does an economy pay the typical woman compared to the typical man? The pay gap doesn't say everything about a country's social institutions, economics, or politics, but it matters and it gets attention. So figure 4.2 asks how a country's gender pay gap relates to that country's birth rate: Are these two measures linked? Or does the evidence permit more variation and flexibility?

We plot the difference in median earnings between women and men. A number like 17 percent (the U.S. statistic) says that the typical,

Figure 4.2. Lower birth rates aren't associated with a smaller gap between male and female pay, among richer countries

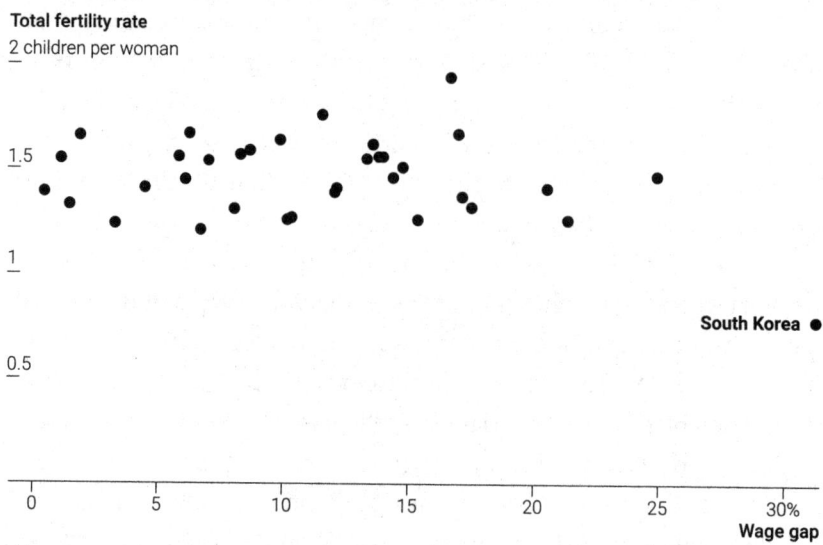

middle-of-the-earnings-distribution man who is working full-time makes 17 percent more than the typical, middle-of-the-earnings-distribution woman who is working full-time.

We use data on countries in the OECD, which is a group of thirty-eight of the world's richer countries—the United States, many European countries, some richer East Asian countries, and a few Latin American countries like Chile and Mexico—all of which score highly on measures of human development. Fertility for nearly all of the countries in the figure falls between 1.0 and 2.0. That's the right range for understanding this relationship in rich, present-day, below-replacement countries. These data are not informative of, say, historical societies or preindustrial times, but those settings aren't relevant for our questions here, which are about the present and future.

What does the evidence say about fertility and fairness? Is there a tight connection?

What the figure shows is . . . nothing. There is no relationship. Japan, Spain, and Italy, for example, have the same total fertility rate of 1.3. But the pay gap is 21 percent in Japan, 7 percent in Spain, and 3 percent in Italy. Ireland has one of the highest birth rates in Europe, 1.8, which it combines with a low pay gap of 2 percent. France and New Zealand have about the same birth rate as Ireland, both with a pay gap over 9 percent.

What if a statistician tried to fit a line to these points, to plot the average relationship? It would be flat, meaning there is no correlation between birth rates and pay gaps. And more important: Many of the points would be far from that average line. Ignoring the outlier South Korea, variation in the gender pay gap explains less than 0.2 percent of the variation in the birth rate among these points. That's two parts out of one thousand. That's a technical way of saying that birth rates, in these data, depend on *something else.*

What if we compared U.S. states instead—and even better, changes over time within each state? The economist Melissa Kearney and her coauthors did that in 2022. They found a similarly patternless cloud of points. Birth rates have not fallen any faster, they showed, in U.S. states where the gender pay gap has closed more quickly.

What if we compared developing countries, instead of OECD countries or U.S. states? We can't use the exact same pay gap measure because "work" means something different in a richer country than in a poor country, where work is often informal and so no directly comparable data exist. But consider neighbors Bangladesh and India. In their most recent demographic surveys, Bangladesh had a birth rate of 2.3, slightly higher than India's 2.0. Yet women in Bangladesh were a little more likely to be literate and a lot more likely to work for pay than in India. So once again, there's no tight link tying better work opportunities for women to lower birth rates.

And in our graph of OECD countries, why did we ignore South Korea? So that nobody would be distracted by an outlier. But it would only strengthen our case to include it. Off to the bottom right, South Korea has the most highly unequal gender pay gap, and it has the lowest birth rate. And although the graph doesn't plot this, not quite as many women work for pay in South Korea as in other rich countries.

All by itself, the one data point of South Korea (or any other country) wouldn't be evidence of much. It is certainly *not* evidence that backsliding on fairness would be a foolproof way to raise birth rates, because the relationship it shows is the opposite.

If we didn't drop the South Korea outlier, then the trend line fit to this cloud of data points would claim that a fairer society goes with higher birth rates. Maybe it does—or could someday. We have heard experts argue that South Korea has low birth rates *because* its high gender inequality especially penalizes mothers. Narae Park is an economist in Seoul and a coauthor of some of Dean's research. She told us that, even though South Korea's economy has grown quickly, "cultural norms have not changed as quickly." Women there are well educated, on average, but if they have a baby, women are the primary caregivers, Park says. So Korean women hesitate to get married and have children because they have much to lose, and because unequal norms mean that they can expect to lose it. If Park is right, then building a more equitable South Korea would be a needed first step toward stabilization there.

What about broader measures of wellbeing? Sweden and Denmark are the two countries at the top of the EU's Gender Equality Index, which includes more than pay. It incorporates indicators like time use, power, health, and violence against women. Both countries have higher birth rates than the two countries at the bottom, Greece and Hungary. So that means that among these countries, people are choosing to have more children in the places with better records on equality.

While we were writing this book, we heard the same thing from Jessica, a twenty-six-year-old from Peru. She said that she will never get married and have children because men where she's from are too macho. And they never take care of children, she said. A data point from South Korea, statistics from Europe, and testimony from Peru are not final social scientific proof, but they all suggest the same way forward. Fairness isn't incompatible with stabilizing the population. Fairness might be the only way to stabilize the population.

Is a birth rate of two compatible with fairness at home?

The economist Claudia Goldin wrote about gender inequality in elite careers in her 2021 book *Career and Family*. Some jobs and professions, Goldin said, are especially greedy because the greatest rewards are only available to somebody who is ready and willing to work all the time. With no children, both spouses could choose to work a greedy job. But in a two-parent family, it may be logistically plausible for only one to do so. Both mom and dad can't say yes to work travel in the same week. Two parents can't each work a twelve-hour day if the day care is closed, or the kid is sick. "As college graduates find life partnerships and begin planning families," Goldin explains, "in the starkest terms they are faced with a choice between a marriage of equals and a marriage with more money."

Goldin's insight was that even a small tilt toward dads in elite, greedy careers could generate a very large gender gap in top pay. There is statistical evidence to support this theory. For example, the average pay gap grows wider once women reach the age where the conflict between having a career and being a mother becomes sharp. Women whose careers are rocketing at age thirty are often tumbling back down to earth by forty, by which time, for many, the unstoppable force of a greedy job has pressed against the immovable object of a needy toddler.

Goldin's achievements are especially elite. She won a Nobel Prize in 2023. But not everybody has elite, greedy careers. Most families don't even have one such elite earner. Even so, Goldin's theory and statistics do say something important about everybody: Part of what happens in the job market depends on what happens in the home. For richer and for poorer households, what happens at home is unequal, too.

It's hard for statisticians to see behind the closed doors of a family, but the U.S. Bureau of Labor Statistics tries. On a typical day in 2021, the BLS reports, "21 percent of men did housework—such as cleaning or laundry—compared with 49 percent of women." On a day that she does housework, the average woman spends 2.7 hours on it, compared with 2.1 hours for a man. In families with children younger than six years old, the average woman spends 1.2 hours physically caring for the child, compared with 0.5 hours for a man. In this statistic, that means not also doing something else: the BLS is counting only *dedicated* feeding, washing, dressing, chasing, wiping, redressing. Women spend over twice as long as men, in these families, on what the surveyors call "education-related activities" and "travel related to care of household children." The table has a footnote in the box that should report how much time average men spend attending children's events on weekdays. The note explains: "Estimate is approximately zero."

Of course, those statistics don't apply to *everybody*. Perhaps you are a father reading this, and you are the stay-at-home parent, while your wife brings home the bagels. Or maybe you are a single dad. Or maybe your child has two dads and zero moms. If so, you are the statistical exception, not the rule. Statistics will never reproduce the texture of everyone's life (or the texture of anyone's life, in particular). But these data cut through the personal details and exceptions to tell us what's true overall.

The clearest reason why stabilization need not be bad for women is that men could and should do more parenting and housework, across the many years it takes to raise a child.

> **It takes more than nine months.** It takes many years to make a new person. That means there's plenty of time for men to even things out.

Males cannot get pregnant. But they can do so much else: They can clean breast pump parts, get up at 3 a.m. to soothe a crying baby, cook the evening meal even though they're tired, process the laundry from floor to drawer, and there is plenty more. Fathers can pack snacks, handle the calls and messages from day care and school, and be the parent a two-year-old looks for, whines at, or *needs* to show a toy. Dads can drive to swim lessons, tumbling class, and birthday parties, even when it's inconvenient. Men can choose to take the work and the responsibility and the risks (to careers, attention, clothes, sleep) that go into making a two-year-old, a three-year-old, and a four-year-old. Plus, of course, the "big kid" years, then preteens, tweens, and teens. So before anybody expects more parenting out of women, they should expect more parenting out of men. If you stumbled across this book in a future archive, we hope this paragraph is a confusing anachronism. (*Did fathers not parent back then?*)

While we're at it, everyone else should do more parenting, too. You started out as a helpless baby—a digestive tract with adorable eyes and ridiculous limbs. If everybody has a widely shared interest in the population stabilizing (and we're assuming for this paragraph that everybody does), then everybody should widely share the burdens of making it happen.

To spell that out: There are about forty years in working-age mid-adulthood. If somebody raises two kids, then they have a little kid for, say, ten of those forty years. So that makes a quarter of adulthood, on average, doing the intensive work of parenting little kids and leaves three-quarters available to offer some support to the people doing their quarter.

Goldin is right that, on top of the cultural habits of inequality, there are powerful economic incentives to choose an unequal family. It is no solution to ignore those incentives. We'll write more about what non-parents (and people who are at the moment not parenting little kids) could do in Part IV. For now, anyone who feels skeptical about the possibility of a future in which care work is more broadly shared has all the more reason to expect that depopulation is a very likely future.

But wait, some unequal burdens of motherhood are inherently biological and can't be changed. Right?

Women, if they are pregnant, might get miserable, unrelenting nausea for months. Men, if their partners are pregnant, will not. That's unequal. It is one reason that perfectly equal parenting—dividing the exact same burdens and joys in two—would be impossible.

Moms and dads and parents and nonparents will never have the same, equal experiences. In any foreseeable future, parenting will indeed be unequal. Women carry the baby, give birth, and face the risks of giving birth—some bigger (death) and some smaller (never being able to have a big laugh again without peeing a little). Women either breastfeed or don't, neither of which is uncomplicated and painless.

In a world of stubborn inequality, this sort of biological difference might feel especially intractable. There's nothing anybody can do to change the fact that evolution gave our species sexual reproduction. So there's nothing anybody can do to change these inherently unequal burdens. Right?

Well, no. Biology doesn't get the last move. Funders, doctors, and researchers get to decide what to do about it. For example, there's already Diclegis, first approved a decade ago for treating morning sickness. And some dedicated researchers are doggedly pursuing treatments for the most severe forms of nausea and vomiting during pregnancy. Unfortunately for women's health, what funders often decide is to spend money elsewhere. It's an old and unresolved problem that more research funding is available for men's health than for women's health. "Before the NIH Revitalization Act was passed" in 1993, an editorial in *Nature* recalls, "it was both normal and acceptable for drugs and vaccines to be tested only on men—or to exclude women who could become pregnant."

Funding is not the only challenge. There are other headwinds against medical trials with pregnant women and fetuses. Ethical review boards ask more questions. There's something right about that. But we suspect that there would have already been more progress at making pregnancy better if review boards put an appropriate amount of weight on pregnant women's wellbeing. It is a *choice* to not work harder to make pregnancy better. You can make a lot of research progress without giving anyone any experimental drugs or doing anything scary.

Choices are about priorities. Choices by researchers, choices by research-funding agencies about what to pursue and whose wellbeing to worry about, choices by academic departments about who to hire and who to promote are all about priorities. There are many ways that pregnancy and its biological equipment cause health trouble for women that they do not cause for men. And there are many potential discoveries and innovations that could make pregnancy better or improve women's health, but so far remain undiscovered. Nobody chose to do, fund, or reward the research that might have led to them. This situation is a problem, but it points to an opportunity. We should and could choose differently.

•

Let's return to where we started. It was indeed an important question that our colleague asked: "Who is going to *have* the babies?" But we might ask other, different questions, too: "Who would work to raise the children?" is a different question. "Who would support that work?" is a different question yet again. And here's one more question: Whose job is it to do the work of changing parenting, changing our economies, and changing our priorities (in culture, in science, and everywhere else) so that women and men who want to can choose to parent an average of two children in a good, free, stabilized future? That question is at the heart of this chapter. We say it's everyone's job.

Some good ideas would be simple. Investing in science that can prevent nausea in pregnancy would directly make women better off. Some good ideas will be hard. Changing social priorities would be worthwhile, but there is inertia that maintains the unequal structures that separate "care work" from "important work," for example. And care work isn't just about parents. What non-mothers and nonparents and not-yet-parents and not-yet-grandparents contribute is a social choice. That means these sorts of changes won't be simple, but they are an option. They are possible.

This isn't just happy rhetoric. On the contrary, it's a challenge with no guarantee of success. As we explain in Part IV, the future of parenting will be *chosen parenting*, so stabilization will only happen if it sounds good to the billions of individual decision-makers—that is, to the potential parents. There is no unavoidable conflict between good lives for women and avoiding depopulation. But there is a lot of work to do.

Chapter 5

Adding new lives to an imperfect world

What if there isn't enough to go around? Specifically, what if there wouldn't be enough for everyone *if* humanity chose to stabilize its numbers rather than to depopulate? What if depopulation is the only way to avoid creating lives full of want and suffering?

If the planet is indeed overstuffed to the point of misery, that would be a good reason to embrace depopulation. Is life for future generations likely to be so bad that we'd do a favor to children by not having them?

Like you, we have never lived in the future. But we can compare facts about the present with the facts about the past. Our present isn't perfect, and the future won't be, either. Sometimes when humanity has taken three steps forward, it's taken one step backward, too. But the facts are clear:

> **There can be enough for everyone.** The data tell us that lives are better now than lives were in the past—even though there are now many more lives around. Fears of a depleted, overpopulated future are out of date.

This chapter confronts the gloomy view that most lives in the future won't be worth living. That gloomy view about the prospects for humanity's future relative to humanity's present is often rooted in a misunderstanding of wellbeing in humanity's present relative to humanity's past. Yes, there are lives that we all should work to improve. But the chances for a good life for a child are at least as high now as they have ever been, in all of human history. Ever more parents can expect good lives for their children. It's true in Texas, it's truer than ever before in Uttar Pradesh, and it's true averaging over the whole world.

We are hardly the first to see that life is getting better and write about it. You've already heard from Hannah Ritchie about environmental progress in chapter 3. In chapter 4, Gail Collins told of the improvements for American women. We personally learned the story of better lives for the global poor back when one of our PhD advisers was Angus Deaton, whose life's work is carefully studying the wellbeing of the poor.

But whenever anyone tells the truth that global living standards have been improving fast, the pessimists race to doubt. Some object that the economy is undeniably getting worse, that everyone is further away from having enough money to afford a good life than in generations past. Others object that even if incomes are rising, talking about money focuses on the wrong goal, ignoring the truly important markers of sufficiency and wellbeing. So we're not going to focus on rupees or dollars in this chapter, even though more rupees would make Preeti, her baby, and their nurse, Seema, better off. We're going to focus instead on improvements in health, nutrition, and survival. These metrics of wellbeing are objective, straightforward, and can be measured and compared around the world and over time.

We start with one of the oldest, most common tropes of insufficiency on an overcrowded planet: food.

More mouths to feed

Mike was having breakfast with his family on a Saturday morning a couple years before he wrote this book. He was dividing up some pastries to share with his father, Bob, his son, Emmet, and April. "Let me ask you something," said Bob. "These people saying we need to increase fertility rates—what are they thinking?" A fair question for his economist-demographer son. Bob shook his head while Emmet had a big bite of zucchini bread. Mike had scraped off the cultured butter and flaky salt for Emmet and Bob. Neither of them liked it. He passed the extra to April. "What about famine?" Bob paused as Mike handed over some of the savory-sweet kouign amann, this week with pistachios. "Shouldn't we worry about feeding the people already on this planet?" Bob took a bite and waited for an answer.

Mike understands where his father is coming from. Bob was born in 1943, when the world's population was less than a third as large as today. He grew up poor in the small industrial city of Woonsocket, Rhode Island. He shared a single bed with his two older brothers in a small home. He rarely had a new piece of clothing as a child, taking hand-me-downs from Tommy and Tony—often clothes that they themselves had received secondhand. Bob drank government-surplus powdered milk. And even if his world today is one of abundant baked goods, he hasn't forgotten that basic necessities weren't guaranteed to him as a child and aren't guaranteed to others today. Mike promised to think about Bob's question and bring back some answers. Bob's question and our answers became this chapter.

Generations of Americans, including Mike's father, formed their views on population in the shadow of Paul Ehrlich and his 1968 book *The Population Bomb*. The book opens this way:

> The battle to feed all of humanity is over. In the 1970s and 1980s hundreds of millions of people will starve to death in spite of any crash programs embarked upon now. At this late date nothing can prevent a substantial increase in the world death rate . . . [humanitarian aid] programs will only provide a stay of execution unless they are accompanied by determined and successful efforts at population control.

Ehrlich's announcement of a population bomb was not intended as mere scholarship. It was a call to action that he hoped would be met with a policy response. The book's cover threatened "population control or race to oblivion." The prescriptions have changed from 1968. It is no longer fashionable to advocate for "population control." (Beyond fashionable, it's no longer socially permissible in many groups.) But the catechism of Ehrlich endures. It is an article of faith, for many, that we must curb population growth or face endless famine.

How not to solve famine

Ehrlich and his intellectual heirs imagine famine as a biological or arithmetic inevitability. The productive capacity of the Earth is limited, they say, so as the population grows, something's got to give. If there were fewer people, then there would be fewer calories needed to feed them and therefore less famine. The concept is intuitive, mathematical, and tidy. But as a matter of historical fact about human populations, it is false. Famines, in modern times, are not caused by humanity's inability to produce calories.

Famines today are *political* events: most often driven by armed conflict, though sometimes driven by the terrible policy choices of the regimes in power. This observation has been made many times. The formulation by Nobel Prize–winner Amartya Sen is the most well-known. According to Sen, no democracy has ever experienced a famine. That is not because democracy can prevent droughts, floods, or crop blights—though good governance could lessen the pain of these. Democracies are accountable to voters. So if there is food to be had—and in today's world, there always is food somewhere—then democratic governments will deliver it. Some have quibbled with Sen's categorical claim. India has enduringly combined elections and chronic under-nutrition, for example. But the people who dedicate themselves to addressing famines understand famines as political events.

The famine-focused charity Oxfam is not focused on bioengineering higher-yield grains. Nor is it lobbying to convert more of the rich world's acreage to farmland. These would be sensible top priorities if the ultimate cause of famine were that too few calories can be grown. Oxfam's country director for Somalia put it this way in 2013, following a terrible famine there: "Famines are not natural phenomena, they are catastrophic political failures."

The most straightforward way to debunk the notion that the world doesn't produce enough calories to feed us all is to see what has happened to the availability of calories as the population has grown. Figure 5.1 plots available calories per person from 1961 until today, using data from the UN Food and Agriculture Organization.

Mike showed this figure to his father, Bob, to answer his question. The figure goes as far back as the available data allow—to a few years before Ehrlich pronounced in 1968 that the near future could not avoid

Figure 5.1. Increasing calorie availability per person, from Ehrlich until now

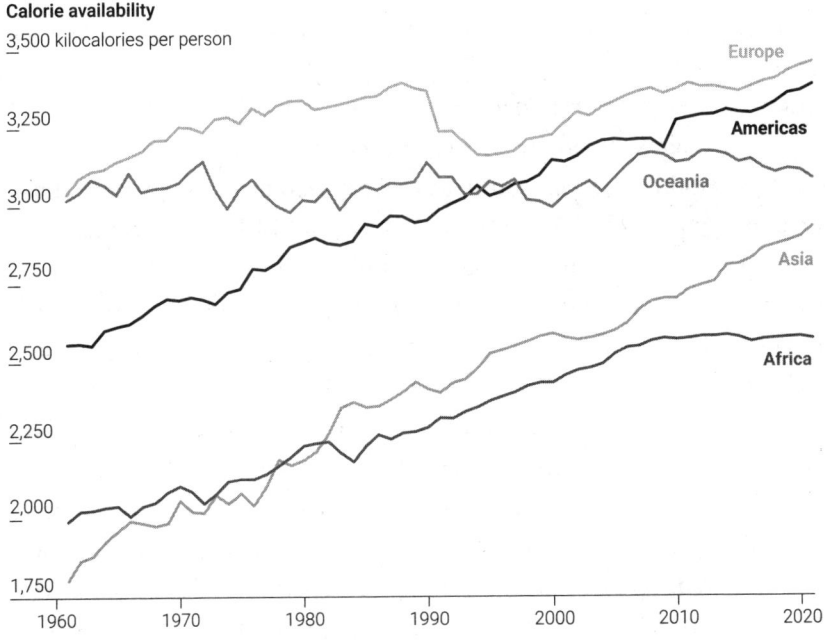

famine. Between 1961 and 2020, the world's population more than doubled, from 3.1 billion to 7.8 billion. Population growth happened on every continent, although at varying rates. Growth was slowest in Europe and fastest in Asia. And in every continent over the past sixty years—the slow growers and the fast growers alike—per capita calorie availability has increased. Increased! Bob changed his mind when he saw this chart.

Ehrlich had the facts backward. Humanity did not starve to death in the 1970s or the 1980s. We "survived the population bomb," as demographer David Lam announced, tongue-in-cheek, in his 2011 presidential address to the Population Association of America. By Lam's accounting: "World food production increased faster than world population in every decade since the 1960s." Globally, we now produce about 50 percent more food per person than in 1961.

Inching toward healthier childhoods

There is an easier way than counting calories to see that nutrition has been improving. We can measure the history of global nutritional success in the heights of populations around the world.

The average person in developing countries is shorter than the average person in richer countries. The difference is especially large for older generations. An average American will feel tall standing in a group of older adults from a developing country. The older adults were children when food was scarcer than today. When people eat well during childhood, they grow toward their full height potential, which is short for some and tall for others. But when calories are scarce, or when infection or diarrhea claims them, our bodies stay smaller. People who might have been tall grow up to be short. People who might have been short grow up to be shorter. There isn't much systematic genetic difference in height potential around the world. People's genes don't set them up to be much taller in, say, northern Europe than they do in Asia. Adults are short in the poor world today for the same reason that Europe's ancient graveyards contain small skeletons: because of what people ate when they were children and because of the nutrition that they lost to disease.

This imprint of early-life nutrition matters beyond the surface-level irrelevance of height itself. The same poor nutrition that can keep us from reaching our genetic height potential affects our cognitive development, too, and leads to physical ailments later in life. For that reason, an important tool of the trade for demographers focused on health in developing countries is a tape measure. Dean is often reminded of Ehrlich's alarmist book because, a few pages after his jarring introduction, Ehrlich confesses to being frightened by "people, people, people, people" in the dense interior of old Delhi. Based on Ehrlich's description, Dean pictures a spot that couldn't be too far. If you get down from the Delhi Metro at Chandni Chowk, you might find the people, people, people, people Ehrlich feared. Nearby, there is an alley where pre-owned electrical outlets are sold. Through it, you can find Dean's favorite shop for baby scales, measuring tape, and other supplies for research and practice in infant healthcare.

Here is what researchers' tape measures show: Compared with past decades, children in India are visibly taller. The average Indian five-year-old, for example, is 0.7 inches taller in the most recent data than in data from only fifteen years earlier. Figure 5.2 shows a large and fast improvement that has nothing to do with genetics. It's a healthier, cleaner, better-stocked environment where children are better nourished.

Ehrlich dramatized his overpopulation fears in India. Still today, too many babies in India's disadvantaged states start life underweight and at risk because their moms are undernourished—even in the same multigenerational households where other household members aren't undernourished. (Those households aren't democracies, which might be the start of a response to Sen.) The recent history of global malnourishment is one of many fact patterns that combines the dual truths that *things are better than they used to be* and *we have work to do.*

Figure 5.2. Children in India (like people everywhere) are taller than they used to be

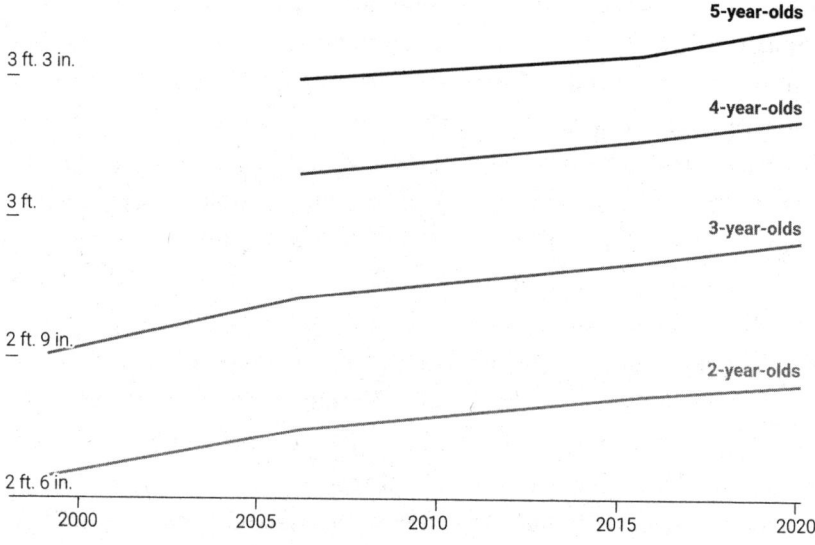

Child height

Whether people are happy and have good lives is the most important thing. That's hard to measure for populations today and wasn't measured for populations in the past, so we cannot plot a graph of happiness across the decades or centuries. But we can plot the calories and inches, and we can know whether people's basic material needs are better met today. Whether you measure progress in food production or in the size of children, nutrition has only been getting better—including at the center of Ehrlich's bogeyman fantasy.

•

Further increasing food production would be a false solution to hunger, even in poor places. It would also be a false solution to food insecurity where you live. Like us, you probably get your food from a well-stocked, hygienic grocery store. It's called H-E-B or Walmart in Texas and Lulu Hypermarket in Lucknow, the capital of Uttar Pradesh. But stocking those shelves even deeper wouldn't address hunger in your city or town. In the U.S. and similar economies, we would not think that increasing domestic agricultural output would end the need for food pantries, SNAP (food stamps), or other poverty-relief programs. So why make that mistake when considering other places?

Thinking that hunger is a problem of calorie availability is like thinking that racial or caste or gender discrimination in labor markets is a problem of not enough good jobs to go around. These are serious problems because they are problems of politics, economics, and societies. We would not lack the material abundance to address them if there were a political will.

Tungsten shortages and other childhood fears

In *The Population Bomb*, Ehrlich did not stop at famine. He predicted material want of every kind. Raw materials would become scarcer and scarcer as our ravenous species scoured the Earth, devouring and discarding and devouring again. In the 1960s, the concern was commodities like oil and tungsten. If we were to adopt Ehrlich's fears in 2025, we might worry about running short of the copper needed for electric car motors or lithium for batteries. If we had adopted Ehrlich's posture in the middle of the nineteenth century, we might have been distressed over dwindling whale oil supplies. How will we keep our lamps burning?! Ahab used his last breath to curse at Moby Dick. A century and a half later, high school readers need a lesson in economic history to understand why anyone would want to harpoon a whale in the first place.

Ehrlich's primary intellectual opponent on the public stage was Julian Simon, an economics professor. Where Ehrlich saw a world of meager crumbs to fight over, Simon saw innovation and adaptation. In Simon's formulation, human ingenuity was the ultimate renewable resource. Simon claimed that raw materials would only become *less* scarce as our technology advanced.

Simon offered Ehrlich a wager in 1980. After ten years, Simon bet, the inflation-adjusted prices of natural resources would fall below their 1980 levels. This would mean that the scarcity problem had improved. Simon was so confident in his claim that he offered Ehrlich the choice of which materials the bet would cover—food, minerals, whatever scarcest resources Ehrlich liked.

Ehrlich took the bet. Ehrlich did not choose any foods, despite his warnings of certain famine and starvation. Instead, Ehrlich and his expert advisers chose chromium, copper, nickel, tin, and tungsten. They created a basket of these commodities worth $1,000 in 1980. If the inflation-adjusted price of the basket rose by 1990, Simon would pay Ehrlich however much more the basket cost at 1990 prices. If prices fell, then Ehrlich would pay Simon however much less the basket cost.

Mike was a fourth grader at the end of the 1980s, a little before that bet would resolve. He had no idea about it. But he was terrified about the global supply of tungsten. A school lesson that year raised the alarm that tungsten was running out. It seemed an obvious and intractable problem. Tungsten, with its high melting point, was the only suitable material for incandescent light bulb filaments. Mike knew from first-hand experience that light bulbs often burned out (particularly when you melted crayons against the bulb of your little red desk lamp and *particularly* when you burned your fingers and then knocked over the lamp, jerking back your hand). Mike went through a lot of bulbs. Soon, there would be no bulbs available. No bedtime stories, no melting crayons. There is a certain kind of kid who can fixate on a problem like that. Mike was that kind of kid. He spent a lot of nights lying in bed, staring toward his night-light, thinking about tungsten.

Tungsten did not run out. When the bet ended in October 1990, Ehrlich cut a check to Simon for $576. The basket was over 50 percent cheaper in real terms. Advances in mining and smelting brought down the prices of chromium and nickel. Tin, copper, and tungsten got cheaper as we found alternative materials to do their jobs. What Mike's father calls a tin can today contains no tin but plenty of iron, one of the most abundant metals in the Earth's crust.

There's even more silicon in the Earth's crust than iron. A century ago, all that silicon was not all that productive. It is now. The invention of the silicon semiconductor changed that abundant raw material into an abundant *resource*. It has become Mario Kart and smartphones and Zoom calls with distant loved ones and internet recipes for chocolate chip cookies and algorithms to better detect breast cancer in the radiology lab. Innovation has conjured up an abundant and valuable resource from the literal dirt beneath our feet.

And lest we be misunderstood, humanity's changes and innovations were not merely in physical sciences. We've learned how to better organize our societies, how to better look out for one another, and why we should include more voices in public decision-making. Parliamentary democracy, copyright law, pollution fines, kindergarten, and universal suffrage are all *human ideas*. New electoral systems, markets, and school systems can be built, today, upon the experience of what has been tried before.

A new child is a bet on a life worth living

So we aren't really in danger of running out of food or tungsten. But that doesn't mean that any child is certain to live a healthy and happy life. Here's how one writer captured the fears she felt when she wondered whether to become a parent:

> A deep sense of grief and despair came crashing over me when I considered what it would mean to deliver a child into this world—a world dominated by a small group of greedy humans who are walking with open arms into ecological dead zones, mental breakdowns, and conflict over dwindling resources. (Britt Wray, in *Generation Dread*)

As dads ourselves, we know and respect this fear. Like many twenty-first-century parents, Dean and Diane first saw what would become their children as blobs on a sonogram screen. Their second baby came after several miscarriages and failed IVF. So they were in awe when a sonogram in the basement of a hospital in Lucknow revealed good news after so many disappointments. Dean and Diane knew what to look for: the right number of beats per minute, the right distance measured from crown to rump. At prenatal visits these days, new parents choose among many tests. But none of them tell you what you want to know. "Is my child going to be happy?" "Will my child have a good life?"

Dean and Diane had a hard time deciding whether to have children, when, and how many to have. For much of each year, they work in India trying to help babies there have a healthier start to life—today with the new KMC program, where Seema works, and in other efforts in decades past. They knew that joining their family, and all that entailed, might not be an easy life for their own child. It's not only the challenges of two schools and two homes and two languages and two cultures. It's not only the air pollution and long flights and extra illnesses and cars without seat belts. As their kids grew, they would eventually understand and possibly share in the sadness their parents sometimes felt before the difficult realities of their work, which includes contemplating and witnessing innocent deaths. How would this affect the kids? Could they be happy, nonetheless?

There was no certainty—for Dean's children or any others. Every new baby is an uncertain bet. Most babies born in rich countries now have good chances at good lives. That's not a guarantee: You never know in advance how your child's life will turn out. Dean and Diane decided to go for it. They decided the chances at good would outweigh the risks of bad.

What progress looks like at an Uttar Pradesh hospital

If you were unmoved by stories about the price of tin and chromium, that's okay. We don't care about the prices of commodities, either, not really. We care about what the prices signal: scarcity and abundance, and what all that scarcity and abundance means for people. We promised to not get hung up in this chapter on dollars and rupees. So let's get back to more direct measures of human flourishing, like health and longevity.

In the KMC ward, Seema keeps track of everything at once. After writing down one baby's weight and oxygen level, and while she's teaching another baby's new mom how to tie on a cloth KMC wrap to keep her baby in place, Seema has an eye on Preeti, in the corner, expressing breast milk into a silicone cup. Preeti needs to get out twenty milliliters this time. But she's only on track for ten.

Seema breaks the news: It's time to hook up the breast pump. Breast pumps are a recent improvement to the care in this hospital—recent enough that Dean's family has to bring replacement parts in their suitcases as they travel back and forth between Texas and Uttar Pradesh. Preeti is still getting used to the idea. "What, you're going to milk me like a cow?" she tries to joke—not quite masking a real reluctance to strap on that contraption.

But Seema knows how to assuage Preeti's concern. With a quip, Seema gets a smile and gets Preeti hooked up. Eventually, her baby drinks enough milk out of the feeding cup and goes back to sleep. Extra milk goes in the fridge. Seema notes a problem solved on Preeti's clipboard.

The KMC program is powered by nurses—by moments like this one. Before the KMC program, there weren't enough nurses or beds. So even vulnerable, tiny newborns went home to poor villages, without moms trained in how to breastfeed or keep warm these very fragile babies. Seema's skill and compassion makes progress every week toward another neonatal death averted, toward many decades of likely life years lived. That improvement is one way the world is getting better.

Seema's next task is to check on a mom in the bed by the wall. In the first few days after her baby was born, she was quiet. She seemed angry. As the days have gone on, she has offered her breast to the baby more often. She is starting to bond more.

The baby's father is not warming to the situation. A poor man from a village, he wouldn't be insubordinate to Seema. She's a nurse in a government hospital, after all. But he is quite willing to vent his unhappiness at his postpartum wife. The KMC ward is a shared space, so Preeti and the other moms are trying to stay quiet and stay out of it. But now the father has told Seema that they should all stop trying to save the baby: "If she lives, she lives, if she dies, she dies."

Seema knows what the problem is. She told her manager that this one is, sadly and despite her best efforts, a Code Pink. "Code Pink" is the nurses' professional way of discussing, within the hospital, the fact that many families do not want to try to save their baby girls because they are baby *girls*. The project needed a sanitized term and that's what Dean came up with. The nurses have adopted it. Code Pinks usually leave against medical advice for the babies to take their chances at home.

Unfortunately, this is a common story. Today there are about 109 boys aged five to nine in India for every 100 girls. Boys and girls are conceived in proportions that are closer to equal. So these numbers tell us that the lives of girls are more likely to be prevented or allowed to end.

The gap that remains is a terrible loss. If girls in India were as likely to reach their fifth birthday as boys, then there would be an extra half-million lives to be lived, born every year. This gap exceeds the total number of births each year in Venezuela, in Italy, in Zimbabwe, or in Australia and New Zealand combined.

We're optimistic that humanity will choose to build a good, free, and fair future for women, men, and everyone. But Uttar Pradesh reminds us that there is work to do. So why be optimistic? Because as bad as it is, matters are slowly improving. Today there are 109 school-age boys for every 100 girls. A decade ago, in 2015, it was about 110 boys per 100 girls. A decade before that, it was about 111. That's not fast enough—indeed, it's a call to action—but that trend is one way that the present is better than the past and a way the future can be even better than the present.

You've got to admit it's getting better

A more systematic review of the evidence tells us that life and health are improving overall, across the globe. Life expectancy is a useful measure of flourishing because it is possible to construct with the barest data. If we know the death counts and population sizes by age group, then we have it. That means we can make like-to-like comparisons over a wide range of times and places. Even in the poorest countries, today's government statistical agencies have the capacity to collect or reliably estimate this. And for times before modern statistical agencies, we can get some idea of longevity from exhuming data from whatever records exist. The records tell a story of progress.

> **Vital progress.** People are living longer, healthier lives than ever before.

The gains of health and longevity over the last two centuries have been astounding. In 1800, global life expectancy at birth was less than thirty years. By the time *The Population Bomb* was lobbed, it had risen to fifty-seven years. The most recent figure is seventy-three. Humans have gained an average of 3.7 months of life per year since the date Ehrlich released his ideas over global population centers. Richer and poorer, women and men, humans are living longer.

The greatest gains have been among the most vulnerable. That's true globally and also among the disadvantaged groups within the much-advantaged United States. The first paper Mike published as a PhD student was in the journal *Demography*. It was a U.S.-focused paper called "Black-White Disparities in Life Expectancy," and the data in it ended before 2000. In the decade after, white U.S. life expectancy climbed, but Black U.S. life expectancy rose twice as much. Life expectancy was lower for the Black U.S. population in every year for which there are data, but the gap has narrowed.

Part of the long arc of progress toward living healthy lives has been due to public health, sanitation, and nutrition. In the past decades, but not really before Mike's dad was born, medicine has been making lives better, too. Today, we have protease inhibitors to prevent HIV from developing into AIDS. We have insulin that keeps diabetics alive. We have vaccines against polio, which was a leading cause of permanent disability in children. There are adults alive today in Uttar Pradesh who live with the effects of polio infections in their childhood. But soon there may not be, because polio is now eradicated almost everywhere. We have treatments for anxiety and depression. We have Diclegis to make morning sickness more bearable. We have gene therapies that can arrest and reverse congenital blindness as it develops in young children. And so much more. And so much more on the near horizon. And so much more on the distant horizon, the years and decades that children born now will live through. People who in the past would have died or been discarded by society can live full lives today because our technologies (and our societies) have improved.

Even the simplest drugs represent a major improvement in the human condition. The over-the-counter painkiller naproxen (Aleve) is a wonder drug for managing flare-ups of musculoskeletal pain. Naproxen was not available at any price when Ehrlich was on TV in 1968. Today, one pill costs about four cents. In 2024, the average (non-farm, private, U.S.) wage was $35 per hour. For someone earning that wage, the cost of a naproxen pill is less than five seconds of work. That pill relieves suffering without adverse side effects. It is effortless beyond the dreams of kings of old. And of course medical advances are not only drugs. Technologies like physical therapy, standing desks, and videos to learn better stretches all serve to calm or prevent musculoskeletal pain. Not everybody has these yet, but ever more people do.

A little better all the time

Since 1968, humanity's efforts to feed itself have not ended in failure. But people today—even if they couldn't imagine telling a poor woman in India how many children she should have—ask themselves updated versions of the questions that Ehrlich's book asked everyone. Why bring a child into a world of failing social and economic systems and a ravaged environment? Who could want that for a child?

Let's look at other measures of flourishing. What about education, female empowerment, and deaths from natural disasters and climate change? In Dean's undergraduate class, students take a poll Dean borrows from Hans Rosling's 2018 book *Factfulness*. Dean hands out the questionnaire in the first minutes of the first class day, before going over the syllabus and before introducing himself and learning the students' names. It includes questions like these about what is happening around the world. Take the quiz yourself if you like:

How many of the world's one-year-old children today have been vaccinated against some disease?

☐ 20 percent
☐ 50 percent
☐ 80 percent

How did the number of deaths per year from natural disasters change over the last hundred years?

☐ More than doubled
☐ Remained about the same
☐ Decreased to less than half

Worldwide, thirty-year-old men have spent ten years in school, on average. How many years have women of the same age spent in school?

☐ three years
☐ six years
☐ nine years

For each question, most students choose the most pessimistic answer, the first option from each set of answers above. But the correct answer in each of these is the last option. And in the years since *Factfulness* was published in 2018, the world has continued to get healthier, safer, and better educated.

Weeks later in the course, Dean asks the students the following: *How much worse or better do you imagine your life would be if you were born in Europe in medieval times?* By now the students have spent some weeks in the course and understand what it is about. They see through the exercise. A perceptive student volunteers the answer that life is better now, of course! Even compared to living as medieval nobility, life today is preferable: flush toilets and modern medicine and so on. More important, she explains, we would be likely to end up being peasant laborers in that scenario, not members of the landholding nobility, as portrayed in some TV drama. Life would be hard and uncertain. Some others nod along. Yes, Dean agrees.

But there's another misdirect here by Professor Spears. In medieval populations, the probability of dying before age five was close to a third (or maybe it was closer to 40 percent; nobody has great records before the 1800s!). So, Dean explains, the fact that you were imagining your experience as being *alive at all* (perhaps toiling as a peasant without naproxen to ease your pain) was too optimistic. A third of you would have died as children.

Squaring the record of progress with the bad news that bombards us

Maybe the progress of the past seems irrelevant. Many people seem worried that some things have gotten worse locally and over the short run of their recent memories. What about, for example, the increase in adult deaths in the United States beginning around 2020, led by increases in COVID deaths, accidents, and deaths of despair? In 2020 and 2021, U.S. life expectancy fell. It was big news in U.S. media. Figure 5.3 plots the fall. It echoes an earlier, steeper decline during the 1918 pandemic. The recent life expectancy drop was alarming because it is the opposite of what we have come to expect and what most of the figure shows: a trend of improvement.

What does this latest worsening imply about whether life for coming generations will be worth living? The figure tells us that the drop in life expectancy makes U.S. death rates resemble what they were in the 1990s. Would anyone reasonably think that people experiencing the survival risks of 1990 (or 1980, or 1970, or Bob's 1943) were leading lives not worth living? Would they have been better off not existing?

Perhaps a better worry is that this downturn is just the beginning. Things will keep getting worse. Such a concern dominated despairing headlines and editorials at the time we were writing this book. We can learn from history. It would have been wrong in 1918 to predict that life expectancy would continue its crash. It is wrong to do so today.

Figure 5.3. Life expectancy in the United States

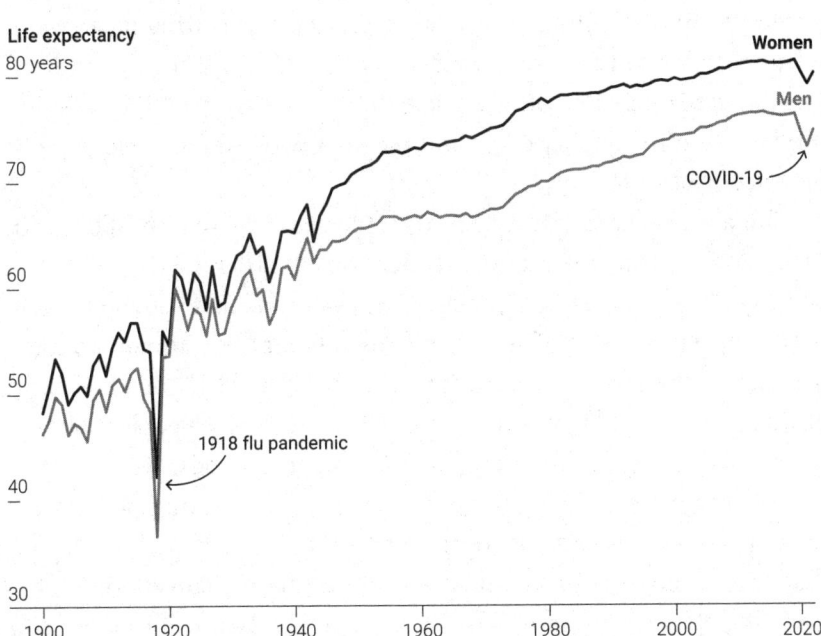

Deciding that history has turned against improvement in human well-being because death rates worsened for a year (or two or five) would be like denying that our planet is on a long-term path of global warming because we had an unusually cold December one year.

And what of the idea that our children will live on an uninhabitable planet due to environmental catastrophes? You've already seen in chapter 3 that the trajectory for particulate-matter air pollution has meant that the present is better than the past and the future is likely to be better still. According to World Bank data, global average exposure to particulate air pollution has *fallen* over the last decade. An opinion piece in today's paper might lament that the air pollution from wildfires canceled outdoor summer play for children—the writers nostalgic for the better days of their own childhood, when wildfires were fewer. But we shouldn't let such nostalgia overwhelm our good judgment of the historical facts.

Anyone who would prefer to be born to a random life in 1970 (when children were breathing in leaded gasoline fumes) or in 1870 (when children in richer countries were breathing in coal dust) or in 1770 (when Britain's polluting industrial revolution was getting underway) or in 1670 (when the best estimates say that over a third of children everywhere stopped breathing altogether before age five) is not being serious about the quality of air and the quality of life available to people, then relative to now.

Climate change is a scarier prospect because we've only started to turn the corner on greenhouse gas emissions. Neither the United States nor any other country has implemented solutions that yet come close to the appropriate size of response needed to address climate change. Disasters caused by climate change are already very bad for some people in some places. They will get worse for many more people in many more places—more heat deaths, more fires, more floods.

Still, these two things can be true at once: A warming planet will make the future poorer, with more suffering and premature death, than would happen in a future without climate change. And: The warming planet that our children and grandchildren will inhabit will be richer, with less needless suffering and less premature death, than our great-grandparents could have imagined. Everything that leading climate science tells us is consistent with both of these facts.

It does not deny the seriousness or urgency of climate change to recognize that it is an extreme, but not unlimited, threat. Exaggerating the risks does not help the serious work that needs to be done. The entire planet will not become "unlivable." Climate change is not a reason that future generations would prefer not to live—not if we today value our lives and if generations of the recent past valued theirs.

Recognize an imperfect world, but don't deny hard-won progress

One reader of our *New York Times* article wrote to express this feeling: "Let's be honest, the innovations of the last century have not really done much to improve us." For many comments, we can see where readers are coming from and sympathize, even if we don't fully agree. But denying the improvements of the last century diminishes the suffering of people who endured the premature deaths of their children and other loved ones in those earlier times. It dismisses the abject poverty that covered much of the world and has since been lessened. And it disrespects the generations of people before us who have worked toward—and succeeded in—making some corner or other of the human experience better. Perhaps worst, it suggests falsely that we are powerless to prevail against the big challenges that confront us now. It says that human effort and ingenuity cannot make things better. We say: They can and have.

The fact that *there can be enough for everyone* doesn't excuse anybody from the work of making sure everyone gets what they need. Just the opposite: We have a duty to build abundance and to share it.

We don't say that idly. It is why Dean and Diane work with the KMC program and Mike works for the White House. It's why Mike's spouse works for the City of Austin, trying to expand housing and make her community more resilient. It is the sort of life of service we hope for our own children. The imperfections of our times are a call to action. Maybe you feel that way, too.

Yes, wildfires, floods, droughts, and other climate-caused catastrophes are already getting worse. Yes, there was a global pandemic and there are deaths of despair and addiction. Yes, even as poverty has declined, there's still a lot of it. Yes, our rich world should devote urgent attention to each of these challenges. We, your authors, chose our profession because we *needed* to contribute to understanding and solving these problems. We recognize the urgency of these problems even as we recognize that life is better for humans today, and will be better tomorrow, than it ever has been. If lives like yours are worth living, then the large majority of future lives will be, too. Mike checked, and Bob is happy for his life. Powdered milk, hand-me-downs, and all.

·

Some people will read this chapter and remain committed to the belief that a few decades from now, when children born today will reach mid-life, life will be terrible. Others may believe that even life today is bad and not worth living for the typical person. Does the evidence say that life expectancy will increase over the coming decades? Oh, bother. Longer lives are larger portions of a bad meal.

We and these readers may never come to agree. But there is one crucial way in which we share the moral commitments of those who think that a bad future could be a good reason not to have a child today. They argue that our generation, we who are born, should not create lives that we expect to be bad. We agree that whether a life should be brought into this world *depends on the quality of life likely to be lived.* Whether to create a life depends on the facts and circumstances. "It depends" not only because of the effects on other people (although that matters, too) but also because of the quality of life *for the person who lives it.*

This is an important agreement. It is a first step on a radical path toward recognizing that creating lives (or declining to create them) can make the world a better place because of the goodness or badness *in those lives.* Chapter 8 will walk that path. For now, this chapter has shown something worth knowing. Do *you* think lives of the present and recent past (lives like yours) are lives worth living? Then, if you could peer into the future, you could expect to judge future lives to be worth living, too. So, if you're a parent or you might be, go ahead and have normal parent anxieties. (We all do!) But cast off the dread.

PART III

The Case for People

Chapter 6

Progress comes from people

Before economists had computers, statistical significance tests, or ball-point pens, we had Thomas Malthus. In 1798, when there were about a billion humans, he published *An Essay on the Principle of Population, as It Affects the Future Improvement of Society.* Malthus wrote that a larger population was bad for the future improvement of society. Several billion people later, economists now have evidence, theoretical tools, econometrics, and other resources that Malthus never saw. Today's economists think differently from Malthus, but the popular notion persists that a larger population is worse for each. More quantity of life, less quality of life. Right?

That was certainly Ehrlich's view. And for one reader of our *New York Times* article, judging population decline is easy. "Honestly, a world population of 2 billion, with our current technology, or even greater efficiencies, sounds like a paradise." But this reader hid a big assumption. *Would* we have the same technology and efficiencies if there were only 2 billion of us? Economists in our century don't think so.

In the last chapter, we confronted the worry that a larger population has lowered average living standards. But as often as we hear this worry, we never hear it from economists whose expertise is in the big-picture economics of long-term material progress. They believe the opposite.

> **Populous is prosperous.** A more populous future would raise living standards. Mainly this is because people contribute to the ideas, creativity, experimentation, and technology that benefit others.

Economics gives us two insights that help explain why a more populous world would be more prosperous for each of us: *idea creation* and *fixed costs*. This chapter is about idea creation. More people means more of the discoveries that people make—more progress over the long run. The next chapter is about fixed costs.

Over time, living standards are improving because new people keep adding to our species-wide, shared stock of know-how, creativity, and understanding. It's why Preeti's baby and our kids can expect much better lives than their great-grandparents' generation had. To see this, we will start where Preeti's baby did: with the power of a good idea.

•

Preeti and her baby are still in the Uttar Pradesh hospital where Seema, Reema, and their boss, Kavitha, work. Preeti's baby was born five weeks ago and weighed just 1,070 grams (2 pounds, 5 ounces) at thirty-four weeks of gestation. Out of 3.7 million babies born in the United States in 2021, only one-half of 1 percent weighed so little. Such a tiny baby is vulnerable.

The KMC ward is more comfortable and restful than returning home to daughter-in-law duties in the village. But it's boring if things are going well. Preeti is grateful for her baby's growth, but it's a long haul. That's why Seema's job is part nurse, part lactation consultant, and part cheerleader. Preeti smiles and pauses to joke with Seema as she paces—baby tied on—through the ten-bed room that has been her home for weeks. Preeti sticks it out another day.

And Preeti's baby is on a roll: 1,315 grams today, almost 3 pounds.

As Kavitha went over the morning's clipboards with Seema, they decided to make the case to the managing pediatrician that this one is ready to go home. Seema and her colleagues will visit the baby at home over the coming weeks and call Preeti's mobile phone often. But Seema and Kavitha agree: The baby is eating, Preeti is implementing the plan, and staying in the hospital risks infection. "There is nothing new we can teach her," Kavitha concludes. And they need the bed for someone else.

What Preeti has learned is Kangaroo Mother Care. KMC is a lifesaving technique—a process—to care for low-birthweight babies in places where expensive neonatal intensive care does not exist. Caregivers learn to keep the baby warm, fed, and safe with continuous skin-to-skin contact and breastfeeding.

This chapter is about progress. So why are we talking about skin-to-skin contact between a mother and her baby? Because a powerful driver of progress and prosperity is the accumulation of knowledge and technology.

KMC is a technology. It was invented in 1978 in Colombia. Underweight babies can't generate much body heat. So without a constant and well-calibrated external source of warmth, an underweight baby can quickly die of hypothermia. Some pediatricians in Bogotá did not have the incubators that modern medicine in rich countries relies on to do the job. So they devised a substitute—the process now known as KMC. Of course, KMC itself is a formalization and refinement of practices tested over history: snuggling a cold, hungry baby to a mother's chest. But details matter. The doctors who invented KMC and the nurses who have refined it found that it helped to keep the baby tied in place (so it doesn't slip off), with skin-to-skin contact (so nothing blocks the mother's warmth), and with mom lying tilted up (so the baby doesn't suffocate or get squished). The process was tweaked and refined, and eventually quantified.

In 2021, the *New England Journal of Medicine* published a huge experiment from Ghana, India, Malawi, Nigeria, and Tanzania. The study confirmed, with the scientific rigor of a randomized control trial, that this process technology works. It showed that babies around the size of Preeti's were 25 percent less likely to die in their first month of life if their mothers were taught to do Kangaroo Mother Care immediately: "relative risk of death, 0.75; 95 percent confidence interval [CI], 0.64 to 0.89; P=0.001" in the formal language of the journal. That improvement is compared against the condition in the control group: starting life with "conventional care in an incubator or a radiant warmer." A radiant warmer is a pretty good technology in itself, so KMC outperforming it means that it is vastly outperforming simply sending a premature baby home to a village.

KMC is an important way that the world has improved, and it is only one of many ways. Somehow, we've made everything more abundant as the population has soared. Is that history a fluke? Chapter 5 told us *what* happened. It didn't tell us *how* or *why*. It's time to understand the how and why so we can see what we might lose as humanity's numbers recede.

Progress comes from people

Economists did not have a very clear theory of where material progress—what they call economic growth—comes from until the last few generations of research. For decades, the leading models of material progress emphasized the accumulation of physical capital. Physical capital is tools and machines and structures that workers use to make the things we value. These models did many things well, but one of their most important lessons was to show us what was *not* possible. Progress could not be sustained by capital accumulation alone. It had to be driven by improvement after improvement in our know-how and efficiency. But how? The models told economists that economic growth had to come from technological change, but they could not tell economists where technological change came from.

That changed in the 1980s. Paul Romer was an economist working at the University of Rochester. He worked out a new way to understand innovation. He recognized that Kangaroo Mother Care, an idea from Bogotá, Colombia, could be replicated in Uttar Pradesh, India. Romer, to be clear, maybe never heard of Kangaroo Mother Care, in particular. What he recognized was a more general fact. Once an idea is invented somewhere, it can be reused elsewhere. Once humanity discovers that tungsten makes good light bulb filaments, develops the cohort-component method of population projection, or learns to recognize mastitis in a breastfeeding mother, others can put that idea to good use.

Decades later, Romer was awarded a Nobel Prize for this insight— for helping to uncover the *how* and *why* of economic progress. He built the first of a generation of models articulating how the positive force of discovery could generate sustained increases in living standards.

The key concept that unlocked theoretical progress was that a good idea does not get used up. It gets copied and reapplied, endlessly. "Ideas can be shared," Romer explained during his 2018 Nobel Prize award ceremony in Stockholm. "I don't mean the kind of sharing where we take turns. This is the sharing where everybody can use something like the Pythagorean theorem at the same time."

This is the economics of "non-rival innovation." *Rival*, in economics jargon, describes something that, if or when one person uses it, another person cannot. Any one cookie can only fill one belly. Any hand tool can only augment one hand at a time. Any particular antibiotic pill can only treat one person's infection. But the recipe of the cookie, the design of the tool, and the formula of the antibiotic can work infinitely many times. Recipes, designs, and formulas are *non-rival*. No matter how many cookies are baked or hammers are made, the knowledge remains available, valuable, indestructible. Ideas—whether technologies, process improvements, political theories, inspiring or clarifying works of fiction and art, or anything else—are valuable because they can be used or experienced over and over and over again.

Kangaroo Mother Care is a non-rival process innovation. The government of India can, and has, promulgated the technology to hospitals across India. Other governments have, too. All the knowledge is out there for free. The World Health Organization publishes *Kangaroo Mother Care: A Practical Guide* on its website. The Cleveland Clinic repackages the same information for a U.S.-centered audience, where it adds that it's best to put away your phone during skin-to-skin time. The World Health Organization and the Cleveland Clinic cannot occupy the very same offices or serve the very same sandwiches for lunch or pay the very same dollars in employee wages. They need their own offices, lunches, and budgets. But they can publish the same advice.

Through Seema, Kavitha, and their team, KMC kept Preeti's baby alive. The most important input was Preeti's time, effort, and love. But the second most important input—a necessary one—was the KMC process that Seema deployed. A doctor in Bogotá already developed that process, once and for all. It need not be rediscovered each time it is put to use. Now, no matter how many babies are saved in Seema's KMC ward, Kangaroo Mother Care continues undiminished.

The fact that ideas, processes, formulas, and knowledge are all non-rival is, to use more economic jargon, a *really big deal*. Economics is supposed to be about scarcity, but here in the engine room we've found a fuel that never gets used up. It's the gift that keeps on giving. It is the deep reason why more for somebody doesn't have to mean less for somebody else. So the first step toward understanding why we have better healthcare, hand tools, and desserts today than a few hundred years ago is recognizing that ideas and technologies are non-rival.

The second step is recognizing that *people* discover ideas. People create inventions. People make things better, in ways large (a new vaccine against tropical diseases) and small (a better cup of coffee). Economists call this "endogenous economic growth." *Endogenous* means "created from the inside." Ideas do not come from outside the economy. They come from us. The activities that people do inside an economy make the ideas that propel the economy forward.

A prize-winning idea: More of us generate more ideas. And that can mean better lives for each of us.

The most obvious examples are in rich countries at the techno-logical frontier. But high tech is not the only tech. Progress happens wherever people are solving problems. One of the most productive tech-nologies ever conceived was invented in Bangladesh in the 1960s. There, in a hospital focused on cholera, doctors first mixed oral rehydration salts. This simple mix of salt and sugar, dissolved in water in the right proportions, transformed humanity's ability to prevent children from dying of diarrhea.

Today, anyone, anywhere can make *use* of the simple formula. And it can make children feel better even in milder scenarios. In Uttar Pradesh, you can mix it from what is already in your pantry. In Austin, you can buy a convenient, pretty bottle of Pedialyte with added grape flavor. Richer children in Austin get a better, tastier version than poorer chil-dren in Uttar Pradesh. But children anywhere today can benefit from the recipe. That benefit didn't exist for any child born before the 1960s— that is, most of the children ever born. The formula exists because some *people*—in this case, cholera doctors in Bangladesh—found it.

This fact about ideas is not something special to a place or a par-ticular economic structure. Ideas get reused whether they first occur to someone living in a capitalist society, or whether they first occur to someone living in a communist society, or in some mercantilist or feu-dal society of centuries past. Ideas get reused when they are posted on-line for free, published in textbooks, or protected by teams of lawyers defending patents. When a student in India today reads her textbook late at night by the bright, cheap, reliable light of an LED no bigger than a sesame seed, the words don't disappear from the same textbook being read in the sunlight on the other side of the planet.

There's some good news and some bad news

So the good news is that drinking up bottles of Pedialyte does not use up the recipe. Filling the beds in the KMC ward does not crowd out the technique of KMC. The bad news is that those recipes, formulas, and techniques would never have been available to anyone if nobody found or created them.

The world is facing an unprecedented economic experiment. What will happen to progress—economists' "endogenous economic growth"—if there are fewer and fewer people to discover new ideas? Not only fewer scientists and inventors, but fewer teachers and librarians and research assistants and all of the people who support their work and all of the people who make their work possible by selling them groceries and caring for their aging parents or children or driving their buses? What if there is less of all the activities that people do that could uncover the next KMC or oral rehydration?

Until recently, most economists hadn't thought to ask this question, because they had been busy studying a history during which the size of the population was always increasing. But Chad Jones, another economist who has led the way in understanding long-run economic change, recently noticed what you now know: that depopulation is coming. So he looked to the future, rather than the past. Jones has written a lot of calculus over the years that has helped him answer this question, but we can summarize his discovery simply:

> **A fact about facts:** Facts don't get used up, but they might go undiscovered.

Because people create ideas, fewer useful ideas will be created in a depopulating future than on a stabilized path. Economists are famous for disagreeing with one another. Not here. As Michael Peters of Yale wrote in the opening sentence of a recent article in one of the economics profession's leading journals: "Virtually all theories of economic growth predict a positive relationship between population size and productivity." More people mean more ideas generated and shared more widely, benefiting each of us.

Without people to do the discovering, innovating, and testing, less creation will happen. Less advancement. Less progress. If fewer people are born in the future, then we may miss out on the team who would have made the next leap in geothermal power or plant-based meat or anxiety treatment or pop music or anything else of value. The fewer people who remain to be born will each be worse off than they could have been.

Sometimes proponents of a smaller, emptier planet reply that we could simply invest more in the people we have. We could guide society to produce more scientists and engineers. Yes! We should! (And more creative nonfiction writers, too!) And we should do that also in a world with a stable population, rather than a shrinking one. And we should be doing it even now, while our population continues to grow for a few more decades. There's no reason not to have fewer subsistence farmers and more PhD researchers in our abundant future. Easier work lives and more advancements to enjoy is a win-win. And things are heading that way. Whether the global population peaks and then shrinks in the next hundred years, or whether the population reverses course and stabilizes, you should bet on the idea that the world will have more PhDs and other markers of advanced training per capita a century from now than today.

But the total matters, not the fraction, when counting the innovations we produce. A larger future is a future with more *total* innovators. If 50 percent of a 1-billion-person population were engaged in some kind of innovation, they'd produce fewer innovations than 10 percent of a 10-billion-person population set to the same task. Stabilizing instead of depopulating would mean there will be more total opportunities to discover new ideas that could be shared the world over to improve life.

Even recognizing that fewer people means fewer ideas understates the problem. Technological progress is *cumulative*, Romer explains. Ideas can multiply each other. Later ideas can interact with ideas that came before. Baseball, starting in 2023, has a pitch clock because basketball invented its shot clock in 1954. This was nine years after the three-pointer was first tested in a game between Columbia and Fordham, itself devised fifty-four years after basketball was invented in 1891. This, in turn, was forty-six years after baseball's 1845 Knickerbocker Rules, which codified an even older game. If we miss out on some entry in the Great Registry of Human Ideas, then we may lose or delay the key ingredient in a whole lineage of innovations and improvements.

We're not done yet. More progress would be better.

But the future is going to be rich, right? Should we really worry if it is not so very, very rich? A demographer friend who is our longtime collaborator asked us, "Can't we still maintain our living standards with fewer people?" It's a fair question to ask. But aiming for *maintaining* living standards rather than *improving things for people everywhere* aims too low. There are still problems to solve. There are still too many people in poor countries and rich countries whose living standards, health, and opportunities could use improvement.

It can be hard to fathom what we might lose if progress slowed because our population dwindled. It can be hard to foresee all the advances that a depopulating future might miss out on. To get a sense of this, without venturing into detailed predictions of future technology that will inevitably look ridiculous, let's instead reflect back on history. Maybe we can't see clearly what we would lose if progress slowed now. But we can see what we would be missing if the progress of our past was delayed or lost.

Start here: If progress had not been made in the last fifty years—if we had merely *maintained* the living standards of 1975—we'd never achieve a clean energy infrastructure in time to avert the worst long-run climate disaster. Before the 1980s, the world had not produced a solar farm as large as one megawatt—not enough to power even one thousand homes. The technology was too immature to scale. But since then, advances in solar have been bounding forward. Photovoltaic capacity in the U.S. today is more than ten thousand times what the first plant could produce. Wind has gone big, too. Today, it's an important source of electricity generation in the central United States (especially

Oklahoma!—where the wind comes sweeping down the plain). That's because technological improvements have made wind commercially viable. There is no clean energy future, no answer to carbon emissions, without technological progress.

If progress had halted seventy-five years ago, we wouldn't have the oral contraceptive pill—the pharmaceutical technology that has proven so important to human flourishing and reproductive freedom since its creation that we could have simply said "the pill" and many readers would have known which pill we meant among the tens of thousands of different tablets and capsules available today. We wouldn't have wanted to stop or slow that technological progress seventy-five years ago.

If progress had frozen one hundred years ago, we'd be missing a lot more still. Joys large and small. Sports broadcast over TV, including basketball's shot clock and, now, baseball's pitch clock. Modern bikes. And bike helmets. And the hospital recordkeeping and epidemiological research to know how useful bike helmets are in preventing serious injury. Phone calls with distant loved ones.

We'd miss chocolate chip cookies, too, which were invented by Ruth Wakefield in 1938. She was working on perfecting her butterscotch cookies and had a new idea for cookies with little bits of chocolate that would not melt. Wakefield owned the Toll House Inn, where her innovative cookies were first served. That is why you still see a Toll House logo on bags of Nestlé chocolate chips.

The 1943 musical *Oklahoma!* was an early implementation of the novel idea of a "book musical"—the now-familiar concept of an integrated musical theater story told over two acts. What came before was something more like a collection of amusing songs and dances without a plotline. A traveler in Act I of *Oklahoma!* sings, "They went and built a skyscraper seven stories high." Kansas City, from his 1907 perspective, had gone about as far as it could go. Rodgers and Hammerstein's joke, of course, was that audiences in 1943 knew otherwise. They had marvels that the fictitious crowd of Oklahomans could only dream of in 1907. Eighty years later, we do, too.

And the risk is not merely that progress will never come, that there are cookie varieties and pills and plays that would never appear. Perhaps progress still happens in a depopulating world, just slowly. But it matters if solutions come less quickly than they could. We expect, for example, that humanity will one day have much better tools to fight cancer than it does now. That's good. But those tools can't reverse the cancer deaths that took three of your authors' four parents before their grandchildren could know them. *When* progress happens matters.

People seventy-five years ago did not have everything good. Good thing progress continued. People fifty years ago did not have everything good. Good thing progress continued. We now do not have everything good. So it matters whether progress continues.

It would be quite a coincidence . . .

The most recent evidence can trace genetically modern humans back to three hundred thousand years ago. If the story of humanity were a book as long as the one you're reading now, then the last two hundred years would be the last paragraph on the very last page. A lot has happened within that paragraph.

Massive advances in technological progress and living standards (life expectancy, health, nutrition, safety, shorter workdays, less precarious lives) happened within the last two hundred years. Massive growth in population happened within the last two hundred years.

It is no mere coincidence that photovoltaic cells came now when our world is filled with so many people, nor that the vaccine against cervical cancer came now when our world is filled with so many people, nor that indoor, climate-controlled jobs came now when our world is filled with so many people. It is cause and effect.

In the 1990s, economist Michael Kremer assembled evidence on population size over an even longer window than the Spike, drawing on archaeological and anthropological evidence. His systematic analysis showed how population and progress aligned for as long as *Homo sapiens* have been around.

But couldn't the causation go in the other direction—from techno-logical progress to a world full of more surviving people? Yes! It goes in both directions. Progress helps babies to survive the start of life, to grow up to be adults. Those grown-ups then contribute to progress.

The relationship between people and prosperity is a virtuous cycle of acceleration. That is part of what Malthus missed, but modern econ-omists understand. As the economist Oded Galor wrote in *The Jour-ney of Humanity*, "The astounding ascent in the quality of life in the past centuries has in fact been the product of an abrupt transforma-tion." What was the transformation? It was humanity's escape from Thomas Malthus's demographic trap. "Ironically," Galor explained, "just as Malthus completed his treatise and pronounced that this 'pov-erty trap' would endure indefinitely, the mechanism that he had iden-tified suddenly subsided and the metamorphosis from stagnation to growth took place." In the past few hundred years, progress acceler-ated. People are why. Children, their health, and what they learn are why. If the future depopulates, rather than stabilizes, then a link in this virtuous chain will break.

A brief history of light

"Progress" can feel abstract. So let's shed some light on the idea. Unless you happen to be reading this book on a park bench or at the beach, you are probably using a cheap artificial source of light to see the words. Maybe that is a fluorescent tube in an overhead fixture, maybe the LED backlight on your handheld device. Cheap light is new, on the scale of human history, the scale of the Spike. The progression from expensive light to cheap light writes the story of technological progress in sesame oil, whale fat, and diodes.

The illuminating history of light was told to economists by William Nordhaus in a 1994 research paper. Nordhaus didn't write this paper to make a point about population. He was out to find a better way to measure improvements in living standards over time. But we can make our own use of his study, nonetheless. Great ideas are like that. They get reused.

Here was the problem Nordhaus wanted to solve: Economists cannot compare our GDP per capita against a past when nobody wrote down numerical prices. Nor would it make sense to compare goods whose quality was transformed over time. There's no comparison between a modern apple and the bitter, mealy, worm-bitten crab apple of Europe's long-ago past, or even between a modern apple and the early domesticated apples grown in the Tian Shan mountains of Central Asia five thousand years ago. Today's apple is three to five times the size and selectively bred to delight us with its color, sweetness, and crispness. And it's delivered just in time to make those features pop on the shelf. Products and services are different today—often much better—than in the past, even when they carry forward the same name.

So Nordhaus found an example "product" that humans have consumed for a long time and for which there was a common unit of measure. He could make a better than apples-to-apples comparison. Nordhaus compared lumens to lumens. In a departure from standard econometric methods, Nordhaus gathered a bunch of stuff—wood, vegetable oil, animal fat—and personally lit it on fire. He measured the light with a meter.

Here's the story Nordhaus told: Over a million years ago, *Australopithecus* (an early ancestor of *Homo sapiens*) began to use fire. For tens of thousands of years, people laboriously made light by burning animal or vegetable fat in stone lamps. Around 3000 BCE, Egyptians and Cretans knew how to form these into candlesticks. By 1750 BCE, Babylonians were burning sesame oil for lighting. Stop reading for a moment and imagine making your light that way (or otherwise having no artificial light at all). Such light would have been too precious to use for any but the most important purposes.

Over the next few thousand years, oil lamps slowly improved. Candles did, too. Tax records from 1292 Paris list seventy-two candlemak-

Figure 6.1. A history of bright ideas

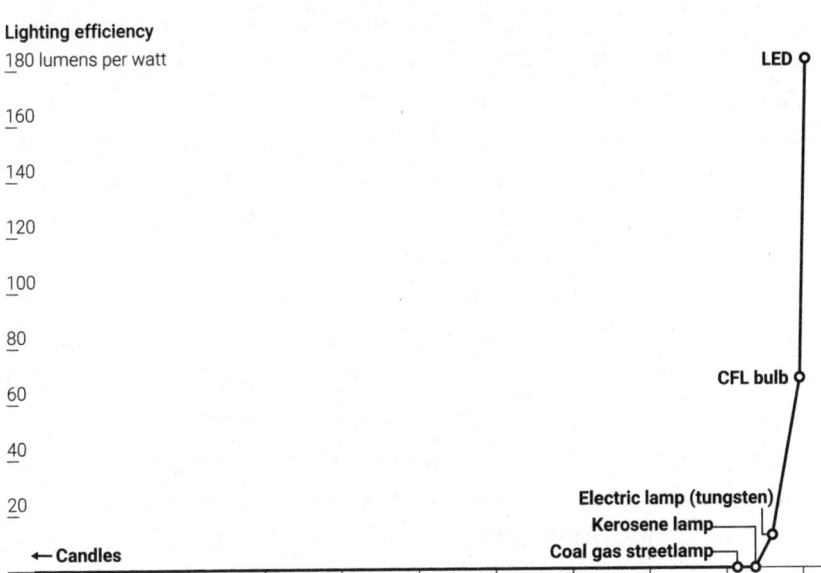

ers. In 1792, coal-gas lighting began to appear. Notice that the dates in this history are accelerating, fewer years passing between the innovations. Then, in the 1800s, new technologies improved candles. Light was still too expensive to use thoughtlessly. But progress advanced by the decade, not the century: gas streetlights in the 1820s next, then kerosene lamps in the 1860s.

And then electrification. The Royal Society of London saw an electric-discharge lamp in 1860. Edison's incandescent lamp glowed in 1879. The twentieth century saw fluorescent bulbs. And Nordhaus's catalog ends in the 1980s, with the marketing of the compact fluorescent bulb, more efficient than the tungsten filament bulbs of Mike's childhood, using less energy to produce the same light output. In his Nobel lecture, Romer explained that today an hour's worth of labor can buy 350,000 times the amount of light as an hour's labor in the time of ancient Babylonian sesame lamps.

The story did not end there. Since Nordhaus published his paper in 1997, LED lamps have transformed lighting again. They last longer than all the past alternatives and use even less energy. And even though the point of comparing lumens to lumens was to find a consumer good that didn't get better over time, that turns out to be too hard to do. Lighting has changed. Now your lights won't flicker. They can be cool or warm, dimmable or not, according to your preference. Instead of refilling the oil each night, modern lamps, once set in place, last for years or perhaps even a lifetime.

The point of this story is not merely that living standards have improved over time. That's true, no doubt, but look closer at figure 6.1, our plot of Nordhaus's data. It wasn't a steady climb. The picture is of a long period of stagnation and then explosive growth in innovation (and explosive growth in what an hour of labor buys). If that pattern looks familiar, it should. It's the shadow of the Spike's upslope.

Now, that matching pattern is not *proof* that larger populations cause more innovation in the same way that the randomized control trial of Kangaroo Mother Care is proof of its efficacy. The challenge of macroeconomic history is that, unlike in a clinical trial, we can't randomly assign one world a large population, another a small population, and then watch a history of humanity unfold on each. But, wow, would it be quite a coincidence if population didn't matter for this history of invention.

What else can we learn from the brief history of light? If tomorrow, an engineer in Brazil or Taiwan were to devise an even better light bulb, nobody living elsewhere would worry that they could never get access to it. Of course we all would. That fact is so obvious that it doesn't even make sense to ask the question. Important breakthroughs diffuse across the world. Sometimes the Nobel Prize for physics recognizes "experiments with entangled photons," or "the discovery of a supermassive compact object at the center of our galaxy." But in 2014, the physics prize went to Isamu Akasaki, Hiroshi Amano, and Shuji Nakamura "for the invention of efficient blue light–emitting diodes which has enabled bright and energy-saving white light sources." Akasaki, Amano, and Nakamura did that work in the 1990s in Japan.

Nursing students throughout the developing world now stay awake, almost costlessly, to study Kangaroo Mother Care and other innovations, by LED light. Almost none of them have been to Japan.

Progress is not a procession of occasional geniuses

The history of light is not the story of a Great Man. Individual contributors might make for interesting biographies and sometimes for thrilling movies. But most progress in science, technology, and society is the lift of many hands and many minds. The efforts of the three 2014 physics Nobel Prize winners who made breakthroughs on LEDs mattered, but not because without them humanity would never have had LEDs. They didn't have all the ideas; they didn't do all the experiments. One way to see this is to notice that clever insights, inventions, or discoveries, waiting just beyond the next frontier, have often been produced by two researchers or teams at about the same time.

Before LEDs, Thomas Edison worked with a team to make better electric lights. He had a lab full of scientists and machinists and glassblowers. With their contributions, Edison patented an incandescent light. But William Sawyer and Albon Man also received a U.S. patent for a similar incandescent lamp, and Joseph Swan did, too, in England. These inventors built upon the materials science, physics, and chemistry of other scientists. Indeed, others had been making various filament materials glow with electric discharge for at least a hundred years prior to Edison's light bulb. And they had the time to do so because they ate food grown and delivered and probably cooked by somebody else.

A group of people can solve a problem together, even if they all make mistakes, even if none of them individually grasps the solution until it is finally assembled. Progress may sometimes leap forward because of an exceptional thinker or doer, but don't let that be a distraction from our point. The argument and evidence of this chapter is not that we need larger populations because every baby is a lottery ticket that might win us a new genius. Genius has nothing to do with what we're saying here.

> **Strength is in our numbers, not just our rare luminaries.** Non-rival innovation is so powerful that even without outliers—even in an alternative universe in which everyone was equally (unexceptionally) intelligent, adventurous, creative, kind, and organized—progress would depend on population size.

The reason is that, even in that alternative universe, ideas would still *accumulate.* Many people have ideas—sometimes big ones, but most often tweaks. Henry Ford did not invent wheels, engines, or cars, but he and his company did implement some very useful processes to make these. So it's not just the Ludwigs van Beethoven and the Maries Curie and the Henrys Ford. It's the many other Ludwigs and Maries and Henrys who matter for human progress. It's anyone who has an idea worth remembering.

And if someday human creativity is no longer needed?

People have made ideas, and ideas have been a foundation for progress. What if someday ideas come from somewhere else, so people, as innovators, become obsolete—or at least redundant? What if, perhaps soon, AI can begin doing the thinking and discovering that humans have done to get us to this point in our history? If that happens—if computer intelligence will substitute well enough for human creativity—then, the argument goes, maybe a few humans could get along fine with computers instead of one another.

Maybe. Nobody knows exactly what new technology will bring, so of course we cannot rule out this possibility. But neither can anybody rule in this possibility as a near-enough certainty. Maybe it will be a

very long time before AI will be good enough to do all of the important thinking that humans do. Maybe that will never happen. Maybe
AI will be much better than humans at some tasks, but humans will
enduringly be much better than AI at others, so that machines will
augment human thinking and labor, as they have in the past. If so,
progress would still depend on us—a new chapter in an old story.

That's a lot of maybes. So let's not bank on AI making up for all the
progress that could be missing from a smaller future. Just like it would
be irresponsible not to plan for a future when AI can do much of what
humans can, it would be irresponsible not to plan for a future when
AI can't.

.

We close by acknowledging something this chapter hasn't addressed
and that this book won't address. The most common worry that one
hears today about the economics of depopulation is that too few workers or too many retirees would foul up government budgets or the
labor force. Maybe so. Or maybe our societies can solve these problems
without stabilizing the population. Yes, the U.S. old-age dependency
ratio (the number of people sixty-five and over relative to the number
of people twenty-five to sixty-four) will double over the next seventy-
five years. But it has already doubled over the past seventy-five years,
and that doubling hasn't brought catastrophe. It is right and fitting that
think tanks study, that wonky discourse attends to, and that finance
ministers and legislatures manage these changes. But these well-worn
concerns and arguments aren't our case for people. Here in this book,
the case for people is bigger.

Why do we have LED lights, but our ancestors lived in the dark?
Because some people alive today know how to make them. The crucial
ingredient is the knowledge. Advancement in science and technology
is the basic force that economists have identified as the reason why
lives today are so much better than lives with animal-fat candles, no
pain relief, no antibiotics, and no land transport except by foot or hoof.
Life has become much better. It could become much better again in the

future. Of course, we today can no more precisely imagine those future lives than the seventy-two candlemakers of thirteenth-century Paris could imagine ours.

But as long as we are dying of cancer and infections and low birth weight, as long as we are inhaling air pollution, as long as so many people in the developing world are working so hard for so little—as long as these and other challenges loom—we can see important room for improvement. To get to the present, someone needed to do the discoveries and make the inventions. Someone also needed to organize and teach what was already known. To get to a flourishing future, someone will need to do these things, too. The past two centuries were a revolution in better living standards as our population climbed. We should not be complacent about upsetting a cart full of so many apples.

Chapter 7

Dodging the asteroid. And other benefits of other people

Preeti is home now. That doesn't mean the work is done. Nurses from the KMC ward will visit and call for weeks to make sure that her still-tiny baby is eating and growing, and that skin-to-skin care and feeding are going well at Preeti's mud-and-brick village house. Even so, everyone is optimistic.

For weeks on end, Preeti stayed in the KMC ward because she wanted her baby to live. And yet, some outsiders, usually sitting comfortably in the air-conditioning of a rich city, question this goal. Aren't there too many mouths to feed in Uttar Pradesh? Isn't that why these families are so poor? Wouldn't the mother be better off, they ask, without this child?

Preeti does not think so. She wants her baby. And we have already seen in chapter 5 that, for centuries, living standards have improved while the world has grown more populous. But the skeptics—even if they do accept what we've learned in chapter 6, that the reasons for those improvements are the innovators who have come before—cannot shake the feeling that sharing this planet with others is a zero-sum game, like dividing up a pie. Player One can only win if Player Two loses. There's only so much wood, wheat, stone, sheep, and brick to go around. More agricultural land dedicated to your needs means less for me. The same with mineral resources. And energy. And everything else.

The last chapter said that more people bring more ideas. The spread of ideas improves living standards over time and generations, making lives today, which come after a populous history of humanity, better than they would be if there were fewer people in our past. This chapter asks a different question—about the population economics of the here and now. It asks whether it is better to live alongside more people, alive at the same time as us. Does having other people around mean competition against getting what we want, or would some wants and needs only be addressed in a big world?

> **How not to get a slice of pie.** Having fewer people around would mean there were fewer people who want exactly what you want. And that might be a problem for you getting what you want. Your neighbors are not eating your pie slice. They're the reason someone is baking.

How our needs and wants get satisfied

If what you crave isn't pie, but a bowl of shio ramen, then you are more likely to find it locally if your locality has other people who crave the same thing. That's because without many paying customers, the ramen restaurant wouldn't exist at all. Your neighbors aren't slurping the noodles out of your bowl. They are filling it up. If what you crave is a lighter bicycle (or a bicycle with a slick belt drive or a bicycle with a gratifying pedal assist or a bicycle with a safe seat for a toddler co-pilot), then be glad that there are enough other people who want one, too. They make it worthwhile for someone to design, produce, and sell that bike.

If what you want is to watch a movie or a concert, or to access specialized immunotherapy treatment, or to use software tailored to your needs, or even to survive an asteroid headed toward Earth (we will explain), you may indeed fare better if there are other people who want the same thing, too.

Fundamental to the economics of bigger being better is the problem of fixed costs. Fixed costs are "fixed" in the sense that they are the costs of doing something, rather than nothing, regardless of how much of that something you do. At the ramen shop, fixed costs are the cost of being in business, no matter how much the shop sells. They include the rent for the building, the stove and cookware, and the earnings the owner gives up by not spending their time and attention doing something else. (The ingredient costs and payroll costs for workers are not fixed, in contrast; they increase as the shop serves more and more customers. Economists call these "variable costs.") If a restaurant has only a few customers, it won't be able to pay its fixed costs. It will close.

Or it might never open in the first place. Small towns hardly ever have a great Ethiopian place and a great Indian place and a great Korean place. But big cities often do. That's because scale overcomes fixed costs. If you have many customers, your fixed costs will seem small. Fixed costs matter because if a business has many customers, the average cost of making each product is lower. And then it's more likely that the business can exist, producing something that people want, at a price they can afford.

Businesses make the easiest case studies to highlight fixed costs, but it's not only businesses. "Bigger means better" is the idea behind National Public Radio, too. NPR wouldn't be able to generate the same quality of broadcasts and podcasts without its large base of member supporters. That's because the cost of producing a show is the same regardless of how many people listen and contribute.

Every scalable activity has some costs that are fixed and some costs that depend on the scope of the project. Fixed costs are a universal force that rewards bigger scale with cost-saving efficiency. Why are there fewer movies, music, and high-budget television shows in German than in English? One big reason is that the German-speaking market is smaller. Why have scientists found a vaccine against RSV, but not a vaccine against sealpox? One reason is that millions of people get RSV each year. Few people face a risk of sealpox. It's primarily seal handlers at aquatic mammal rehabilitation facilities who are unlucky in their encounters with an infected seal.

What the scale effects of cities can teach us about the scale effects of humanity

Median home prices in Austin are more than twice what they are in the smaller city of Tulsa, Oklahoma, where Dean grew up. Why spend so much money? Simple: to be around so many people. The basic economics of cities is this: *People pay to be crowded together.*

The advantages of having neighbors are not the only reason why the rent is so damn high. Many urban policies could and should be changed to expand housing supply and bring down prices. But! The rent could *stay* so high (under bad policies or good) only if someone is willing to pay it. Even as urban housing costs rise, more and more people are leaving rural areas and heading to the city. The global urban population grows by two hundred thousand people every day.

Do cities have downsides? They sure do. Some critics point to noise, others to crowded spaces or difficult parking. But when people move to cities—to take that new job, to attend a university, or to chase some dream their small town can't support—they are saying that the upsides of city living outweigh whatever downsides they perceive. Every time someone chooses to pay more to move toward other people, they reveal that having more people around is better for them, overall and all things considered.

The economics of cities can help us understand how a larger population produces benefits via specialization, trade, and scale. The point, in this chapter on what depopulation could mean for living standards, isn't the cities themselves. Cities are a useful microcosm for learning about the benefits of larger populations of other kinds.

Figure 7.1 tells us that cities are accomplishing something. The graph starts in 1960, as far back as the World Bank releases an estimate of global living standards that corrects for inflation. In 1968, when oral rehydration solution was invented in Bangladesh and Ehrlich's book was published in New York, 36 percent of humans lived in cities. Now 57 percent do. And while the fraction of us living in cities has almost doubled, living standards worldwide have almost tripled. The graph doesn't show this, but we know from Part I that over the same decades, child deaths fell, life expectancy grew, education soared, and so on. Urbanization accompanied flourishing.

Of course, figure 7.1 is not a simple case of cause and effect. Improving living standards, improving productivity, technological and social change, and denser living are all supporting characters in one big, complicated story of the last half century. What the graph shows is that when people have more options—which is one thing that having more money means—they often choose cities. People choose one an-

Figure 7.1. Better together: Living standards rose as the world urbanized

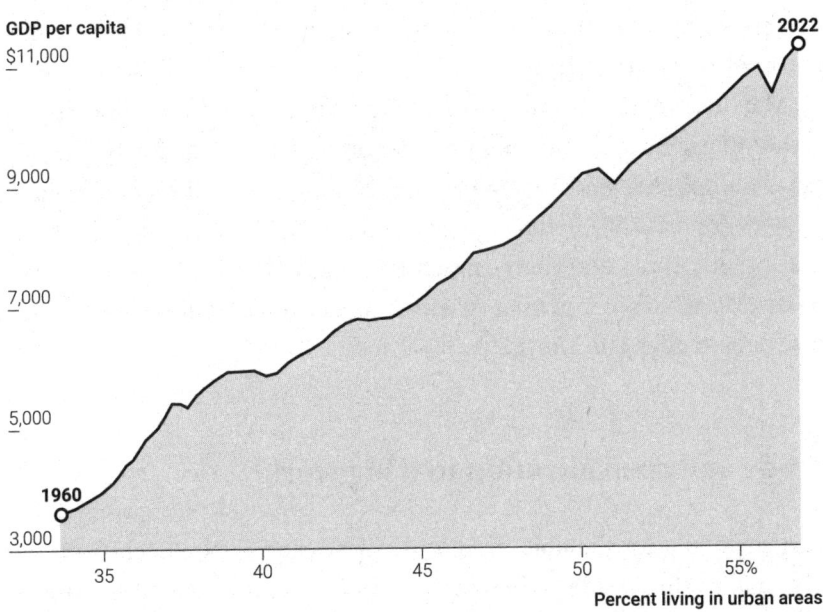

other. The rent is so damn high, in part, because other humans are so damn valuable. We pay just to be near them.

So what *are* people good for, economically speaking? We have already seen one benefit: People have valuable ideas. But you do not need to move to Bogotá to warm a baby with Kangaroo Mother Care. You don't need to move to Japan, where Akasaki, Amano, and Nakamura improved the LED, to read by its light. So what else? Why do we move to cities?

For starters, people move to cities to be near people who might hire them—that is, for jobs. We, your authors, did. We both moved to Austin for its university. But work is only a half answer. The reason that high-paying jobs are more likely to exist in cities is that people are more likely to be especially productive when working in close collaboration with a wide variety of other people—both people who are like them and people who have different, complementary skills.

Another fact behind the global trend toward urban living is this: All of that productive *making* becomes someone else's *using* or *enjoying*. We are all sellers sometimes (if only when we get a job and sell our labor) and buyers sometimes. Cities offer more that we can buy. Cities offer more customers and residents, which means more reason to build that park, music venue, sports stadium, or museum. And cities make one another easier to find.

Maybe someday soon people will no longer need to collocate together to get the benefits that physical proximity brings today. Maybe new technologies and new ways of organizing will let us collaborate at work (or leisure!) better at a distance. Even if so, that won't prove that other people don't have much to offer. It would mean only that observing what's happening in cities would underestimate the value that people offer one another.

Trade and specialization in a big world

Larger populations enable more trade between people. Each transaction makes things a little better than they otherwise would be. If it is not obvious to you what is so good about trade, imagine trying to produce everything you use and enjoy yourself. Your food, your clothes, your medicines. Your flush toilet, your electricity, your hot water. Your pediatric vaccinations and firefighting and traffic lights and train lines. Your computer, and the music that streams from it. All while being the only person looking after and educating your own children. Trade means that we can pick up someone else's book when we want to learn something new or be entertained. (Not everyone needs to do their own demographic research.)

A core idea here is *specialization*. Specialization allows tasks to be done by people who are good at them. Over time, specialization empowers people to become experts who are good at some very narrow *something*, and to spend their time doing it. There is more for everybody if we each concentrate on making what we are good at and then trade with one another.

And here's the point: Doing something specialized only makes sense if enough people want you to do it (and are willing to support your efforts). That's fixed costs again.

Medical care is an important example because everybody values being healthy. Enjoying the very best ramen bowl is not one of the most important things in life. Making sure you and your loved ones have the care they need for their gravest illnesses might be. Scale effects make it possible for a doctor to specialize in treating just your condition. She can find enough patients to make that a productive way to contribute her time and talents. Indeed, how to provide high-quality healthcare and keep hospitals open in rural places is a big challenge in U.S. policymaking. There are too few patients to pay the fixed costs of a big hospital or to motivate a specialist to move there.

Dean went back to Tulsa when his dad, and later his mom, had cancer. When he sat with them waiting for and waiting through their infusions, they chatted with the other patients who had traveled in for treatment from smaller Oklahoma towns. Tulsa has enough people to make the scale economics of a big cancer center make sense. Jenks, Skiatook, Claremore, Glenpool, Bristow, Vinita, and Nowata don't.

•

Seema's KMC ward is in a government medical college in the district's capital city. One reason it is able to save underweight newborns is that Seema knows how to help. She is not merely a medical professional. She is not merely a nurse. She is not merely a neonatal nurse. She is a neonatal nurse skilled in the particular set of compassionate, low-resource, peer-reviewed techniques called Kangaroo Mother Care.

But we still need to go one level deeper: The KMC ward is able to help *any* babies only because it is able to help *many* babies. Part of Dean's contribution to the KMC ward is shopping in Lucknow and sourcing supplies from friends in Sweden, but a bigger part is as a research and funding partner. He is codirector, with Diane, of the nonprofit that makes the case to philanthropies that the KMC ward is worth paying for. Central to Dean's pitch is how cost-effective the KMC ward is at saving lives.

The main cost of the program is the salaries of nurses like Seema and their managers and support staff. That averages out to a few hundred dollars per baby in the program. Statistics show that the program prevents at least one death for every ten babies admitted. No one knows ahead of time which of these very fragile babies would survive even without the attention of KMC nurses. So ten babies and their mothers are helped in order to save one. That means that on average the program prevents a neonatal death for a few thousand dollars (in addition to whatever other good it does for the admitted babies and their moms). That is *very inexpensive* compared to the other lifesaving strategies that philanthropies and governments know how to do.

The cost per baby can be this low only because there are so many babies already together within the government medical college. Twenty years ago, only about a fifth of births in Uttar Pradesh happened in a medical facility rather than at home. Now that's flipped. Less than a fifth happen at home. That's great progress for mothers' obstetric care and for newborns' vaccinations. And it means this hospital sees thirty births a day on average. That's a lot: A hospital in Texas made the national news in 2021 for a "rare and exceptional" 107 births over a four-day stretch (working out to twenty-seven per day).

Someone who sees the economy as a zero-sum game might take the crowds and stretched, hardworking staff at Seema's hospital as signs that there are too many patients for the hospital to support. But consider this: Out of an average day's thirty births, most will be ready to go home, but one or two will be candidates for the help that the KMC ward can provide. That's a flow that keeps the KMC program just the right amount of busy. Before it became normal to give birth in a facility, rather than at home, could the KMC program have worked? No. It never would have been practical to hire a nurse and send her ranging across the district to track down a low-birthweight baby, even if she might eventually find one in some village. So underweight babies would have faced their poor odds of survival at home, without Seema's specialized care.

What makes the KMC ward so inexpensive per baby is that the costs of the managers and specialized software and nursing shifts (responsible for a whole room at a time) are *shared* among so many babies. Starting up a KMC ward is a fixed cost. Scale effects make it possible and cost-effective.

Incentives for innovation depend on scale, too

If more people move to your neighborhood, it might be able to support a new noodle place. That's fixed costs. But that restaurant didn't invent shio ramen. The difference between the scale effects of making and the scale effects of inventing is why we separated chapter 7 (this one, about fixed costs) from chapter 6 (about people growing humanity's stock of ideas that don't get used up). It's worth understanding that these are two different ways that more populous means more prosperous.

And now that you've understood that, we're going to mix it up, because these two economic processes—non-rival innovation, from the last chapter, and fixed costs, from this one—interact. How? Innovation is a fixed cost, too. Just like it makes more sense to open a restaurant where more people are going to eat, it makes more sense to do the work of inventing something that more people are going to want. In the short run and locally, entrepreneurs will start fewer innovative restaurants in small towns than in cities. In the long run and globally, innovators will start fewer companies and clinics, fewer drug trials, fewer writing projects—less of everything else, if there's a smaller market for their creations.

So to understand this consequence of depopulation, we need to step back from our experiences as consumers of things and ask why innovation happens—electric vehicles, plant-based meats, a cochlear implant. Once invented, these get mass-produced because enough someones out there want them. But these technologies cost a lot to *develop*. That's above and beyond dishing out bowls of a tried-and-true recipe. Humanity can only afford the up-front investment in all that engineering and refining because it can eventually be spread across many buyers.

Manufacturing one smartphone can cost a few hundred dollars. But *inventing* the next smartphone may cost hundreds of millions. That's why billionaires use the same smartphone that you do. Maybe theirs is covered in a gold case or encrusted with diamonds—your authors can only guess how billionaires bedazzle their things. But we know that it's the same phone inside. No tech company is willing to put up the fixed costs of developing a new phone if the potential market is just a few hundred people. Billionaires don't get their own smartphone models because even the exorbitant price that a billionaires-only phone could command wouldn't cover the fixed costs. Selling 100 million phones at $1,000 each can recoup R&D expenses that selling a handful of billionaires-only phones at, say, $1 million each cannot.

Or how about a different phone, tailored to the battery-life needs and durability requirements of the poorer regions of the world? The prospect of 50 million units at $50 apiece sold across Africa and South Asia still outperforms the billionaire product.

The power of people. Millions of poor farmers and traders in the developing world can spur innovation that all the billionaires in the world cannot.

A former Apple CEO led one effort to produce such a phone in the 2010s. Many companies now compete to develop smartphones tailored to the needs of the global poor—and still no companies are making a phone for the billionaires. We get to have nice (meaning incredibly powerful and capable and productivity-enhancing) phones only because we have a lot of neighbors on this planet.

Because scale matters, a depopulating planet will be able to fill fewer niches. In a back-and-forth with other readers about our Spike article, one commenter wrote:

> Well, at some point you don't have enough people to support modernity. Markets, factories, supply chains all require a certain minimum number of producers and consumers in order to work. A world with 1/100th of the current population would not have iPhones, Airbus jets, or Baldur's Gate; there simply wouldn't be enough consumers to support the production of those things. "Oh but I don't care about—" yes well, shrink the population enough, and at some point it won't be able to produce things you do care about, like laptop computers and publishing houses and cancer medication.

Things you do care about

What might we miss in a smaller world? No one can say exactly, because depopulation in a technologically advanced world has never happened before. But we can make a narrower case study of some recent innovation.

COVID brought fame to messenger ribonucleic acid (or "mRNA") and to the biotechnology that uses it. In the few years since BioNTech and Pfizer's mRNA vaccine was first approved in the UK in December 2020, researchers have been hard at work on other mRNA innovations. Moderna (whose name is a contraction of "modified" and "RNA") first became widely known for its COVID vaccine, but the company has a broader mission to make mRNA medicines. Others do, too. New vaccines have been developed against RSV, a virus dangerous to newborns. HIV and malaria vaccines are being researched now. mRNA treatments for cancers and genetic diseases are in the pipeline, too. (Still no sealpox vaccine.)

This is all very new. mRNA medicines hardly existed before 2019. mRNA itself had only been discovered seventy years before. All prior disease vaccines that had been put into circulation used different technology. Even experimentally, these types of vaccines were almost unknown: In 2013 there had been a trial of an mRNA vaccine for rabies; in 2015 there had been a test of a flu vaccine. The supereffective mRNA vaccines for COVID were an invention just in time.

Reaching this point took the work of many scientists in specialized roles—and large, branching roots of other people supporting them. One innovation modified the chemistry of messenger RNA to keep the body's immune system from destroying an mRNA injection before it can do any good. The biochemist Katalin Karikó developed this modification (pseudouridine) with the immunologist Drew Weissman in 2005. It was a long, lonely road. She was demoted at the University of Pennsylvania when she couldn't find grant funding. Still, she kept working toward making mRNA useful. But Karikó shares credit: "Everyone just incrementally added something—including me."

Another crucial step was managing to encase the mRNA in a tiny bubble of fat so it could get safely into the body's cells and go to work. In 1987, a grad student named Robert Malone experimented with a version of this, using fat droplets to send mRNA into frog embryos. By 2001, these fat drops were refined into a four-component recipe for "lipid nanoparticles." These particles make a vaccine practical and viable at scale. The first drug that used them was approved in 2018.

Even if the ultimate linchpins of the first mRNA vaccines were the efforts of a bare handful of lead scientists, and even though the 2023 Nobel Prize in Medicine went only to Karikó and Weissman, there were many contributors and a large infrastructure that supported them. Pieter Cullis, a biochemist whose labs pioneered the lipid nanoparticles, agrees with Karikó that many collaborators, scholars, technicians, and workers made the vaccines happen: "We're talking hundreds, probably thousands of people who have been working together to make these [lipid nanoparticle] systems so that they're actually ready for prime time."

The appearance of niche economic specialization is new, on the long timescale of humanity. At the start of the industrial revolution, specialization might have involved eighteen separate job functions to produce a pin. Today, it involves countless thousands, all existing contemporaneously, to develop (never mind globally distribute) an mRNA vaccine—not only the lead researchers in their labs, but the postdocs who support them; the logistical staff of clinical trials (trial numbers NCT04470427 and NCT04405076 in the case of COVID vaccines, among other studies leading to these); the network of researchers with adjacent expertise to provide peer review, interrogating and validating scientific claims; the teams of scientists and administrators at the National Institutes of Health and the National Science Foundation to evaluate applications and award funding that this research requires; the dozens of university roles that administer the grants and support the researchers; the hundreds or thousands who trained all of these people. And not only these, of course, but the engineers and industrial designers who made the lab benches, microscopes, centrifuges, and autoclaves; makers of the statistical software to analyze and graph results and makers of the typesetting software to publish findings. On and on and on.

Would new miracle mRNA medicines have existed in a much smaller population—say, 1 billion people instead of our 8 billion? Of course, many things would be different in a world one-eighth our actual size, but let's focus for now on this one potential difference: In a world of 1 billion people, would we have been likely to get the mRNA technology we now have? We think the answer is far from a definite *yes*.

If you need to bake six cookies, but your recipe is by the dozen, it is easy to halve it: a half cup of sugar instead of a whole cup. Sugar is sugar in a teaspoon or a tablespoon or a cup. Some activities scale like cups of sugar in cookie recipes. But many important ones do not.

We specialize. We collaborate with others who specialize in something else. We share costs of big projects. We learn from each other—not just from the words on pages of old textbooks, but from our ultra-specialized collaborators here and now. Because we, your authors, improved one another's ideas iteratively, we would never have been able to produce this book if each were trying to write it alone, even given twice the time. (And we asked a lot of other people for help, too. You can find their names in our acknowledgments.)

Four people working together can move a heavy piece of furniture that would stay put if, one after another, each gave their best shove individually. All the truer for complex feats of biological engineering, like shoving messenger RNA into cell cytoplasm.

From billions to millions to zero?

So we have seen that fixed costs matter for noodles and phones and high-budget television, yes, but also for vaccine recipes and neonatal wards and cancer treatment. Here is something else important, a consequence bigger than big. Some day humanity will go extinct.

We hope it won't be for a long time. Maybe the sun will burn out first. Some observers note that if humans stay around for a span typical of mammalian species, then we've got between a half million and a million years left to go.

But, of course, we're not a typical mammalian species. We have figured out how to radically lower our mortality rates and how to radically lower our fertility rates. Which of our fellow mammals does that? No other species has figured out cardiac bypasses to extend the lives of adults or vasectomies and intrauterine devices to choose the number and timing of their offspring. These facts tell us not to count on the extinction risk of the typical mammalian species.

And these facts raise the possibility that we humans have something special to worry about. Humanity could hasten its own extinction if birth rates stay too low for a long time. This was the risk that we quantified in chapter 1 when we tallied that, if global birth rates go below two and stay there, then four-fifths of all human births, ever, are already in today's past. No other mammal species chooses that.

We saw in Part I how fast we might go from billions to millions. But that didn't tell us how, exactly, the millions might ever become zero. So let's sketch out some ways that a larger population might offer protection that a smaller one could not.

When it comes to avoiding certain types of catastrophic risks, scale matters. The problem of an asteroid hurtling toward Earth boils down to just another problem of fixed costs—for your economics professor authors, anyway. Let's sketch that out. We are picturing cinematic, violent extinction risks, big enough to kill us all. The important word is *all*.

> **Some problems are like asteroids.** A larger population would have a better chance at resolving some shared threats, like one big asteroid that could wipe everybody out.

The type of risk we are envisioning here is not the type of risk that arises because some person dreams up the doomsday machine that ends us—the next child born might become the grand villain, after all. Consider here risks that come from something other than people. Risks that are coming, if they are, whether humanity is ready or not and no matter how many of us there are. A large asteroid of the kind that wiped out the dinosaurs. A continent-wide supervolcano. A pandemic as contagious as the measles and as deadly as rabies. But don't get snagged on the details of any particular scenario. These particular catastrophes are offered as metaphors for any risks that would work like this:

> **A threat with a fixed cost:** A threat has arisen that will kill all humans (however many) unless a large cost is paid to escape it (such as by deflecting an asteroid) within a certain time period.

This large cost is *fixed* because it must be paid to deflect the asteroid whether "killing all of us" means killing a few million or killing a few billion. Which would be more able to pay the fixed cost in time: a larger population or a smaller one? A stabilized population or one that had been depopulating for a couple centuries?

A tiny bit of arithmetic goes a long way here. Imagine two futures. In both futures, living standards have climbed marvelously, so world income per capita is $70,000 (about what it is now in the United States). But in one future there are 10 billion people alive to enjoy it, and in the other there are only 10 million people, one for every thousand in the larger future.

Toward both worlds, the big and the small, the same planet-killing asteroid is coming. Suppose we can deflect the asteroid, but it will take more than a moon shot. It will take a $10 trillion investment, paid in some necessary number of researcher hours, some necessary amount of ore newly mined out of the Earth, some necessary number of fabrication hours, and so on. With that investment, we can build enough rockets and guidance systems, and we can crash-course train enough astronauts and ground support in time to nudge the big space rock to bypass Earth.

Great! Ten trillion dollars is a lot to pay, where "pay" really means diverting material resources and labor efforts from other valuable activities in our economies. Maybe there are no new cars or trains or airplane models built for a few years, as emergency industrial powers are used to bend people and steel toward the engineering and manufacturing needs of the global effort. Maybe some lifesaving medicines are discovered a few decades later than they would otherwise be because research careers are diverted toward outer space. Maybe for some reason chocolate chips are scarce for a while. But survival of the species is worth it. Led by the biggest economies, governments of the world get together and start contributing, in the ways that governments can, especially by taxing and then spending and building.

How much will the effort tax our economies? Well, in the 10-billion-person global economy, it would require about 1.5 percent of all human activity to be redirected to this Asteroid Shot. (That's 1.5 percent of the

$70,000 per capita income, 10 billion times over, to get to $10 trillion.) Some folks will gripe, and some will deny there's an asteroid at all. Governments will mismanage some of the funds and activities. Some billionaires will build their own rockets. It will be messy. But we might just pull off an average 1.5 percent tax hike, globally, and complete the effort.

What about the 10-million-person global economy? That works out to a tax rate of (let's see, move the decimal three places . . .) 1,500 percent. Uh-oh.

Even if every human activity were immediately and fully redirected to the shared cause of flicking away the asteroid—and even if somehow we kept on being able to function without anyone doing agriculture or day care or garbage collection or maintaining the wind turbines, and even if no resources were wasted on errors or corruption or arrogance (good luck!)—we would raise only $700 billion (100 percent of $70,000, 10 million times over), falling 93 percent short of the $10 trillion investment needed to mount humanity's most important rescue party.

So the larger world has the better chance of avoiding catastrophe. At least, it does for the types of cases that fit the fixed-cost model. That's not merely asteroids. The model also captures developing a new vaccine against some new plague, where the same fixed cost is a smaller per-person cost when the population is larger. We could build the rocket ships or light the space lasers or develop and test the vaccine with a smaller average sacrifice from each of us—if there were enough of us.

And even before the asteroid appears on our tracking systems, a larger population already produces an advantage: It supports faster technological progress. Cures sooner, discoveries earlier, burdens lifted before they are borne too long. If an asteroid is coming, it's coming whether we're ready or not. We're more likely to be ready if science and engineering has progressed further by the time it arrives.

The upshot is that at least some existential threats would be more likely to be survived by a larger population. There might not be enough of us around to pull off a defense against a supervolcano or asteroid or whatever threat pops up. Just like every other possibility for existential risk out there, we can't know or even imagine the details that might prove decisive. But we can know this: Maybe we will someday face a threat that we could better surmount if there were more of us to contribute.

The economics of asteroids also apply to less cinematic civilizational threats

Let's work through the logic of fixed costs one last time, because this is an important case: decarbonization. In chapter 3, we saw that climate change is too urgent for depopulation to make much difference in the decades that matter most. The reason is timing. The world needs to reach net-zero carbon emissions more quickly than any intentional effort could bend the curve of population growth. But what about after that? What is the next environmental goal after net-zero emissions?

Once we reach that milestone, there would remain the important task of taking carbon back out of the atmosphere: sequestering it, for example, in reforested areas or geological formations or via some other "negative emissions" technology we have not yet discovered. The possibility of negative emissions at scale at some future date is no excuse to do less to address climate now. But even if some miracle delivered net-zero emissions today, greenhouse gas concentrations are *already* too high because of humanity's recent past.

As we write, carbon in the atmosphere stands at about 425 parts per million. NASA figures that's about 145 parts per million more than when our industrial revolutions began dumping carbon into the atmosphere by the gigaton. Possibly by the year our flows of emissions reach net zero, there will be 600 to 700 parts per million. Maybe it will be some different number, but it will be *some number*.

> **Another threat with a fixed cost:** Once humanity has stopped net emissions of greenhouse gases, there will remain a stock of greenhouse gas in the atmosphere, unless and until a large cost is paid to remove it.

So the inescapable decision that future generations will face is whether to clean carbon out of the air, and if so, how much to invest in the effort. Whatever size cleanup job we leave to future generations will be a fixed cost to them. What exactly is *fixed*? *Fixed* doesn't mean "solved," remember, it means "numerically unchanging." Here, the amount of greenhouse gas will be numerically unchanging no matter how many future people are around to clean it up. They won't get to choose the greenhouse gas concentration that they inherit, but they will have to deal with it.

Because our carbon footprint will someday be somebody's fixed cost, the logic of scale effects applies. A bigger economy—not bigger on average, not bigger per person, but bigger overall—will more easily and more quickly afford the costs of removing that carbon. One more ton of carbon sequestered for each person in a 10-billion-person population requires less individual sacrifice and does more good than five tons sequestered for each person in a 1-billion-person population.

That was an unexpected insight from the research team we assembled to assess the climate impacts of population scenarios. Working through the math and the model revealed how a bigger population (not now, but far into the future) might actually be helpful for making progress on climate. A richer, more populous future will face less carbon dioxide already in the atmosphere *per person*, per inventor, per worker, and per dollar or rupee in the economy. Chapter 3 showed that depopulation barely changes the size of the fixed-cost problem that we leave future generations because it kicks in too late. But depopulation would slash the resources they have to cope. What matters against a global fixed cost is the total size of the global economy. So once the task switches from emissions reduction to emissions cleanup, many hands could make light work.

Uncertainty is no excuse

But are asteroids really coming? And could humanity really become small enough that we lose the niches that would otherwise produce the next immunotherapy to fight cancer, or even lose the ability to produce what niche immunotherapies for rare diseases we've already discovered? (Could any company even stay in business producing them, if a smaller population meant that there were only ten potential patients a year who needed the medicine instead of one thousand?)

We don't know. We do not know what is going to happen over the centuries. No one can say with certainty what such an unprecedented future as depopulation might bring. But we can project with certainty that *if birth rates remain low,* then humanity would become quite small—perhaps vulnerably small—on a timeline of centuries.

·

Whatever it is you value that humans make and do, was there less of it a century ago, when there were fewer of us on the planet together? Vaccines? Streaming, high-budget television? Books or newsletters by a writer who is just your style? Social statistics and ideas about how to use them to build better communities? If so, the Spike warns you not to be confident that a few hundred million people will pull it off in a small and shrinking future. Nobody knows what a complex, interdependent modern economy would be able to produce when there are so few people to fill its niches. The appearance of niche economic specialization in human society is so new, on the scale of the Spike, that nobody should pretend to know what would happen without it.

Chapter 8

More good is better

One consequence of depopulation is so quiet that it would be easy to skip past it without noticing. Many billions of lives that could be excellent and full of wellbeing and joy would never be lived.

Would that silence be a peace to welcome or a loss to mourn?

Religious traditions have their points of view. The Quran asks Muslims, "How can you disbelieve in Allah—when you were lifeless and He gave you life?" This question suggests poetically that not yet existing is a missing-out similar to no longer being alive. The God of Abraham famously charged Eve and Adam to "be fertile and increase, fill the earth and master it," implying that life—existence rather than nonexistence—was a good to be pursued. Thich Nhat Hanh, a Vietnamese Buddhist teacher, said, "The greatest miracle is to be alive."

But it's not only the religious who say that human life is valuable. For many secular humanists, the chance to be alive is the greatest good luck. The astronomer Carl Sagan, an agnostic, thought "we are rare and precious because we are alive." Sagan, facing an early death from cancer, chose to be thankful for the goodness that he had: "Far better, it seems to me, in our vulnerability, is to look Death in the eye and to be grateful every day for the brief but magnificent opportunity that life provides." And although some say that philosophy is learning to die, novelist Ursula K. Le Guin thought life was what mattered: "We don't live in order to die, we live in order to live."

What about bigger stakes than a single human life? Most thinkers—secular and religious alike—would agree that human extinction would be a tragedy. Something important would be lost if all of humanity were gone tomorrow. Something even greater would be lost if all *life*, human and not, were gone tomorrow. Wellbeing needs, well . . . being.

This chapter asks: What does it matter if another person gets to be born to live a good life? What does it matter if they don't? What does it matter if billions don't? As we stack up consequences for parents, for the environment, for technological progress and living standards, should we also give some consideration—not everything, not zero, *some* consideration—to the would-be people who would exist if the population stabilizes and not if it declines? Or should we care only about the wellbeing of people here and now?

Questions about values—questions beyond the graphs and numbers—surface whenever someone asks about the long-term future of the human population. Climate scholars and activists raise them. Our university colleagues raise them. The readers of our op-ed raised them. They can't be settled by presentations of statistical facts. But they can't be avoided in any honest and complete assessment of stabilization versus depopulation.

Nor can we leave unexplained our position in this book, which is: Yes, population size matters, and yes, progress toward a better future matters, and no, that does not motivate or justify pushing people into having children they don't want.

So in this chapter we ask these questions, and invite you to consider the ethics of depopulation. Our belief is that the chance to live a good life counts for something. To affirm this benefit is to say that depopulation matters beyond what it means for the trajectory of the economy, for balancing a government's budget, or for geopolitical power. The solvency of public pension programs is not the only thing at stake. Population is people.

Our piece of a big question

There are many ways to reach the understanding that it is a good thing when a good life is lived. It is possible to feel it. It is possible to reason to it, stepping through logic and details that arrive at this conclusion. A niche research subfield of economics and philosophy called "population ethics" does exactly that. This chapter introduces only as much population ethics as we need to compare depopulation against stabilization. It doesn't aim to settle everything, nor to survey everything that any expert has ever written. Seeing this is big enough:

> **More Good is Better.** It's better if there is more good in the world, other things being equal, and worse if there is less. That includes good lives: It's better if there are more good lives.

"More Good is Better" may sound like a meaningless truism, but if a good life is a good thing, then it has teeth. It says we shouldn't care *only* about the quality of lives, but also how many people get to enjoy them. This idea affirms that if we could wave a magic wand and add one more good life to the future, and if we could do so without costing anyone else anything important, then adding that life is better than choosing not to. It would make the world a better place overall. And so, if one possible future would contain more good lives, with their good experiences, then that counts as one benefit of that possible future.

When we write "better," we are talking about the wellbeing of everyone. The idea of making the future better, overall and impartially—not merely better for you and your friends—has many names and flavors. When we write "better," we mean what the U.S. Constitution calls "the general welfare." We mean what economists call "social welfare," what philosophers of ethics study when they do "axiology," what the heroes mean when they talk about "the greater good," and what the villains pretend to mean when they invoke the same phrase. We mean the kind of overall betterness that health or environmental

159

economists in government agencies ask about when they weigh gains to some (say, the health benefits of removing lead from water service lines) against losses to others (somebody's tax rate and somebody else's inconvenience of having streets temporarily torn up) and assess what is overall *better*.

We believe that the general welfare matters and that everyone should care which future would be impartially better. That is not the same as believing that betterness or social welfare is the *only thing* that matters for any policy or social question. The same U.S. Constitution that seeks to promote the general welfare also lists rights and rules that the government is not allowed to disregard. Anyone who agrees that the general welfare is *among* the things that matter for society's biggest policy and social decisions can agree with what we say in this chapter—that More Good is Better.

When we write "good lives," we mean "good lives overall, on net." We know that there are many ways to have a valuable, good life, so we are not being prescriptive about what a good life means. All sorts of experiences, bodies, traditions, or capabilities could be part of somebody's good life. Some people would say that a life is good if the person whose life it is says so. Others would insist that a good life needs certain resources, or depends on the situation, or has to be great to count as "good." It's okay that everybody doesn't agree about what a good life is. What matters for what we have to say here is merely that there is such a thing as a good life. We say that it would be better, all else equal, if the future held more of whatever good lives are.

As we go through this chapter, we'll start from several commonsense notions. First, we hold this truth to be self-evident: Impartiality is ethically right. Impartiality means that a future in which some person named Abe is doing great, someone else named Bhimrao is doing well, and a third person, Chen, is struggling is every bit as good or bad as a future in which Chen is doing great, Abe is doing well, and Bhimrao is struggling. If asking about the general welfare means anything, it means being evenhanded.

Some cynics say that nothing matters. They say that even though some future or another may be better *for them*, there's no such thing as a future that is better or worse *overall* when it comes to population—or climate, equity, freedom, security, or anything else someone else might value. We won't entertain this cynical view.

We'll also dismiss a subtler nihilism. It worries that—even if we can say what's better or worse when it comes to some unchanged set of people—there is no meaningful better or worse about futures in which different lives are lived. It's hard enough to judge, someone might say, when a policy has winners and losers among people here now. But population change? Two futures with different numbers of different people—one in which Carlos and Debbie are born generations from now and another in which Erica, Francisco, and Gautam are born generations from now? Some would say that we can't judge, that nothing is better.

We disagree. Why? Because every social or policy question that matters is about futures in which different people are born and different lives are lived. That fact doesn't make judging what might be better among possible futures some impenetrable puzzle. All of us make such judgments all the time. Every big shift in our societies (civil rights, no-fault divorce, Medicaid, electric lights) has had some impact on what people have chosen for their family lives—and therefore on which people later came to exist.

So we can judge, for example, that improving educational access for girls (and everyone else) in developing countries over the past century was good. Saying that *improving education was good* is a judgment that compares scenarios with different sets of people in them. That is because a whole generation of better-educated girls grew into women with different outlooks, different family-planning goals, and different childbearing patterns. And so different children were born at different times and in different numbers, compared to some alternative history in which educational access had not improved. Nearly all of us understand the statement "improving educational access for girls in developing countries was good" as both sensible and correct, even though it compares scenarios with different numbers of different people in them. We don't stop asking which futures would be better just because to be a different future is to be a different set of people.

We have set the pieces on our board: There are such things as good lives. Some futures would be better than others and some futures would be worse. Every consequential policy or social change affects which people later come to be born. And when we ask which futures would be better, we must answer impartially. Now we are ready to face the question that this chapter is for, whether More Good is Better.

A blank space

Imagine a photo of a large group of people. You're in it, too. It could be your family, if you're the type that gets together for extended family gatherings. Maybe for you, the photo is a group of friends on a camping trip or at a bachelorette party or on a sports team. Maybe you don't have to imagine. Maybe you have this photo propped on a shelf or saved in your phone.

Now imagine that half of the people in the photo with you never existed. They wouldn't die because they never lived. You couldn't miss *them*, in particular, because you never met them. You would be part of a different team, a different family, a different class, a different group of friends. There would be a different photo, but those missing people wouldn't be in it. They wouldn't be anywhere. Would that be worse? What if it were not only your group that was cut by half, but the whole world? Would the universe be a little less bright for the billions it was missing?

Humanity's numbers might decline or stabilize. In this book, you have seen the graphs that chart these possibilities. Here is what is hard to appreciate, what's hard to really, deeply feel from a figure on a page or a number like 8.2 billion: The numbers aren't just numbers. They are people. What's missing in the blank space following the downslope of the Spike is *people* who someday could be as real as you are, with experiences and aspirations and joys and sorrows that matter just as much as yours do.

The problem with a blank space is that people don't see it. Here are three comments that readers posted when we published our article about the Spike:

- "I was alive in the early 1970s when the world population was half as much as it is now. I don't recall thinking we had too few people then."
- "World population in 1955 was ≈2.5B people. Today around 8B. I wasn't alive in 1955, but, from what I read of that time and hear from those who were, it was a pretty nice time to be alive, no 'shortage' of people."
- "I remember a planet with less than half as many people and it was wonderful. I loved every day, especially when I could be away from people (and this was much easier). If I wanted a job as a young person, I just walked into a business, filled out an application, and had a job. Getting into college, I had many choices and I do not remember it being at all stressful."

We understand why these readers thought so. But there's a blind spot hiding here. Perhaps these readers were imagining or remembering some of history's more privileged lives, among those that were lived in the twentieth century.

Let's look at 1955. World life expectancy at birth was only fifty years. One in five babies died before turning five. Angioplasty to clear blocked arteries, combination chemotherapy to treat cancer, and synthetic insulin to treat diabetes were not yet available. So people lost loved ones when today they don't have to. In the United States, neither civil rights nor the gender revolution had yet made the progress toward a freer and more equitable society that would come over the following decades. In India, life expectancy at birth was in the thirties in 1955. The Dalit movement to reject the caste system by converting to Buddhism would not start for another year. In China, the Great Leap Forward was just about to commence and kill tens of millions. In 1955, most of Africa was still colonized and would not be decolonized for years. Many lives in 1955 were not what many readers, accustomed to the standards of seven decades later, would call "pretty nice."

Not seeing the whole history is a common blind spot. It is not the ethical blind spot that this chapter is about, but noticing it might help to notice another one, a hidden premise that all three comments have in common. It is a privilege that all three readers share.

The commenters are alive. So they write from the point of view of somebody who is alive. (Good for them! Future people should be so lucky!) The population of 1955 was about one-third as large as today's. Among you (the reader) and the two of us authors, only one of us might be here in a world the size of 1955.

It's not a failure if someone does not immediately notice their ethical blind spots, and especially not this blind spot. To the contrary, it's normal. Everybody reading this exists, so we all share that perspective and that privilege. It's understandable not to notice the underlying assumption that the future billions who only *might* come to exist do not count.

But what if they did count—these future people who may or may not someday exist, depending on what we do, you do, and everyone else does? If we evaluate depopulation only from the point of view of people who already are alive—if we hide the assumption that we get to exist—then we ignore the question that this chapter is here to answer: Does it count as a benefit of stabilization that more good lives get to be lived?

Without any representative of the future to complain, it's tempting to ignore or dismiss this question. But this temptation *may* be wrong. Future people can't speak for themselves. If they have a stake that counts, then it's up to us to hear their case and consider their cause.

Two hypothetical futures: Which would be better?

Do the additional lives that would get to be lived count as a benefit of stabilizing the population? To make progress and say anything concrete, we're going to have to be more precise and start smaller. Doing so will let us build up to answering a common question: *Shouldn't we care only about the quality of lives lived and not their quantity?*

To start simple, we're going to ask only about adding good lives, magically without making any other changes and magically without any risk of the added lives being bad. This is our version of a way that the philosopher John Broome found to clarify the question. In the real world, adding lives does have other effects, including on other people. In the real world, some lives have been bad. Both of those real complications matter. And we've just spent several chapters thinking through some of the biggest real-world complications. But we've got to set aside those details for long enough to see whether there is any value in good lives at all, under any circumstances.

Here are the two simplified possibilities (they are also in figure 8.1, where each dot is a person, and dots higher on the page are better lives):

Figure 8.1. Which future would be better, A or B?

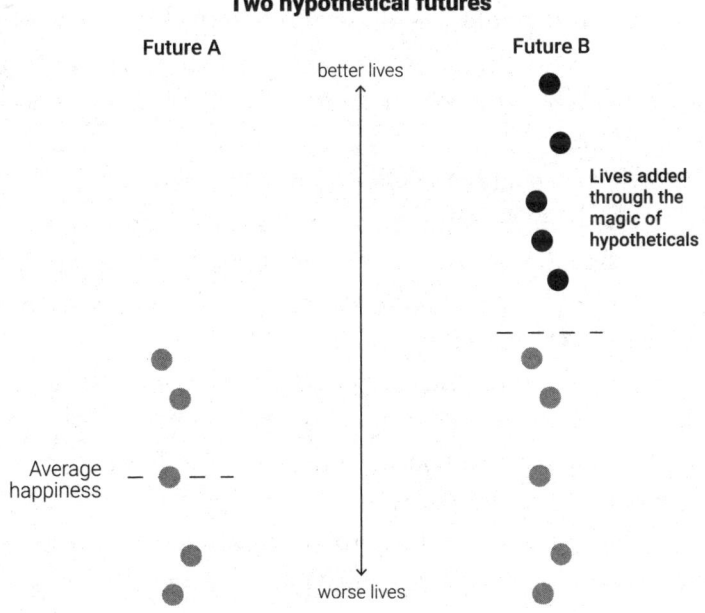

- **Future A** is whatever the status quo is, low birth rates and all. Your life, our lives, and the life of everybody you know about is in Future A.
- **Future B** is built in two magical steps. First, make an exact copy of Future A. That will be half of Future B, with one identical life for every life in Future A. Second, make the other half of Future B wonderful. Each person in this other half is living a wonderfully good life, better than the life of anyone you know about, and better than *any* life in Future A.

Every person and every life in Future A is also in Future B with the same wellbeing, the same ups and downs. But the additional lives in Future B are superbly wonderful and joyful. In other words, Future B is Future A plus an equal number of even-happier lives.

Built from these instructions, Future A and Future B turn out to differ in two ways: in their *size* and in their *quality of life*. Future B has twice as many people as Future A. And Future B has better lives in it, because half of the people are better off than anyone in Future A and the other half are just as well-off. One way of thinking about this is that the *average* life is better in Future B than the average life in Future A. But it's not just the statistical average that's better in Future B. The best life is better in Future B. The median (middle) life is better in Future B, too.

What about inequality? There's no single correct way to measure inequality, but we made Future B so that it matches Future A in having the same Gini Index, one of the standard measures of inequality used by economists. What's more, the worst-off person in Future B is no worse off than the worst-off person in Future A.

The question is, which future would be *better* overall? Because none of the lives that are lived in Future B but not in Future A are anything but excellent, and because nobody is made worse off if Future B happens instead of Future A, we say the choice is easy. Future B would be better than Future A. We find it hard to argue otherwise earnestly.

Perhaps someone would be tempted to say that Future B is worse because it hides some bad consequences for others. But the example is constructed so nothing else is helped or harmed by the existence of the extra people in B. There's no environmental destruction, for example, from choosing Future B. The thought experiment ensures that nobody has to parent babies they don't want to parent in order to get Future B's larger population. It's magic—useful, clarifying magic—that lets us separate the question of this chapter from the issues we've seen in previous chapters.

Perhaps someone else would be tempted to say that someone low on the wellbeing scale in Future B (someone toward the bottom of the chart who exists in both A and B) is harmed because now they have to suffer the unpleasantness or envy of sharing a society with people so much better off than them. But the construction of the example has ruled this out, too. We aren't saying merely that, for the overlapping people who exist in either A or B, incomes or job satisfaction or family lives are held equal across A and B. We're saying, for the people who exist in both, their *wellbeing* is held equal. Perhaps they aren't the envious types. Or perhaps in Future B they get an extra scoop of ice cream to make up for the occasional painful awareness of the existence of people so much happier than them. Or perhaps they aren't aware because the really great lives in Future B happen later, rather than contemporaneously with the bottom half of lives, or on a different planet. You can construct the example in whatever way you choose to keep the thought experiment tidy. And as a magically tidy construction, Future B is the better option.

Comparing stabilization against depopulation isn't as tidy as comparing Future B against Future A. For one, we've sketched an idyllic future where none of the added lives are bad. But of course, suffering matters, too. More Good is Better is an *if-then* claim: If a life would, on net, be good, then it makes things better. So in the real world, we would need to take suffering into account, too. More bad would be worse.

And yet, we have learned something important by stripping away complications. Adding extra, wonderful lives and changing nothing else makes a future better. Leaving those lives out makes the future worse. If Future B is better than Future A (we say it is), and if the extra lives are the only difference (they are; we set it up that way), then Future B is better *because of the extra, very good lives*. More Good is Better.

But wait! Future B is better merely because the lives are better!

Here is an objection that we often hear: "No: Future B is better because *lives in it are better*, not because there are more of them! The wellbeing of the typical person is higher in Future B, for example, because the added good lives pull up the overall profile. It's about the *quality* of lives, their *quantity* doesn't matter at all."

Here's the most straightforward version of an *only-quality-not-quantity* view, though there are others: We could try to judge how good or bad different futures would be only by the *average* wellbeing that people would have. How happy are people on average? How well are their material, social, intellectual, spiritual needs and aspirations met, *on average*? In principle, a smaller population could have better lives, on average, or the other way around. The *only-quality-not-quantity* approach tells us that if we knew about average wellbeing, then we could ignore how many lives were lived.

Our view, that More Good is Better, says that quantity and quality both matter—that we can't ignore how many lives get to be lived. Why do we think that caring only about quality misses something crucial? In part, because following its logic leads to some pretty strange places, and to conclusions we cannot endorse.

If the *only-quality-not-quantity* proposal is right, then adding good lives doesn't necessarily make things better, even if they would be splendid lives. That's because—according to the *only-quality-not-quantity* position—adding new lives makes things better only *if* those lives would bring up the average.

Why only-quality fails: Contrary to the only-quality view, adding lives cannot make things worse as long as the added people's lives are good (in an imaginary scenario with no consequences for any other people).

It is not for you or us to say that a good, worthwhile life, one that all in all brings happiness or value to its owner and harms no one else, is unworthy of existence. But the *only-quality-not-quantity* approach mistakenly disagrees. The *only-quality-not-quantity* position tells us that it would be better (not fine, not good enough, *better*) if some people never exist, even if they would love their lives.

Here's why that's wrong: Imagine a child born in Uttar Pradesh, maybe next year. This particular child is lucky. She is poor by your standards, but her family loves her. She manages to avoid serious illness. She is happy and healthy as a child and enjoys her siblings. She rides the tide of improving gender equity to a school she loves attending as an adolescent. She finds a way to a job she is proud of, maybe as a nurse. She still enjoys her siblings as an adult and calls them walking to and from work. Her parents give her say in her arranged marriage. It turns out to be a good match. She is friends with her sister-in-law. She enjoys becoming a parent. She's healthier and wealthier and safer than most women who grew up in the same part of the world in decades and centuries past, even if she's not as healthy and wealthy and safe as most people who read this book. In short, she grows up to live a life that is happy, if below average for 2025—a life that she wouldn't trade for nonexistence, after thoughtful meditation on the question.

What if her wellbeing is below average, not only for 2025, but for all time? Did her life make things worse? According to *only-quality-not-quantity*, it would have been better if she had never existed. Not better for her or according to her. She decidedly wants her life! But *the universe* would have been better without her, this view would say, because her existence nudges down the average. This is one way to see that the *only-quality-not-quantity* approach goes wrong.

Let's see that same point again by adding a life to the diagram we've been building. We will make this different from the example of the Uttar Pradeshi woman, by making the added life more splendid than any life so far lived. Now imagine, in figure 8.2:

- **Future C** is just like Future B, but adds one more person. This person's happy life is better than yours (the reader's) and ours (the authors'). They love their life. It's very good. Really it's quite amazing by your standards. But, in this example, that one more very good life is not quite as good as the average life in the very excellent Future B.

Oops. Adding that extra happy life in Future C pulled down the sky-high average of Future B. So according to the *only-quality-not-quantity* view, Future C is worse than Future B.

The *only-quality-not-quantity* approach is not merely *indifferent* to adding this good life. It instructs us that adding a good life would

Figure 8.2. Now which future would be better, B or C?

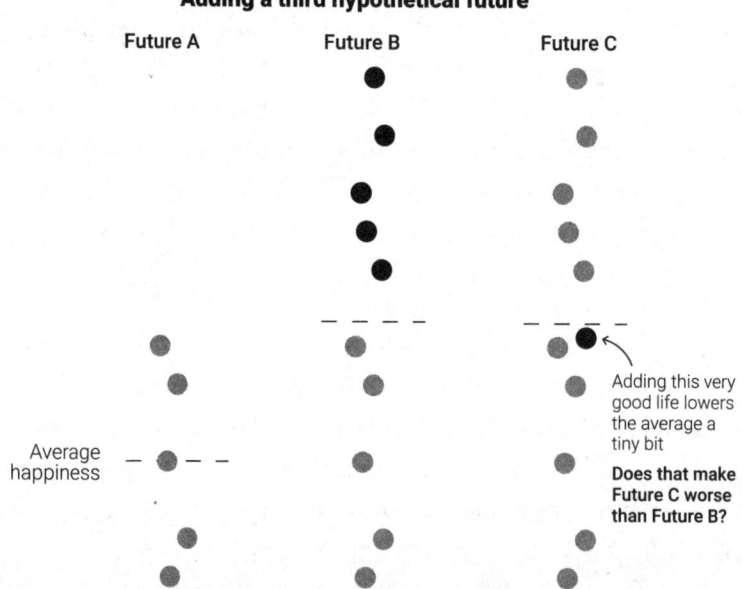

Adding a third hypothetical future

Future A   Future B   Future C

Average happiness

Adding this very good life lowers the average a tiny bit

Does that make Future C worse than Future B?

make things *worse*, in this case. It says this even though the person added to Future C would be happy to be alive. Even though nobody and nothing else is harmed.

How could adding a good, happy life—a life better than yours and better than any life ever lived so far in humanity's long history—make things worse, if nobody else is harmed or affected at all? Our answer is that it can't, so the *only-quality-not-quantity* view, even if it sometimes points in the right direction, must be wrong as an overall, infallible guide to what is good.

To be clear: It's not that a person *couldn't* think Future C is worse than Future B or *isn't allowed to* because of some contradiction of formal logic. When we say "it's wrong to rank Future B as better than Future C" or "it's wrong that adding that very good life makes things worse," we're not saying that a robot couldn't be programmed to disagree without frying its circuits. We mean that somebody who has thought through the implications shouldn't disagree.

This is a possible *person* we are talking about here. They would live a very good life that they would be grateful for. Why should anyone say no? What reason to deny that person a life could they give (in this imaginary example with no costs or consequences for anyone or anything else)? What arguments would they present to the judge in some cosmic court? What would they tell this potential person's lawyer or fairy godmother? So yes, it's possible to think Future B is better than Future C, but we don't think anyone should.

Focusing only on quality leads to the same set of problems however one defines quality. Instead of the average, what about deciding what would be best by comparing the median person's wellbeing? Or the wellbeing of the worst-off person only, ignoring everyone else? Any *only-quality-not-quantity* formulation turns out to fail a basic test by recommending that some people with good, valuable lives make matters worse, just by existing.

Do you see that as a problem? We do. That's one reason we say that the *only-quality-not-quantity* view is wrong. We began this section by considering the possibility that "it's about the *quality* of lives, their *quantity* doesn't matter at all." But doing that would lead us to preferring that some great lives that had no negative impacts on anyone else would never happen. So we conclude that caring *only* for quality just can't work as a tool or an indicator to judge whether depopulation would be better than stabilization.

We say both quality and quantity matter. That still leaves plenty of open questions. For example: How *exactly* should we weigh quality against quantity when there is a trade-off to make? That is a big question, but not one we need to answer in this book. As a practical matter of facts—facts about health, mortality, education, income, leisure time, security, and many other indicators—a bigger world has proven to be a better world (on average and by most other quality criteria that one might prefer). So, for the real-world choices that lie ahead of humanity, stabilization looks better than depopulation, whether we narrowly consider only quality or whether we say that More Good is Better, which means that both the quality and quantity of good lives count.

Who does Future B make a difference for?

There's a story that helps us see that More Good is Better. You may have heard a version of it before, but it's worth hearing again.

In the hour before dawn, walking along the beach after an overnight storm, you see someone picking up starfish and gently throwing them back into the ocean, where they can survive. Many starfish are stranded on the beach, as far as you can see in either direction.

"Why are you doing that?" you ask.

"This one's still alive. It may live, if the offshore pull is strong enough. I can help them."

"But there are too many!" you object. "You'll never make a difference!"

The person stoops again and plops another star into the water. "It made a difference for that one."

Loren Eiseley, an anthropologist at the University of Pennsylvania, wrote the first version of this story in the 1960s. Like Kangaroo

Mother Care, the Pythagorean theorem, and other non-rival innovations, Eiseley's story has thrived and its applications evolved. So the version that you might have heard could be a little different from the story Eiseley wrote in *The Unexpected Universe*.

Eiseley's story captures an idea called "independence" by the economists who study social wellbeing. The lesson from the starfish story is that in an evaluation about which of two futures would be better (throw back a single starfish or don't), you shouldn't worry about what won't change or be different across those two futures (the many others on the beach that will never be helped; the many more others in the ocean that don't need help). You should think only about the *differences* between the two options. And if those differences are only good—if the consequences are good for everybody touched by a policy, by a charitable program, or by your actions—then, independently of anything else, that's enough to know what would be better.

The extra lives in Future B and the added life in Future C have a lot of *good* in them. In particular, they are *good experiences for the people who live those lives*. These people would like their experiences. And that's all. The mere existence of these added lives does not make matters worse or better for anybody else, in our simplified scenarios, so we don't need to consider the unaffected people in our evaluation of what future is better. Evaluations like average wellbeing fail because their judgments are affected by unaffected people—or starfish.

Future C is better than Future B, which is better than Future A. More Good is Better, when all else is equal. We've seen this by considering magic examples where good lives just pop in. To keep going, we will have to turn off the magic. To grapple with the ethics of population, we need to consider both magical scenarios and real-world consequences.

Wouldn't a kajillion lives be even better?

If an additional life would be good in a clean and simple thought experiment, does it mean ever more lives would always be better in the real world? Our answer here is pretty simple. No need to go through complicated scenarios or imagine a Future D. Believing that something is good just doesn't mean the same thing as "It would always be better to have any imaginable amount more, whatever the costs and consequences."

The one comment with the greatest number of recommendation upvotes at our *New York Times* article was this:

> By this logic, we should all be having as many kids as possible. Why stop at 2 kids, when I can theoretically have 25? Think of all the potential joyful lives I am suppressing by not having as many children as biologically possible.

Because so many readers agreed with this objection, we must take the blame for leaving the misunderstanding open. Of course it would be worse if everyone had twenty-five kids! It's beyond our imagination exactly how it would wreck lives, society, and women's health if the only thing that anybody ever tried to do was to parent another kid. It would be bad enough indeed if someone who absolutely didn't want any children ended up with even one.

Even if a stabilized future would be better than a depopulated one, it doesn't mean more babies are always better than fewer. It's a mistake to confuse "something would be good" with "something would be the only good thing and should be our only goal to the exclusion of all other goals." It's good to feed hungry people; it's good to teach children; it's good to heal the sick. That's all true, even though a dollar, a minute, a thought spent on one of those good goals is not spent on the others. None of these is the one and only thing we should do, to the exclusion of all other goals and values. Each of the last five chapters has considered something that matters.

It's probably not a good idea to eat an entire pie. But it might sometimes be a good idea to eat one slice (unless you're allergic, or happen to have no taste for pie). There's no conflict here. The fact is, even if stabilization is better than depopulation, it doesn't follow that a kajillion lives would be better than a few billion. (And what about beyond the facts? What if we again turn on the magic of far-flung hypotheticals? Could a kajillion lives ever be the best plan? That question goes beyond the practical question that this book is here to answer. But many scholars are captivated by it. If you're interested in the philosophy of a hypothetically enormous population, then after the conclusion of this book, you'll find a Repugnant Appendix.)

Stand for reproductive freedom, and care about a depopulating world, too

When we talk about values and the ethics of population change, one of the first questions is usually about reproductive freedom. If a world with more good lives would be better, the worry goes, then wouldn't that justify forcing people to have children that they would rather not have? It might feel like there is a conflict between freedom and the idea that More Good is Better. Is standing for reproductive freedom compatible with caring about depopulation? Yes, these ideas are compatible. They are both part of making a better future.

The fact that something would have benefits or be better when people chose to do it does not imply it's okay to force people to do it. Let's start by stepping away from pregnancy in particular. Most of us can recognize that it would be valuable if you saved a life by donating one of your kidneys. That would make the world a lot better for somebody, and a little better overall. But recognizing this doesn't mean that the law should compel you to part with your kidney. The philosopher Judith Jarvis Thomson first spelled out the moral analogy between other people's kidney failure and reproductive freedom. For many obvious reasons, it makes both society as a whole and individual lives better when your body is yours, not someone else's kidney farm.

We could really stop there, but we are keenly aware that when we propose that More Good is Better, someone might bristle in alarm. Wouldn't agreeing to the idea that good experiences in good lives make the world a better place mean that all of us should drop everything to raise more children? Wouldn't it mean that women would be obligated to conceive and birth babies they don't want? No, because there is no actual conflict in believing both of the following two sentences:

It would be *better* if the world did not depopulate.

Nobody should be *forced* or *required* to have a baby (or not to have a baby).

Let's see it through the lens of Seema's work as a nurse in the KMC ward. One way to offer people the benefits of good, happy experiences, loving relationships, and fulfilling projects is to participate in the teamwork of creating their lives. Another way, what Seema does at work, is to participate in the teamwork of *extending* their lives, by saving them from dying in their very first days. Seema's work does not create lives. But saving the lives of babies so close to birth does allow many whole (long) lifetimes of good experiences to happen that otherwise would not.

Seema's profession is her choice. But what if she wanted to leave the KMC ward to take a different job, or to marry and move to a different district, or to stop being a nurse for any other reason? Almost nobody would endorse using the government to compel Seema to stay at her post, continuing to save lives. The obvious truth that "*the government should not try to force anyone to be a nurse*" is perfectly compatible with the idea that "*one way the world could be better, all else equal, is if through the efforts of nurses (and with society's help), more babies survived to live a good life.*"

In the same way, the obvious truth that "*the government should not try to force anyone to be a parent*" is perfectly compatible with the idea that "*one way the world could be better, all else equal, is if through the efforts of parents (and with society's help), more babies were conceived and born to live a good life.*" Trying to force people's big life decisions is an atrocious idea that has nothing to do with the proposition that avoiding depopulation would be valuable.

In the case of nurses and saving lives, it is easy to see this truth because governments, as a matter of standing policy, do not tend to force people into nursing (or any other profession) against their will. In the case of parents creating lives, alarm bells trigger because some governments do force women into bearing children against their will, to say nothing of forced sterilizations. But there is no inherent conflict here, either.

We can respect individual freedom not to be a nurse. And in the same way, we can respect the freedom not to be a mother, or a death row lawyer, or a kidney donor, or an aid worker in a war zone, or a volunteer at a suicide prevention hotline, and so on. And we can do it all while acknowledging that life is good. Of course we can!

If you agree that Seema is not required to be a nurse, then you should agree that nobody should be required to become a parent, merely because life is valuable and More Good is Better. The world is more complicated than that. The threat of coercive reproductive policy—as real and harmful as it is—does not refute the idea that More Good is Better, or even speak to it.

What we can learn from progress on matching kidney donors to patients

So then what *does* More Good is Better mean, in practice? What would it look like to care about the value of life as a society, while respecting individual choice about parenting?

What to do to avoid depopulation is the question for the next part of the book. For now, we will tell a story that offers a preview. It's about the challenges of matching kidney donors to patients in need. Kidneys, we said a few pages back, make a powerful analogy for reproductive freedom. Most healthy people have two kidneys and could do fine with one. So kidney transplants often start from living people who donate a kidney to help a relative. Altruistic kidney donations do a lot of good. They save the lives of people who wouldn't otherwise have access to dialysis (in poorer countries, not everybody does), and they improve the lives of people who do.

The trouble is that a transplant can only happen if a donor matches blood and tissue types with a patient. Donors tend to want to help the people they know and love—a parent, a sibling, a child—but family members may not be a match for each other. For a long time, doctors have understood that they could make more matches happen in pairs: One donor from family X wants to help a relative, but doesn't match; another donor from family Y wants to help a relative, but doesn't match. If the donors happen to line up across families, a two-by-two trade—family X giving a kidney to Y and family Y giving a kidney to X—could happen with four surgeries in one day. That's an improvement, but it still leaves many people out. What are the chances that all four people in families X and Y are ready to go and the two families manage to find each other at that right moment?

That question is the kind that excites Alvin E. Roth. Roth is an economist who studies how people make matches in large groups. A job is a "match" between a worker and a firm. An accepted college admission is a "match" between a student and an institution. A romantic match is a "match." And, a person donating a kidney to another who needs one and shares blood and tissue types is a match. In the 1990s, Roth helped the medical profession improve its tools to match doctors-in-training to medical residencies. When Roth heard about this problem in kidney donations, he realized his tools could help there, too.

Roth and his collaborators used what they had pioneered in the economics of matching to build a new system for kidney donations. First that meant building up databases and processes to help families like X and Y find each other more easily for a two-family swap. Later it meant devising new algorithms that could identify and propose longer chains of donors and recipients. In long chains, your spouse might get a kidney while your spare kidney goes to someone else's mom (with whom you match). Her son would give his spare kidney to someone else (with whom he matches). And so on. Often these chains of dozens of unrelated people could get going because of one "non-directed" donor—someone who didn't have a sick relative and so wasn't asking for a kidney to come back to *their* recipient, in return.

U.S. medical institutions adopted Roth's system. Family members with a mismatched blood type could finally help their loved ones. The waiting time for a kidney fell. Thousands more transplants happened. Lives were extended and improved. Roth won a Nobel Prize in 2012. This increase in transplants created more good, and it made things better.

The moral of this story is not that we expect economists to solve parenting by designing a better tool to match parents to babysitters or romantic partners to one another. The point is that within the bounds of free, voluntary choice, there is often room to make things go better. Before Roth's system, kidney donation was voluntary. After Roth's system, kidney donation was voluntary. Before Roth's system, prospects were worse for people with kidney disease. After Roth's system, prospects were better.

It is unimaginative and untrue to think that respecting free choice means everyone is stuck with whatever happens to be the status quo. What Al Roth and many doctors, nurses, and organ donors have proven is that a smart and compassionate rethink at a systemic level can make for a better future—can even add more life to the world—without overriding anyone's self-determination or bodily autonomy. That's not a plan for avoiding depopulation, but it is inspiration.

·

We told you at the beginning of this book that what needs to happen now is to start a conversation about depopulation on humanity's horizon. Chances are, an hour of reading and thinking is not enough to spark an epiphany about the value in getting to experience a good life for someone distant in time and place. That's okay. This chapter isn't meant to settle the issue. It's an invitation to engage with it. That's hard work. It can't happen all at once.

Being impartial—caring about people far beyond our immediate circle—is hard. And not only for grand questions of the future of humanity. A grounded analogy might be helpful here. Local housing politics often turns on partiality: How much weight should one give to the voices and demands of current residents?

Mike's wife, April, tries to think more broadly in her job in Austin's planning department. She encourages her department and the city's elected representatives to consider not just current Austinites, but also people who only *might* get to join the Austin community, depending in part on what she and her colleagues manage to accomplish.

April tries to keep in mind how different development plans could be a boon to the people who would come to live in Austin, if only more housing were available. They could live closer to their jobs instead of fighting traffic each day to commute and pollute from far-flung suburbs. That's not an easy position to hold: New housing and denser neighborhoods often dissatisfy incumbents—people lucky enough to be here now and have their voices heard. Potential Austinites don't get to show up at the community feedback meetings. Still, April wants to consider their wellbeing, too.

> **Potential Austinites count.** "Better" and "worse" can't only mean better and worse for the people who already live in Austin. "Better" means for everyone.

> **Potential humans count, too.** "Better" and "worse" can't only mean better and worse for the people who are already here or who will be born no matter what else happens. "Better" means for everyone.

Even though More Good is Better isn't the one right idea that settles everything (no one right idea is), doesn't the fact that one future would contain more good than another count for *something*? And if—*if*—together we might find ways to support aspirations for parenting and caregiving that turn the future away from depopulation, without harming one another or sacrificing anything important, then wouldn't that be better? Maybe a lot better?

PART IV

The Path Ahead

Chapter 9

Depopulation won't fix itself

The last six chapters told us that a stable population wouldn't be an environmental catastrophe and that depopulation wouldn't relieve us from the need for urgent action on climate. They told us that gender equity and higher birth rates need not be in tension—that there is no good path toward population stabilization that does not begin with lifting and sharing the burdens that women have borne as they carried humanity up the Spike. These chapters showed us that the world has gotten better, not worse, as our population soared, in part because of the soaring population. The economics of scale and shared innovations mean that we can do more good together than alone. We're not misers dividing up meager crumbs; we're baking a big pie. And the last of these chapters asked us to reflect on whether we can see value in good lives getting to be lived.

The task for these earlier chapters was to understand whether it would be better for the world population to stabilize, instead of decline. When we weigh all the facts, evidence, and argument, we say yes, we should hope to avoid depopulation. More than hope, we should try to avoid it, if we can. But can we? And how?

Or will the situation somehow fix itself? When we show people the Spike, a common first response is to wonder whether fertility decline will somehow stop at two. We explain to them that it won't—because it hasn't. Two-thirds of the world lives in countries where fertility is already below replacement. Fertility decline in those places did not stop at two. So we know that fertility can fall right through two without pausing.

Another response, when someone first hears of low fertility, is that migration will solve things. But depopulation is a *global* phenomenon. Once every country is a low-fertility country, allowing migration will still be a good idea. But it will not add more people to the planetary stock. Migration won't prevent depopulation. Not, at least, if the migrants' homelands happen to be on Earth.

Yet low fertility is still new on the scale of centuries. Maybe things will turn around, even though they haven't yet. If low fertility would "self-correct," so that birth rates rise to replacement on their own after falling below two, then we needn't invest scarce attention or resources to understanding depopulation. There are plenty of other pressing problems in the world, after all. We could all work on something else. And then we wouldn't run the risk that some new law or program or movement, although done with good intent, ends up making things worse. Could it be that—even though stabilization would be better than depopulation—the best response to the warning of the Spike is no response?

> **Don't expect depopulation to fix itself.** We cannot count on automatic stabilizers to avoid depopulation, if humanity does not choose to change its course.

This chapter considers what we should expect to happen automatically and what we shouldn't. Of course, we cannot know the future, but we know enough today to assess the possibilities for an automatic reversal, one by one.

There is nothing natural or inevitable about a birth rate of two

Some may think that it's only natural that humanity will return to an average of about two children per woman and settle there over some longer run. If so, then in its long history, humanity has never yet achieved its natural state. We weren't living "naturally" at the turn of the twentieth century when the global average of births per woman was above five. We weren't living "naturally" a century earlier, when global fertility rates were a little above six. There's no evidence that Bronze or Stone Age humans were living "naturally" at two births, either. And we aren't living "naturally" today, when most populations on Earth have below-replacement fertility.

There are no natural forces that pulled ancient fertility down to two. There are no natural forces that have pulled modern fertility back up to two now in places where it has fallen below it. No natural forces stand ready to activate and automatically stabilize the global population.

In demography, there is no thermostat that keeps births and deaths in balance. So far, the number of births each day has exceeded the number of deaths each day. Soon, the number of deaths will instead exceed the number of births. There is no reason that these two numbers would happen to be the same, so this imbalance is nothing new. Birth and death rates have never held at equal levels over any period for which anyone has reliable data (the last century or so) or even for the longer period for which there is plausibly-in-the-right-ballpark data (the last couple millennia). And where fertility rates have stuck to one number or another, it hasn't been the number two. Fertility in Japan has been bouncing around 1.4 for thirty years. A constant fertility rate at 1.4 means a shrinking population. History offers no reason to expect that a total fertility rate of around two is the outcome that will naturally or inevitably emerge.

The Amish will not inherit the Earth

But what about the Amish? Even if the rest of us are having few children, the Amish are not. They typically have big families—raising five kids or more in traditional religious enclaves in Pennsylvania and elsewhere. Doesn't the logic of above-replacement fertility mean that these populations will grow and grow, making up an ever-larger fraction of humanity, and eventually bringing global average fertility above replacement?

In recent years, Amish women have had between five and six children on average, according to estimates by the sociologist Lyman Stone. In the mid-1970s, there were about 50,000 Amish. Today there are maybe 350,000. These numbers are estimates—there is no census of the Amish population in the same way there is a census of the Austin population, so estimates will have to do. When others have studied the Amish growth rate, they've benchmarked it at about 3 or 4 percent per year. If the Amish grew at 4 percent a year, then a straightforward extrapolation tells us that in another fifty years, there would be 3.5 million Amish. In one hundred years, 17 million. In two hundred years, almost a billion. On and on, until the Amish outnumber the grains of sand on the Earth. Problem solved, a trillion times over.

While writing this book, we heard "What about the heritability of high-fertility culture?" enough that we published a paper about it in the journal *Demography*. That article worked through the math, social science, and history of the idea. It is true that children who come from larger families do tend to become adults who have more children, on average. Parents' fertility is *correlated* with their children's fertility. But it turns out that this fact isn't enough to expect that the Amish—or anyone else—will soon cover the globe.

There are two ways this idea goes wrong. The first is that the meaning of "high fertility" changes over time. "High fertility" groups today tend to have lower fertility than in their own pasts. That suggests they will have lower fertility still in their futures. For the middle of the twentieth century, Stone cites estimates that the Amish birth rate was between seven and nine children. By 2015, it fell below six. The difference between eight-point-something children and five-point-anything is . . . huge.

The Amish are just one example—researcher Isabel Juniewicz suggested it to us. Here's another, which comes from our *Demography* article: Like in many other places, birth rates in India differ across religious subgroups. India's Muslim minority historically has had higher birth rates. Yet, the total fertility rate among Indian Muslims has fallen from 4.4 in 1992, through 2.7 in 2011, to 2.4 in data collected in 2019 to 2021. Muslims in India have a birth rate now below the birth rate for all Indians not much more than a decade ago. No major subgroup in India, whether you define groups by education, or rural/urban, or religion, is avoiding fertility decline.

A few short decades ago, in Pennsylvania or in India, "high fertility" used to mean something like four children. Now it means something like three. Maybe someday "high fertility" will mean two children instead of one or none. And when "high-fertility groups"—whether that means religious minority subcultures or sub-Saharan African countries—fall below an average of two, they'll shrink, too. Just maybe more slowly.

The second reason that high-fertility religious subpopulations offer no sure deliverance is that the links connecting generations are not perfect. For example, in the United States and Europe, younger generations are less religious than older generations. And younger generations in Latin America are shifting away from Catholicism toward Protestantism.

No parent will be surprised to hear this, but it turns out your kids might choose not to inherit your cultural practices and beliefs. (Mike is working hard at getting Emmet interested in board games, and Dean is working hard at getting his kids hooked on rice and beans. These may stick. They may not.) If you do not have a child, take a moment to reflect seriously about your own teenage years or young adulthood. Dean's parents thought that moving to rural Uttar Pradesh was a truly bad idea. He did it anyway. Social scientists find that children make their own plans. An anecdote of a high-fertility subpopulation may be interesting, but it cannot tell us the shape of the future (or even the present) if it excludes the life stories of children who grow up to leave the fold.

We needn't guess about the future while ignoring history. The past contains more high-fertility religious minorities than only the ones that today feel relevant. In the mid-twentieth century, birth rates among the French Catholics of Canada were right up there with today's high-fertility enclaves. They had a larger starting population than do the Amish today and plenty of room to expand within national borders.

Here's an experiment that we would like you to do if you are not in Quebec: If you are reading this book in a room with other people, don't immediately turn around. But listen for a moment for people speaking French with a Canadian accent. Have the French-Canadian Catholics been covering the globe? If the story about the Amish were right, it should have applied to the Québécois Catholics, too. But that population hasn't exploded. So what happened?

Mike's Catholic grandmother, an immigrant daughter of immigrant parents from Quebec, grew up in the United States, along with her eleven brothers and sisters, in a French-speaking immigrant enclave in Woonsocket, Rhode Island. Mike's mother, Suzanne, also born and raised in that enclave, attended a Catholic school. Born in America, living in America, she was taught by nuns in French. In fact, for a while, she spoke only French in a U.S. city where speaking French was a perfectly functional way to get around. Rosaries and crucifixes adorned her childhood home. She attended church every week (some weeks, twice) and was about as Catholic as you could get. But Suzanne grew up to forget nearly all her French, use contraception, and have only two children—though she prayed daily and attended Mass weekly. Her only sibling, Jeannie, retained more French and kept up with regular Mass, too, but had no children.

History tells us that children *do* leave the fold—or at least choose which of their parents' and grandparents' traditions they adhere to. That is one reason why human demography is not just a branch of

Figure 9.1. The tapering Belisle family tree

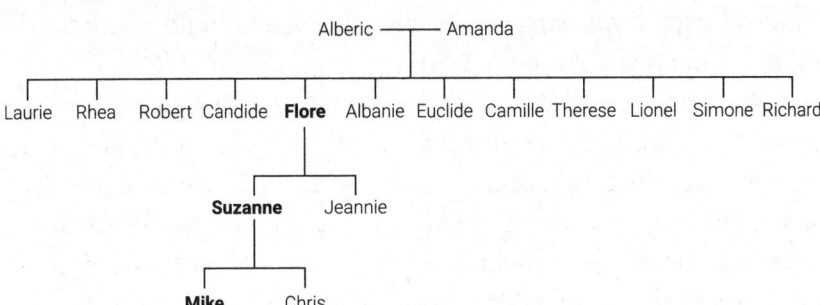

mathematical biology. People aren't bacteria in a petri dish multiplying according to some formula of the temperature and nutrient environment, each twenty-minute generation inheriting the reproductive properties of the prior. People choose. When researchers study the statistical relationship across generations *in people*, it's never a straight, perfect line. Religion, like the rest of culture, is not preserved without alteration through the generations.

For heritable fertility to prevent depopulation, a high-fertility subpopulation would have to hang together, generation after generation, for hundreds of years and ever after. That hanging together would have to persist even after an exponentially expanding Pennsylvania Dutch population ran out of Pennsylvania farmland on which to raise barns. All we can say in favor of the argument that heritable high fertility might come to the rescue is that it is *possible*: The math does not rule it out. But that's pretty far from *plausible*. It's not *likely*. It has never happened. There is no evidence that it is happening, and it's not what anyone should count on.

Doctors cannot cure low fertility

Mike became a father at thirty-two. Dean at thirty-six. In the years since then—we write to you from the vantage of our forties—each of our families has experienced the sadness and frustration of infertility. So we see a lot of value in a world in which doctors could cure infertility. But could they cure *low fertility*?

Infertility is a property of an individual or couple, a medical diagnosis: "failure to achieve pregnancy after twelve months of regular unprotected sexual intercourse." *Low fertility* is a statistical property of a population, the descriptive fact that on average and for whatever cause—including most importantly the cause of *choice*—people are not having very many babies. There's a clear way in which the two phenomena are linked: The biological ability to have children declines in age. When mothers start childbearing later in life, they end up with smaller completed family sizes, so older parenthood is an important statistical predictor of low birth rates. (No country, in any year, on any continent, with an average age at first birth above thirty has ever had a total fertility rate high enough to stabilize the population.)

For the last few decades, in vitro fertilization (IVF) has been empowering some women to have children later, including into their forties. In IVF, eggs are induced to maturation with medicines, surgically retrieved from ovaries, and then combined with sperm in a lab to generate a fertilized embryo to be reimplanted in a uterus. Sometimes the mother's own egg is used, sometimes an egg is donated by another woman. Some eggs are fertilized quickly after they are retrieved. Sometimes they are frozen for years. Sometimes the sperm is injected into the egg's cytoplasm. Sometimes sperm cover the final millimeters on their own. Sometimes the uterus belongs to the child's mother. Sometimes a gestational carrier makes that contribution.

If you are reading this in a rich country and you are older than thirty-five, then you probably know someone who has considered or used IVF or has frozen her eggs, and none of the above will sound like groundbreaking technology to you. Dean's family gave IVF two tries. Overcoming infertility may someday be possible for many more people than it is today. That would be great. But whether this would alter overall birth rates in a big way is a separate question.

Some of the clearest evidence on what IVF has meant for birth rates comes from Israel. In 1994, the Israeli government made in vitro fertilization treatment completely free for all citizens. Within a decade, IVF use increased tenfold. Economists Naomi Gershoni and Corinne Low documented how the wide availability of this technology changed decisions and families in Israel. Women began to get married later. And they had children later, empowered by the opportunity to plan their family lives with more flexibility.

But here's what the Israeli women did not do: have more children. Israeli fertility has been more or less flat over the decades that followed. It was 2.9 in 1993, just before the policy. Ten years later, in 2003, it was still 2.9. And over the longer run? Twenty years later, Israeli fertility was 3.0. Thirty years later, 2.8. The economists warn, in their conclusion, that the politicians who made fertility treatment free in the interest of boosting birth rates did not get the extra births that they were hoping for. "Policymakers should note that the behavioral response to IVF access may cause fertility effects to be [small] or even go in the opposite direction. If women do delay starting families, assured against the outcome of having zero children, they may nonetheless end up with a smaller overall family size, due to the late start." Israeli women used IVF to choose a life of more education and later family formation, not more children.

Elsewhere, it isn't delayed childbearing and difficulty getting pregnant that is causing low birth rates. Infertility in the late thirties is not why average Indians aren't having more babies. Fertility in India is below replacement even though women there mostly start having babies in their early or mid-twenties. Fewer than one in ten Indian thirty-five-year-old women say to surveyors that they want another child. Indeed, women in India are much more likely to seek medical care for permanent sterilization surgery than for help getting pregnant. To be sure, many women in India still face strong pressure from families and others to get sterilization surgery, regardless of what they want. But on average, young women in Uttar Pradesh say they *want* fewer than two children—and they tend to have those one or two children in their twenties.

So the old technology of in vitro fertilization—and pills and shots and the option for younger women to freeze their eggs—probably won't do the trick alone. We live in a world of IVF and egg freezing. And we live in a world of low birth rates. It is by now a historical fact that the former hasn't prevented the latter.

A fictional premise in the sci-fi future of reproduction?

But what about *really* new medical technology, like artificial wombs? Someday, more people—maybe women or men, maybe singles or couples of any sexes and genders—might be able to have genetic offspring at any age of their choosing. Is it possible that breakthrough medical technologies, just on the horizon, will remake the possibilities for reproduction in a way that changes everything?

A 2017 study published in *Nature Communications* described how a lamb was successfully gestated in a plastic bag on a hot plate. Technically, it was "an extra-uterine system to physiologically support the extreme premature lamb." So might advances in sous vide save us?

To get a handle on something so unfamiliar, let's do a thought experiment: Let's apply the logic of the availability of an artificial womb (for those who want it) to the availability of a new contrivance that would eliminate the burden of breastfeeding (for those who want it). Relieving the demands of breastfeeding would be a real boon to some moms. For a small fraction of moms who have a really, *really* hard time with breastfeeding, it would be as monumental as relieving the demands of carrying a pregnancy. For others, it could help relax everyday constraints and pressures, whether waking up in the middle of the night to breastfeed or missing an important meeting because the team rescheduled and didn't take into account your pumping schedule. Would such a technology push birth rates above replacement?

Apparently, no. Fertility wouldn't rebound. The evidence is that we've had that technology—*infant formula*—for a long while. In rich countries, where excellent water infrastructure reduces the risk of contamination, formula has been a safe alternative for decades. In these places (setting aside clinical special cases) healthy babies don't *need* to breastfeed. Sometimes when we explain this to people, they respond that formula is a bad analogy because, alongside the benefits, there are downsides of formula. Maybe it doesn't convey the same protection against infection that breastfeeding does; maybe your mother-in-law will disapprove. Yes, and we expect that, alongside the benefits, there could be some downsides of growing a fetus in a plastic bag, too.

Breastfeeding is great. Formula is great. Our two families took different approaches to this one. Formula might not be for everyone, but it improves life for many, Mike's family included. But formula has coexisted alongside falling birth rates.

Making another person is still hard, even with formula and even with Diclegis to ease morning sickness. Parts of it will still be hard if research priorities shift, as they should, to better support doctors and scientists working to make pregnancy better and safer. The lesson from formula and Diclegis is that maybe expanding humanity's bag of tricks for making babies will raise birth rates a bit, or slow their decline, but it isn't likely to reverse depopulation on its own.

Why not? Let's take technological improvements one step further, as we teeter here on the edge of a sci-fi future, between the normalcy of mixing a bottle of powdered formula and the strangeness of gestating a baby outside of a human body. To clarify our thinking:

> **What if there were a baby button?** Press it, and you get a baby. Press it again, perhaps a year or two later (or right away!), and you get another. Press it as many times as you like. As long as you're willing to raise the kid.

How many times would you press the button? Is the *creation* of babies really the binding constraint for most people? The biggest-picture answer is no, but we should start by saying that for some people, it sure is.

It was for Mike and April, for example. They were married in their college town of Blacksburg, Virginia, not many days after graduating. He was twenty-two. She was twenty-one. They had ambitious plans for their future. They didn't really see how a child could fit into those plans anytime soon, even though they both wanted two or three children eventually. A few years after they were married, she had her urban planning master's degree. Six years after that, he had his PhD and she was working in a planning job. They decided they were ready for kids and were happy when they got pregnant right away. Emmet was born, but having a baby and then a toddler was harder than they had guessed, especially because they didn't want to dial back their ambitions beyond family. So even though they had love and money and support from family and friends, they constantly felt tired and stretched thin. Like many parents of a young child, they never felt like things were under control.

It wasn't until Emmet was seven that they felt like they were ready for a second. They started trying again. A few months passed, and then a year, and then another with no success. They talked about IVF, but didn't pursue it right away, worried that the intensity—shots every day, ultrasounds after ultrasounds, months of organizing their lives around the project of getting pregnant—might mean too much emotional investment in an outcome that might not happen.

And they didn't *need* another. So they kept trying, but both were resigned to the idea that another baby probably wasn't going to happen for them. They were sometimes sad about a life together with a little less life and joy in it. Other times they were excited that they and Emmet could do more together—play, travel, learn—if it would be just the three of them. When Emmet was nine, April took a new job in Austin's city government. Two months later, she was surprised to learn she was pregnant. With the new baby, there would be ten years between their first and second kid. It wasn't the thing they would have planned, but they were happy. But you know the story from chapter 4. That pregnancy ended in a miscarriage, and there probably won't be another.

If there had been a baby button, Mike and April would have pressed it years ago, when they started trying for a second. In fact, they would have pressed it sooner than that. One reason to not get pregnant was that the first pregnancy made April's mind foggy. Her work was important to her and she didn't want pregnancy to compromise her ability to serve the communities that she worked with. A baby button would have erased that concern in a way that transformative medical technology may someday do for others. So if there were a button, Mike and April would have a larger family.

The power of the baby button is that it overcomes *whatever* physical or biological barrier is keeping you from having a(nother) child. Did your family wait too long to get started, relative to the family size you wanted? Are you understandably scared of yet another miscarriage? Does your important work or art or vocation not have the space for you to be pregnant anytime soon? The baby button magically solves all of those problems, plus any other things where there *may* be a problem but nobody quite knows yet. The button gives you a baby—if you choose to press it.

And now to the point: How much would the button bend the Spike? Probably some, but not much, we conjecture. You would push the button only if you want to parent a new baby. The reason why *most* women do not have children in their late thirties is not because they can't. The reason, self-reported by women in surveys, is that by their late thirties, most are satisfied with the number of children they already have, whether zero, two, or some other number.

Between our two families, we have had three live births, four miscarriages, and three failed IVF rounds. We know how hard it can be for people struggling to achieve the families they desire. They deserve both tangible help and loving-kindness. But we also know that people like us are not a large fraction of the global population. Many women are having fewer children not because they are medically unable to have more but because that is the life that they choose. Helping people build the families they want through public investment in fertility treatment is a good idea. And even miraculously effective medical care—even something better than formula, even something better than Diclegis, even the baby button—is only going to create as many babies as people want. Wherever and whenever "as many babies as people want" averages out to less than two, these real and imaginary technologies won't prevent depopulation on their own.

·

In 1930, John Maynard Keynes, famous for his contributions to macroeconomics, made some predictions in his essay "Economic Possibilities for Our Grandchildren." He predicted that a century later (which at the time of writing is roughly now) improving living standards would have led to a fifteen-hour workweek. That, as you know, didn't happen. Today, Keynes's prediction seems silly. But Keynes wasn't wrong that we'd be able to live a 1930 lifestyle on a fifteen-hour workweek with 2030 incomes. We reached that milestone ahead of schedule. What Keynes did not count on was that today, people wouldn't be satisfied with 1930's most amazing lifestyles. Our ambitions expanded as our opportunities and budgets did.

Today, many fertility techno-optimists make a similar error in thinking tech and progress will boost fertility. AI tutors! Robot nannies! Mechanical wombs! Yes, sure. But we've had new tech and big progress supporting pregnancy, parenting, and care work before. IVF! Formula! Disposable diapers! Washing machines! Dishwashers! iPads! The Snoo! We can learn from that.

More time, more money, longer lifespans, and better health have all expanded our opportunities. They, as a matter of historical fact, did not lift birth rates above replacement. It misses a step or two to leap from speculation about future technology that eases biological constraints around birth to the conclusion that we'll all choose to have many more babies. "Technology will make life better and make parenting easier" is not the same as "technology will raise birth rates above replacement." Somebody has to parent the baby for many years once it's out of the bag. Someone has to choose to press the button. Fertility techno-optimism has no answer to why people would start *choosing* children again, instead of all the wonderful competing goals and options that a whiz-bang new world would offer us.

Externalities don't fix themselves

There is one last reason someone might think we should not worry: Because if depopulation really does become a problem, then a government will jump in and fix it. Maybe someday there will be a constructive, compassionate policy response to low birth rates. Our conclusion looks toward what that might look like. But the response that we seek won't be a simple matter of voting yes or signing an executive order. From the vantage of 2025, neither governments nor social scientists yet know what to do. There is no government agency that can implement a desired fertility rate like a central bank can choose a short-term interest rate.

There are two broad ways that governments have tried to change birth rates. They try to coerce people with bans, campaigns, and control. And they try to support people with cash or with social policies that leave people free to choose. Those are our next two chapters.

But before we get into the details of government coercion or government support, there is another question lurking here—one that might explain why no program or policy has yet been ambitious enough to succeed. *Really* supporting parents, *really* empowering people's choices, *really* sharing the burdens of care work, *really* resolving the conflicts and costs of work and family could require *really* big changes, investments, disruptions, and innovations. How much change do society's decision-makers really want?

One reason that decision-makers may not care enough about avoiding depopulation is that much of what would be gained will help people elsewhere and elsewhen. Economists have a name for this type of problem: "externalities." An externality happens when one person makes a decision and another person bears the consequences. Some externalities, like the sharable, non-rival discoveries that come from scientific inquiry, are good. Economists call these positive externalities. Others, like whatever comes out of a factory's smokestack into the air we breathe, are bad.

Environmentalists have long understood the externalities of greenhouse gases. This person's beef consumption, that person's car commute, another person's single-family home blasting an air-conditioning system fed by a coal-fired power plant—these all matter for other people. If my company or my country or my generation emits greenhouse gases, somebody else pays the price. It changes the world for other people, today and in the future. It changes the chances they choke on the smoke of wildfires sparked by climate change. It changes the chances that those wildfires (or floods or droughts) take their homes, maybe their lives.

Externalities ordinarily don't fix themselves. Externalities are economists' classic cases where the sum total of individual, uncoordinated pursuits doesn't lead to the best outcome. Nobody who really knows economics would believe the caricature that economists think the market can solve every problem on its own.

So what do externalities mean for whether low fertility will reverse on its own? Wouldn't governments have an incentive to act? They might face strong incentives to act if citizens demand it of them. But if not, would politicians find it in their political self-interest to confront the issue?

There may be some reasons to think that elected leaders do have such an incentive. In a low-fertility world, an aging population strains social support systems like pensions and healthcare. Too many retirees, not enough workers. These challenges—amounting to an imbalance in government budgets—are not the case for people that we have made in this book. We've said nothing about the problems that come with a high dependency ratio (other than to clarify that we are saying something else). But they are what most people talk about when they talk about depopulation. So if we want to imagine that society's big-picture decision-makers are going to leap into action, then it makes sense to imagine that these well-rehearsed and widely debated reasons are why.

Let's imagine just that. Let's imagine, for the sake of illustration, that elected leaders are concerned about an aging population and that there exists some effective, equitable, noncoercive plan for increasing birth rates among people who want to parent. Let's further imagine that, over the long run, this plan would pay for itself because the children would grow up to be productive workers who paid taxes, grew the economy, had ideas, and generally eased the financial pressures of an otherwise aging population. And finally, let's imagine that everyone— voters, politicians, social scientists—basically agrees on all of these facts.

Even in this cartoonishly optimistic hypothetical, we would be unwise to count on this splendid plan being adopted.

That's because babies are freeloaders. They won't become the workers who could balance society's books for decades. Liberalized immigration and job automation are fast solutions to the problem of too few workers. Increased funding for scientific research is a fast solution to boosting innovation. Restructuring public benefit programs and retirement ages is a fast solution to balancing the books in an aging population. Raising birth rates is a slow alternative to any of these.

Any government or politician that chose the splendid plan to raise birth rates would be working on behalf of future people, not meeting the needs of today's voters. The politician's perspective would have to extend beyond the next election, or even beyond the next decade or two, because their splendid plan would cost money and deepen any budget problem for the first few decades. "What do we want? Change! When do we want it? Phasing in beginning thirty years from now!" . . . is not an effective campaign slogan. And perhaps as bad, that splendid plan would be spending money and effort in part to help people outside of the government's constituency, because progress and innovation shine across national borders.

Whether the population stabilizes or depopulates has big consequences for humanity's future. But that's not what a serious and dutiful politician or bureaucrat worried about the *right here, right now* is motivated to solve. And it's not what potential parents have on their minds when they decide whether or not to have a baby. Babies are little bundles of externalities, so an automatic reversal from our depopulating path is nothing to count on.

It's not Seema's job to worry about population externalities

Here's what is on the mind of Seema, the KMC nurse, and her big sister, Reema. After college and jobs and a master's degree in nursing—an impressive level of education for a young woman from her corner of Uttar Pradesh—Reema got some life-changing news. She had passed the tests and made it through the paperwork. She had been offered a permanent government job as a nursing teacher. It's a goal that she had stalked for a decade, since high school. This secure, prestigious job—far above even Seema's good job as a nurse in the KMC program—means she will be comfortably employed for life. It is the culmination of and reward for her hard work and the many sacrifices of her parents.

After Reema's news came in, after dinner with the KMC team, the two sisters took a walk. To celebrate, they strolled to a cart where a man sells frozen treats. They prefer ice cream, but they economized with bright orange popsicles instead.

Beyond celebration, the walk gave the sisters a chance to talk alone. The new job means it is time for Reema to marry. Her career is now safe: Any future in-laws are unlikely to demand that she abandon a good government salary (which, after all, would go to them, her husband's family). So Reema's future is now certain and bright. What isn't certain is whether she will stick with her plan to have two children. The worldwide consequences of population dynamics have not changed, but Reema's own circumstances have, so maybe she will change her mind in one direction or the other.

Seema's future, meanwhile, has been made less certain by Reema's new job. Sisters in Uttar Pradesh are married off in age order, so Reema's marriage will mean that attention will soon shift to Seema's prospects. There is another sister in between, but the urgency of that decision is closing in. It won't be much longer until her father calls Seema to tell her that she has a proposal from a boy's family.

If Seema gets married, it's the end of her time with the KMC ward. Perhaps she'll get to work in a different nursing job in whatever place her marriage takes her—if she gets to work at all. We might hope she would find a way to keep the job she has, but that is not the reality of her life. One day, Seema will face a decision about whether to push back when her father calls with the big news. But tonight, it's bright orange popsicles under the streetlight with her sister.

Reema jokes: "At least you won't have eight children! Whether you find your salary job or whether your tests don't work out and you stay at home, you'll only have one kid to take care of."

The benefits of population stabilization, we have seen, would be big. But all evening, while Seema and Reema talk about their news and their plans, they never once mention the consequences that their children might have for the environment, for macroeconomic growth, or for asteroid management. They never mention whether the babies whose lives they save as nurses would have those consequences, either. It would be silly to expect them to. They have enough to talk about.

Solving externalities requires collective action

One reader of our Spike article asked: "Show of hands for the women out there who will volunteer to have more babies than they had planned to help out."

It is not a solution to ask anyone to have more children than they want. It's society's collective task to lift the burdens of parents and other caretakers. Externalities need cooperative solutions.

Depopulation is the worst type of externality, of a kind with climate change. It is not merely a national policy issue. It is a global, intergenerational policy and cultural issue. No single person, family, business, country, or generation can solve climate change on its own. No single person, family, business, country, or generation has the right incentives (or the power) to avoid depopulation, either. Like climate policy has been a decades-long political effort at coordination, responding to global depopulation is going to have to be something that people do together.

We hope that this happens someday. We hope that countries and communities and generations coordinate and collaborate to build a future in which more people decide they want to be parents or to parent more children and in which they have the support they need to do it well. But if such a solution is constructed, it will be in the same way that air and water pollution have been successfully fought in many places and in the same gritty way that climate change may eventually be fixed: After decades of research and advocacy, after many careers devoted to overcoming challenges, and after many political fights debating whether anything should change at all—after all of that, and after many failures along the way, we might pull out a win. We might manage to avert the worst climate disasters; we might manage to clear the air; we might keep alive the potential of a populous, prosperous, flourishing future. But not without attention and effort and investment and votes.

Will that happen? Will we find a solution? Not an automatic one, we have seen. The answer is unlikely to emerge from business as usual. We won't find a solution without a concerted, conscious effort. And not without understanding what matters to Reema and Seema and to women and men everywhere, when they choose their jobs and families.

Chapter 10

Government control cannot force stabilization

If parents need to *want* more babies on average for there to *be* more babies on average, then we believe the only path to a stabilized population is through better lives for mothers and fathers, so that billions of individual choices sum up to a rebound in birth rates. For that to happen, parenting will need to become better than it is today.

That's what we, your authors, hope and believe in. But what about a shortcut through government control? Wouldn't rolling back the clock on contraception and abortion access be an obvious response for a politician obsessed with falling birth rates? Couldn't some governments find a coercive way to raise birth rates that skips the difficult step of making lives better for parents? Can't governments control the population?

Most of the politicians and voters who support abortion restrictions, like most of the politicians and voters who oppose abortion restrictions, are not fretting about population-level average birth rates. Many people support banning abortion because they think an abortion does impermissible harm. Many people—including us, your authors—support reproductive freedom because they think nobody should be forced to have a baby who doesn't choose to. But already, some influential voices around the world have begun to say that a reason to restrict abortion is to increase long-run, overall population growth rates.

To some people in some countries, the threat of a successful political movement to strip away reproductive autonomy *for the sake of birth rates* already looms. To others, this possibility feels remote, peddled only in other, distant places, or else at the fringes of their own societies. We can't foresee the next decade's politics—in our country or any other. But we can, as we have done elsewhere in this book, look backward. When governments worried about *over*population in the twentieth century, many, like India and China, reacted with coercion and harm. If governments react thoughtlessly to depopulation—and some governments will—then it could happen again.

In chapter 8, we said that restricting reproductive choice is wrong as a matter of ethics. Another way it's wrong is as a matter of fact, in its presumption that doing so would raise birth rates by enough to escape depopulation. That's what this chapter shows.

The future will be chosen

More than ever in history, and considering the world as a whole, parenting—whether, when, and how many—is a choice.

> **There will only be a future with many children in it if people choose to have them.** Parenting must be attractive if we expect people to choose it—and choice is what will matter in the long run.

No, parenting will never be perfectly freely chosen for everyone. Even if you want a baby, you can't choose which month you get pregnant, whether you have a miscarriage, whether the baby is born premature or overdue, or any of the zillion facts about what kid you get. As long as parenting is something humans do, there will be uncontrollable surprises. So even in places and times where abortion and contraception are freely available, becoming a parent (which usually involves another person's wants and choices, to say nothing of families and cultures) is not an uncomplicated, simple choice. Nobody, parent or not, gets everything they choose.

We mean something specific when we say that choice is what will matter. We mean that, over the long run that matters for global population growth, the average number of babies a whole population has tends to be close, overall, to the average number of babies the people in that population want. And this will only be truer in the future, as the technical tools and social norms spread to empower more people to choose whether to parent or not to parent and how and when.

The limits of control

Many readers of our *New York Times* article, like so many others, believed the familiar story that population control policies were responsible for the below-replacement birth rates that exist today in many places. China's One Child Policy is everyone's ready example (although history has others). Readers wrote:

- "Governments often influence the reproduction rate positively or negatively (China)."
- "China did the world an immense favor in leading the way."
- "Grossly overpopulated places like China have been forced to control them."
- "China had a one-child policy . . . and this enabled China to focus its resources on a more slowly growing number of people. This change seems to have made possible the economic miracle that occurred within China. In my last China visit, I took the elevator to the top of the Jin Mao Tower and had a glass of wine. I was amazed at the wealth I saw in the surrounding neighborhood."

There were many more comments about government-led population control. Some readers, like these, approved. Others disapproved.

What so many had in common is that they *believed* in the power of coercion. They believed that a government can enforce a birth rate.

It makes sense to believe this, based on what everyone has so often been told. In 2023, when India's population became larger than China's for the first time, we read newspaper explainers where sentences like "China's extended 'one-child policy' has resulted in a steep decline in population" appeared without any evidence or proof beyond being what everyone already knows. This belief is typically presented as a historical fact. It is not a historical fact.

Population control has never controlled the population.
Birth rates and population trends are beyond coercive command and control.

Attempting to force fertility has *influenced* birth rates, especially over the short term, but has never actually had enough power and leverage to shove the world on or off the path of depopulation.

That can't be correct, can it? Many of us may not know all the details of repressive population control measures in 1970s India or across the world today. But we know for sure that China's One Child Policy caused the dramatic decline in Chinese births that landed China where it is today. Right?

Let's see. We'll do an exercise, inspired by a conversation we had with a fellow economist-turned-demographer, Jesús Fernández-Villaverde, who has done a version of this experiment himself. It builds on an idea from an earlier study by sociologist Wang Feng and coauthors. In figure 10.1, we'll plot the birth rates for China and several of its neighbors that did not have its One Child Policy: Hong Kong, Romania, South Korea, Taiwan, and Thailand. (No, Romania is not a neighbor of China. We'll explain soon!) We won't label who's who. See if you can identify which country is China, just from a plot of birth rates that span the period of the One Child Policy. If what we've been told about population control is true, it should be easy. China should stand out, with a birth rate that drops away from its neighbors' during the One Child Policy.

Figure 10.1. Where's China? Total fertility rates in China and its neighbors during the One Child Policy

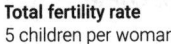

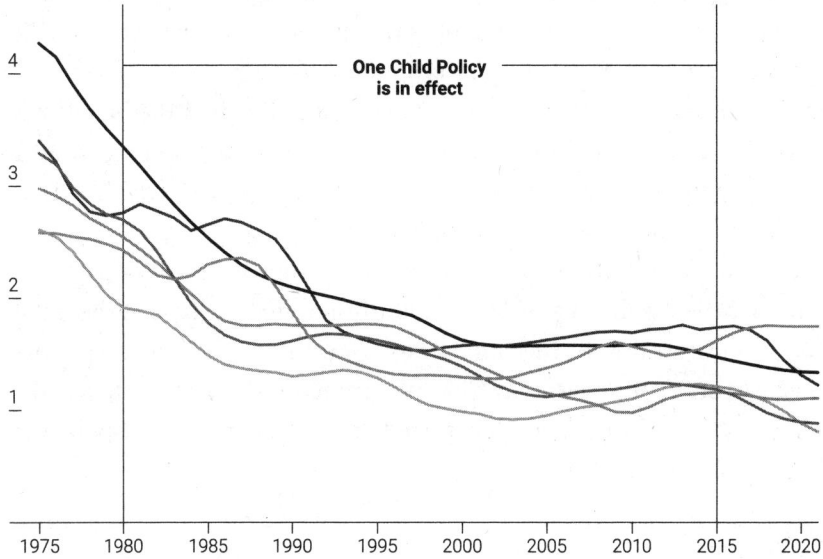

So which country in the figure is China? Leftists, rightists, and centrists; capitalists, socialists, and communists; and people committed, opposed, or indifferent to abortion access all seem to agree that the One Child Policy had a huge effect. So we all should spot it right away. But which is it? Is it the country that started with the highest birth rates in 1979/1980 when the policy started? Or the country that ended lowest by 2015 when the policy ended? The country with the sharpest decline over the decade following the policy's start? Or the country that actually reached a fertility rate of about 1.0 in the 2000s? Maybe we could spot it by looking for a big surge in births after 2015 when the One Child Policy ended, when people were out from under the boot of population policy. But that's curious: It looks like none of these countries surged after China's birth restrictions were officially lifted in 2015.

Each of these countries experienced fertility decline from above- to below-replacement levels over the span of years considered. None stands out among the others in its pattern of decline. We couldn't tell which is China without the labels, and we bet you can't, either. We aren't going to give you the answer. We're not doing this to be annoying. If you really want to, you can look it up on your own. We're doing this so that you remember that right now, without the labels, there's no way to be sure which is China. If the One Child Policy had the big effects so often claimed, then we should all be able to be sure. Let figure 10.1 stand as a monument against the uncritical acceptance of the idea that population control controls the population.

Do not believe the official Chinese Communist Party propaganda line that their policies prevented 400 million births. Believe the data. China was heading in the same downward direction as its neighbors because these countries shared big-picture economic and social trends. That was true before the policy started. It was true during the policy. It was true after the policy.

Credit the changing world, not the repressive regime

Susan Greenhalgh is an American anthropologist who studied population policy in China for decades. For her field research, she lived in rural Chinese villages in the 1980s and '90s. The first page of her four-hundred-page magnum opus notes, almost in passing, that although Chinese birth rates fell significantly since the late 1970s, "much of that decline appears to be due to rapid socioeconomic development, which has lowered childbearing desires to the point that today large and growing numbers of couples, rural as well as urban, want only one child."

By "socioeconomic development" Greenhalgh means forces like rising incomes, extending literacy, and improving health. These forces happened in China and everywhere else, too. So births declined in China, as they did elsewhere. From 1980 to 2000, fertility in China fell by roughly one child per woman, but over the same period fertility in

India fell by 1.5 children per woman. Average fertility in Latin America and the Caribbean fell by 1.6 children.

None of this implies the One Child Policy did nothing. There was significant harm: forced abortions, forced sterilizations. People were denied the basic autonomy to decide when and how to form their families. Some pregnant women went into hiding from the state to build the families they wanted. Millions of children, exceeding their family's quota, were born illegally to Chinese parents and then denied social services and human dignity. The harm didn't end when the policy did. Now decades later, China faces a large gender imbalance (about seven men in their early twenties for every six women) that makes it hard for many to find partners and have the full lives that they hope for.

No doubt, birth rates today are *some different number* in China than exactly what they would have been if this policy had never happened. But if this policy had never happened, then birth rates in China would still be *some number* well below two. To believe otherwise is to believe that China has nothing important in common with its neighbors in Asia—and nothing important in common with other middle-income countries whose economies have quickly grown and whose birth rates have quickly shrunk. To believe otherwise is to believe that in these other places, "socioeconomic development" is why people came to have fewer children, but for China, and China alone, the same pattern at the same time had a different cause.

The historical evidence should give no one confidence that population control is what brought China's birth rate so low. It might have changed the exact path China took to the long-run outcome of persistent low fertility. But the long run—not what happens this year or that one—is what matters for population growth or decline. In the end, China arrived at the same place as its neighbors: the same ballpark, for sure, if not the same patch of grass.

The lesson here is this: When someone starts a chain of logic with "We know that population control has worked before," stop them there. Do not accept the premise. Coercion and repression of reproductive freedom matter everywhere they happen—the forced sterilization of men and women in India during "the Emergency" period of the 1970s *mattered*. But these episodes have never enduringly shaped birth rates in the big ways that we all have been told.

Population control didn't work in Romania, either

And that brings us to Romania. The birth rate in Romania almost doubled from 1966 (1.9 children per woman, on average) to 1967 (3.6). That was because of "Decree 770." Romania's dictator, Nicolae Ceaușescu, wanted more babies. And so after a decade of freely available abortion (more free and more available than the whole United States has ever experienced by a long shot), Decree 770 criminalized abortion in 1967. And for a few years, the abortion ban delivered the babies that the government wanted.

But that was only a short-term effect. After immediately jumping above three for the first three years following the decree, Romania's birth rate began falling again. Fast. By 1971, it had fallen halfway back to where it started in 1966. By the 1980s, Romania's birth rate had fallen three-quarters of the way back to where it had started before the decree—and not because the government backed off. In the 1980s, the Romanian government redoubled its efforts, not only banning abortions, but instituting mandatory pelvic exams for some women at work, all in service of compelling high birth rates. Women in Romania sought and received unsafe abortions and were much, much more likely to die because of pregnancy than in any comparable country.

So much harm and suffering managed to keep birth rates somewhat above the pre-1966 level once they settled down—at least until Ceaușescu was overthrown and killed in 1989. And let's pause there. If a regime is horrible enough that it ends with the perpetrators lined up against a wall and shot upon a popular uprising, then nobody should pretend that those perpetrators have discovered a way to *sustain* high birth rates. Brief impacts for a few years or a decade will not change the trajectory of the Spike.

So, throughout the 1980s, abortion was provided by the state in China and banned by the state in Romania. Look again at figure 10.1. Romania is there, but it's indistinguishable from the Asian countries in the figure. Which one is Romania? If pro-natal decrees (Romania) and anti-natal decrees (China) were each as consequential *for birth rates* as many take for granted today, then you would expect to see big, obvious differences between these countries in the figure. But you don't, because they weren't.

Some people worry that even a public conversation about low birth rates is dangerous. They fear it could embolden the politics that seeks to control people's bodies and families, their most personal decisions. Many governments have tried to force people to give birth. Many governments have tried to force people not to give birth. It's happened because of democratic elections, because of autocratic whims, and because of technocratic computations. It's happened because of homegrown nationalism, and it's been imposed by nations on one another. It's happened in capitalist countries, and it's happened in communist countries.

The fear makes sense. But our solution cannot be to recycle the falsehood that population control controls the population. The myth of population control is worth debunking. Population control is deeply morally flawed. *And* it is ineffective. Both points are important. Forgetting the second part gives repressive forces too much credit.

Dispelling the idea that coercive policy could have big effects on birth rates is important because it's one step in clarifying something big: There's no conflict between freedom on the one hand, and a stabilized world on the other. There's no grim dilemma that we might only avoid depopulation by doing terrible things to one another. Doing terrible things to one another will not avoid depopulation.

The data show that April is not alone

In chapter 4, you saw what happened after April's state government in Texas made pregnancy feel unsafe to her. She stopped trying to have a second kid. Restricting reproductive healthcare in Texas made it harder, not easier, for Mike and April to have the second child they were hoping for.

The novelist Ursula K. Le Guin had three children—because first she had an abortion. In 2004, she tried to remember "what it was like to be twenty and pregnant in 1950." She could hardly remember. She told her audience:

> I can tell you what it *is* like, for me, right now. It's like this: If I had dropped out of college, thrown away my education, depended on my parents through the pregnancy, birth, and infancy, till I could get some kind of work and gain some kind of independence for myself and the child, if I had done all that, which is what the anti-abortion people want me to have done, I would have borne a child for them, for the anti-abortion people. . . .
>
> But I would not have borne my own first child, or second child, or third child. My children . . . the three I bore, the three wanted children, the three I had with my husband—whom, if I had not aborted the unwanted one, I would never have met and married, because he would have been a Fulbright student going to France on the *Queen Mary* in 1953 but I would not have been a Fulbright student going to France on the *Queen Mary* in 1953.

And the rest of us might not have had her novels.

April's story is important. Le Guin's story is important. Every story is important. But let's see what the data say systematically. Figure 10.2 compares birth rates in high-income countries, each of which has a dot. Left to right, countries are positioned from less rich to more rich. Countries with higher 2017 birth rates are plotted higher (we use an age-adjusted total fertility rate from the Human Fertility Database, a reliable source that doesn't include every country but makes sure that our result won't be because of differences in the age of parenting across countries). South Korea is a focal point in the figure because, among the relatively rich countries with this high-quality data, it was the only one classified by the Guttmacher Institute as "abortion highly legally restricted" in 2017.

Each country has its own uniquenesses, including South Korea. So figure 10.2 is hardly a randomized control trial that tells us what happens when you hold everything fixed and change only abortion laws. It would be statistical malpractice if we were attempting to use this figure to make a claim like that. But the figure shows something simple: Fertility is lower in South Korea than in any other country in the graph. South Korea's abortion laws did not bring birth rates anywhere near replacement. Nobody who argues that banning abor-

Figure 10.2. The country where abortion was banned had the lowest birth rate

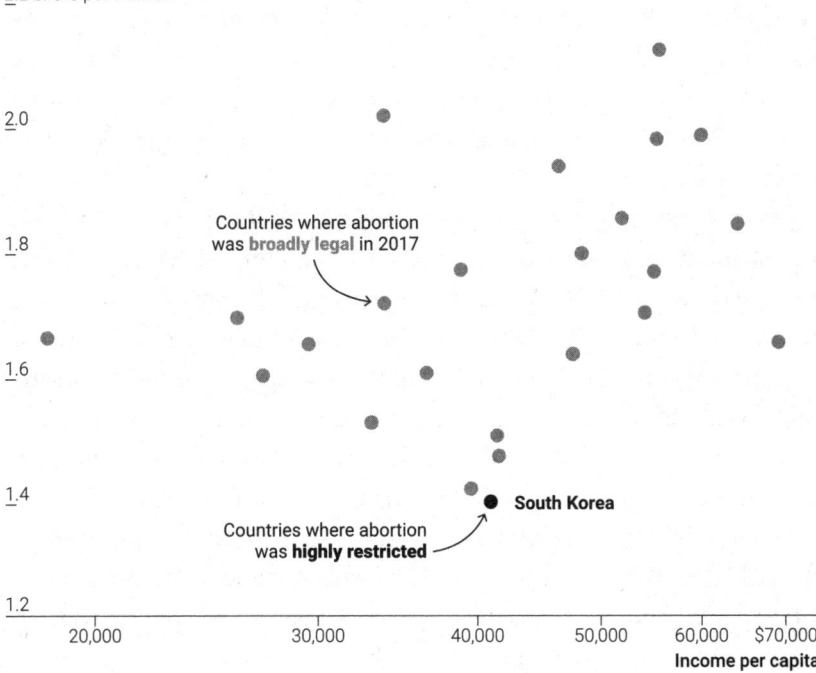

Total fertility rate (adjusted for mother's age)
2.2 births per woman

tion would yield an increase to two births per woman can ignore this contrary evidence.

·

There's another fact about South Korea. It's part of why we believe that reproductive choice is a long-run reality that any response to depopulation should expect. In 2019, South Korea's Constitutional Court declared its abortion ban unconstitutional. It's not just Korea. In Ireland, a 2018 referendum legalizing abortion passed with 66 percent of the vote. In places where governments have made abortion hard to access, many women now find care through telemedicine and receive the medicine they need in the mail. And, of course, Ceaușescu's Decree 770 ended in Romania.

Most women worldwide live in a country where abortion is broadly legal. Only four countries have removed legal grounds for abortion since 1994: El Salvador, Nicaragua, Poland, and the United States. In the United States, the evidence so far says that women are finding new ways to make their own decisions. Data collected by our University of Texas colleague Abigail Aiken show that self-managed medication abortion has risen as a popular, safe option for many women who can't get care another way.

As in every battle for progress, holding the line is an ongoing effort of many dedicated people. Mike works alongside some of these dedicated people in the White House—people who have invested their careers and more in the fight to expand reproductive healthcare for American women. In 2024, they enlisted his expertise in health insurance to set out new rules requiring insurers to cover more contraceptive options for women. At the time, emergency contraception and a newly approved over-the-counter birth control pill had been slipping through the cracks of insurance coverage when these products weren't prescribed by doctors. Moving forward with stronger regulations to fix the problem required that a new economic analysis be completed first. Many people in U.S. politics have worked to expand access to contraception; the economic analysis that helped push the newest proposed rules toward the finish line in 2024 was Mike's part.

Around the world, technological, political, and social changes are continuing an arc that is making pregnancy optional. That is reason to hope and to believe that, in the long run, ever more families will have the number of children they choose, when they choose. To say so does not deny or overlook the work and struggles of the activists and inventors, women and men who are pushing progress forward. Such work is why choice, we believe, is eventually going to win. If so, then one reason why bans won't work is that bans won't last.

Chapter 11

Is cash the answer?

To some, the answer to why people are choosing few children is obvious. Children are too expensive! Just about every parent today, including us, has thought some version of this, filling the cart at the grocery store, paying the day care bill, or considering what college might cost.

When we first wrote about the Spike, one reader left the comment: "People who are having children are having fewer of them because they cannot afford to have more." Many others have said similar things. And not only readers and parents. Researchers who study families often say the same, that children are no longer affordable.

> **The affordability hypothesis.** Is it true that parents are having fewer children today than in the past because they can no longer afford them?

If the affordability hypothesis is right, then there would be no difficulty in knowing how to avoid depopulation. Any government concerned with low birth rates could turn trends around by passing a bigger child tax credit, or paying parents with a new baby to take six months off from work (or a year, or two years), or paying for day care (and aftercare, and anytime care). These changes would make parents' lives easier. But would they stabilize the population?

In Sweden, the government has done something like this. Pro-family policy makes parenting in Sweden much less expensive than in the United States. Healthcare for children (and adults) is free and universal. Day care for little kids is heavily subsidized. Lower-income families may pay nothing at all, and even the richest parents pay no more than about $130 per month for their first child and less or nothing for later children. Not only is day care affordable through government subsidies, there is also investment to ensure that there are spots available. The Swedish government wants parents to keep their careers. So after a birth, parents in Sweden receive about sixteen months of paid and protected leave by law, split between a couple.

Has making children more affordable in Sweden brought birth rates back up to two? No. The average woman in Sweden in 2018 had children at a pace of 1.76 over a lifetime, almost the same as 1.73 in the United States that year. In 2019, both countries fell to 1.70, which happened to be the same as Denmark. Sweden and Denmark each spend twice the fraction of GDP that the United States spends on family benefits. (So do neighboring Norway and Finland, where birth rates are even lower.)

Why doesn't public spending appear to have an effect on birth rates? And if subsidized day care and paid parental leave and the rest don't make a difference, what should we make of it when commenters say that unaffordability is why people are having fewer children? Let's turn to the evidence to make a call on whether the affordability hypothesis is correct.

Strike one: Comparing birth rates in different places

Affordability is about both the price of the thing you want to buy and the size of your budget. Let's narrow in on budgets first. One way that budgets vary is across the march of time. The world has become much richer over the past few decades. Another way that budgets differ is across richer and poorer parts of the world today. All of this diversity in how much money people have provides opportunities to test the budget side of the affordability hypothesis. Do people who have more to spend also tend to have more children?

People are much poorer, on average, in Uttar Pradesh than in Texas. Just over one in ten households in Uttar Pradesh has piped water into their home. A large fraction of homes have dirt or otherwise unimproved floors. And although most have some electricity some of the time, only about half have a TV and less than a third have any sort of refrigerator.

But Uttar Pradeshis are having more children, on average, than Texans, who could afford more of anything costly. In Uttar Pradesh the average woman had 2.3 children in the most recent data, compared to 1.8 in the same year in Texas.

The difference in fertility is not because women in Uttar Pradesh are too poor to afford contraception. They have 2.3 kids, not six, like both of Dean's U.S. grandmothers. Not twelve like Mike's great-grandmother. For many reasons, including the global policy response to HIV/AIDS and the simple fact that markets tend to supply what consumers with any money want to buy, contraception at our point in the twenty-first century is pretty widely available, even in very poor places. Demographic surveys show that 62 percent of women of reproductive age in Uttar Pradesh are using contraception (including a lot of sterilization surgeries, for better or worse). That is pretty close to 65 percent, the number for the United States.

Across the world today, in countries with more money, people tend to have fewer babies. As in any statistical pattern, there are exceptions, but the correlation is clear. The United States and most countries of Western Europe have average birth rates below 1.7. Latin America and the Caribbean, an upper-middle-income region, averages about 1.8. The average is 2.1 births in Southern Asia and South-Eastern Asia together, where economic development ranges from lower-middle income to middle-middle income. And in sub-Saharan Africa, the poorest region, fertility is highest: above 4.0.

There's really no question that poorer regions today have higher, not lower, birth rates on average than richer regions do. There are not more babies in the places where people have more money. We'll call the international comparison strike one against the affordability hypothesis.

Strike two: Comparing birth rates in different years

The international comparison doesn't close the case. Maybe it doesn't make sense to compare India, Indonesia, and Italy: There are too many differences in history and culture that affect both income levels and births. The comparison doesn't hold enough equal. So let's dig deeper. Let's not compare *across* countries. Let's look at changes *within* countries as their living standards have risen over time.

Figure 11.1 plots the changes for the world as a whole and for each country, region by region. Points higher up mean a higher birth rate. Points farther right mean higher living standards. The points-in-time for a country are drawn together as arrows, so each arrow represents a country, showing what has changed. Each arrow starts in 1990 and points to 2021.

The pattern is clear, even looking back only to 1990, when high-quality, internationally comparable economic data are available to build the figure. Most of the arrows go down and to the right. So does the overall shape for each region, and so does the arrow for the world as a whole. People have chosen to have fewer and fewer children as their societies have become richer and richer.

The point is not to deny that children are expensive (they are!), or that parents need more help (they do!). The question that the figure answers is whether the core reason why fertility has *fallen* could plausibly be because parents' budgets have tightened over time. Budgets haven't tightened, and the affordability hypothesis is hard to square with the fact of a much richer world.

So comparisons within the same places over time, as these have gotten richer, provide no support for the affordability hypothesis. Call that strike two.

Figure 11.1. Fertility has declined as living standards have risen

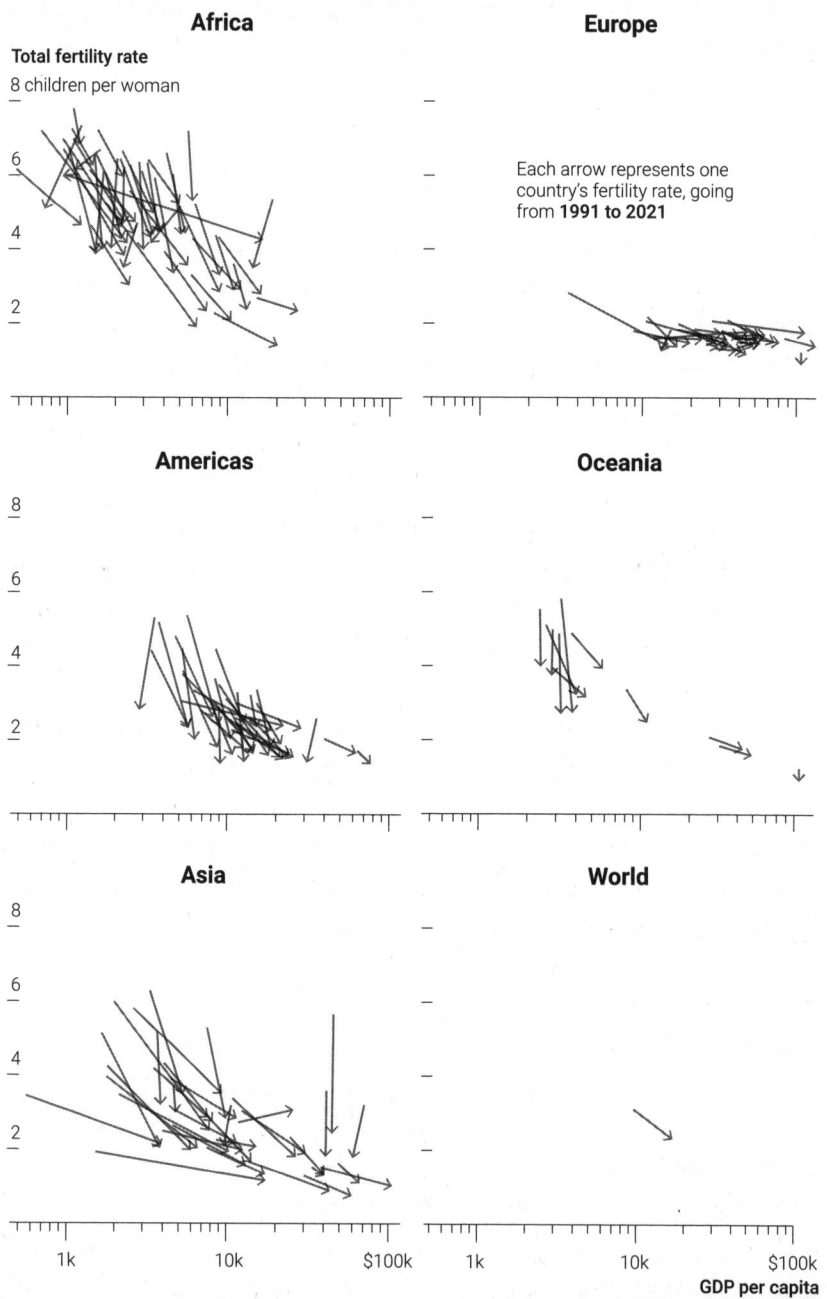

Strike three: Comparing birth rates where prices differ

The last refuge for the affordability hypothesis may be to say that it was never a claim that budgets are smaller than they used to be. It was always about the prices of child-related things climbing fast—so fast that they outpace the world's riches. The problem, in other words, is that the rent is too damn high.

Now, here's a move that may feel like sleight of hand but is on the level: Without bothering you with this detail, throughout this chapter we have been using what economists call "real incomes" whenever we compare incomes across times or places. When economists write *real incomes*, they mean incomes after adjusting for different overall price levels. So if the cost of living had gone up faster than paychecks had, real incomes would have been going down (opposite to the actual patterns). Quite a lot of excellent economics research goes into figuring out how to adjust real incomes for inflation. And about three-quarters of the prices considered in the U.S. Bureau of Labor Statistics' consumer price index—a key tool for measuring inflation—are for items like groceries, transportation, and housing, which all are pretty relevant for starting or expanding a family.

That means we haven't been ignoring prices after all. We've been adjusting for them behind the scenes. But we don't want to be too simplistic here. It's not the case that the prices of all goods and services rise or fall in lockstep with each other, so a single "purchasing power adjustment" to incomes might miss some of this nuance.

Let's go a bit deeper. Prices of mass-produced, manufactured goods like painkillers, solar panels, and televisions tend to go down over time. That's true even if one doesn't bother to correct for the fact that the quality of these goods increased while their prices were dropping. In contrast, products where the main ingredient is people (think nurse visits, not *Soylent Green*) do not get cheaper over time in the same way. That's because relative to other ingredients, people's time is expensive (good!). It may always take fifteen minutes of a doctor's time to evaluate a patient's health during a checkup. And it may always take all of a day care worker's attention to care for a room of eight three-year-olds. Innovation and technology have lowered the cost of solar panels, but there may not be much that management consultants or generative AI can do to optimize the business of preschool. That may change, but it hasn't yet.

The price of people-powered services like these is a notoriously stubborn problem. It's called Baumol's Cost Disease, after the economist William Baumol, who first made this observation with William Bowen in the 1960s. Could Baumol's Cost Disease explain low birth rates? Worker pay is most of the cost of childcare. Because workers today are earning more than they did in the 1960s, childcare workers are, too. Given these facts, there should be no surprise that the price of childcare has risen faster than many other goods in the United States in recent decades.

So is the price of childcare the culprit? Economists Melissa Kearney, Phil Levine, and Luke Pardue took a look at what happened to birth rates across U.S. states when the prices of childcare and other necessities like housing changed over time. Different states experienced different trends in these prices over the last decade. All states' birth rates declined over these years. But did birth rates fall faster in the states where prices grew more quickly, as the affordability hypothesis would predict?

No. In Massachusetts, annual childcare costs increased by more than $4,500 per child. But Massachusetts had the same decline in birth rates as Delaware, where costs increased by less than $1,000. On housing, rents for multi-bedroom apartments increased in D.C. by about seven times as much as in Connecticut or Oklahoma, but these three states all had similar changes in birth rates over the same period. Zooming out from individual data points to take in the patterns across the entire country reveals . . . no relationship. That null pattern was true for other factors they looked at, too, including student debt held by would-be parents. Kearney and her collaborators plot graph after graph, each without any correlation that would say that prices are to blame.

Strike three against the affordability hypothesis. Many potential parents want more children, and many say that children are too expensive. Maybe dumping some huge sum of money on parents would change things. But it's hard to find evidence that births have been falling for decades because children have been getting less affordable. Let's call the affordability hypothesis *out*.

Costs and opportunity costs

If the people who responded to our Spike article aren't right about money, what *are* they right about? There must be something real and important that people mean when they say that they can't afford to have children. There must be something real and important that they are expressing when they choose smaller families. Is there another way of looking at the cost of children that goes beyond money, that shows that children are, after all, costlier than they used to be?

Yes, there is. And a bit of economic jargon can help: *opportunity costs*. An opportunity cost is whatever you give up in order to have something. Money can be an opportunity cost, but so can time, attention, joy, cleanliness, peace, and quiet. Can you eat your cake and then still have it, too? No. The opportunity cost of eating your cake is that you can't continue to have it, even if you got your cake without spending any money.

Emily Oster is an economist at Brown University who studies parenting. In her 2019 book *Cribsheet*, she writes about the big trade-offs that parents face every day, especially when it comes to time: "Our intuitions should be informed by the economic idea of 'opportunity cost of time.'" Time spent focused on a child, she explains, is time not spent doing something else. And so we're making a mistake if we think only about some ideal option, rather than the real choices parents face. Parents worry about how much time little kids should ideally spend looking at screens. But maybe screen time is what the family needs in some moment so that mom or dad can attend to the hundred other things they are doing in support of raising their kiddo well. Oster is writing about decisions made once someone is a parent, but the same idea applies to the decision to become a parent at all.

For decades, researchers have sent surveyors to ask women how many children they would ideally have. In populations with birth rates below two, many women say they would like to have more children than they do—often averaging out to more than two. So what is going haywire? Why aren't people doing what they say they ideally want to do?

The trouble is that "ideal fertility" survey questions do not ask about opportunity costs. They neglect the opportunity cost of time that economists like Oster know are essential. They do not ask about what a potential parent *would be ready to give up* to have an extra child. They ask adults only what they would *ideally* like to have happen, potentially giving up nothing to get it.

Once we understand "too expensive" to be about opportunity cost (rather than only money cost), we can see that there *are* ways that children have become more costly, if not exactly less affordable. Parenting a child, or another child, could mean scaling back educational goals, career plans, or other ambitions. However hard someone is willing to work at their career, however dedicated they are to some personal project or some friendship, if they're getting kids dressed and packing lunches, or doing drop-off and pickup, or handling bath time and bedtime and wake-up time (and wake-up-in-the-middle-of-the-night time), or just being home on a kid's sick day or a school holiday, then there are fewer hours and less energy left to devote to the other things they care about.

In decades and centuries past, there was less to lose by spending time on children. The opportunity costs of parenting today include vacations, restaurant meals, quality time with a partner, streaming any good song or movie ever made, and just hanging out while the dishwasher and laundry machines do their things. Running shoes are better than they used to be, so professors in their forties can squeeze more years out of their knees. (Medicine, including artificial joints, is better, too, so they can squeeze more knees out of their years, if it comes to it.)

The opportunities for work and careers have also expanded, so there is much more to give up at work. That's especially true for women. Claudia Goldin—from our discussion of career and family in chapter 4—was elected president of the American Economic Association in 2013. In her presidential address, she explained that in the late 1960s, only a third of young women expected to spend their adult years in the paid labor force. By the late 1970s, about 80 percent thought they would. This was a revolution in expectations.

A better world, with better options, makes parenting worse *by comparison.*

> **The opportunity cost hypothesis:** Spending time on parenting means giving up something. Because the world has improved around us, that "something" is better than it used to be.

The *affordability hypothesis* that began this chapter was a hypothesis about money costs. And now we've seen a lot of evidence against it. The *opportunity cost hypothesis* is a different story. The basic facts fit. It tells us that we should expect that as jobs pay more and more, and as more and more people have access to education (and sports, and video games, and travel, and mystery novels on an e-reader, and everything else that people enjoy), parenting faces stiffer competition.

Thinking about opportunity cost uncovers some surprising implications. Did hourly pay go up for an hourly worker? If so, then parenting just became more expensive, if parenting means working fewer hours than they could otherwise. Did someone just get good news at their job? Perhaps there is a new chance for a promotion if they work hard over the next year to prove themselves. That good news makes the trade-off of parenting bite deeper. Maybe it makes sense to wait a little longer to start a family. Once we see that costs include opportunity costs, as life becomes richer and more rewarding, children cost more.

And yet, fertility decline is more complicated than improvements in women's career options

It might be tempting, especially after considering the opportunity costs of careers, to think that we've arrived at a grand theory of fertility decline: Low birth rates simply and invariably arrive if and because women attain the freedom and power to pursue careers. But it turns out that this cannot be the one grand theory. We've already seen that fertility is low (or falling) everywhere. Fertility is low where women's careers are soaring, and fertility is low where women don't have the opportunities for anything like what women in Sweden or the United States would understand as a career.

Consider India. The path that India has taken to low fertility is a challenge to this grand theory of fertility decline—and most of the other grand theories of fertility decline, too. Most adult women in India don't work for pay outside the home. Of every eight Indian women fifteen to forty-nine years old, only one has a job classified as "professional, technical, managerial, or clerical," like Seema does. Only one in four has any job at all. The United States hasn't had such a low level of female labor force participation since the 1950s.

The top panel of figure 11.2 looks across the whole world at women's participation in the workforce. It shows that in India, low fertility is happening without a conflict between parenting and women's careers. Birth rates there are below replacement even though most women there don't work for pay. Elsewhere in the same plot, birth rates are much higher and women are working more than in the United States and Europe. There's no simple, universal pattern here.

The bottom panel compares birth rates with the median age at which women in a country start having children. India is an outlier again. Birth rates are below replacement even though women there have their first child in their early twenties, on average. That is much younger than in China, Europe, or the United States. So neither wom-

Figure 11.2. Opportunity costs of parenting are different in India

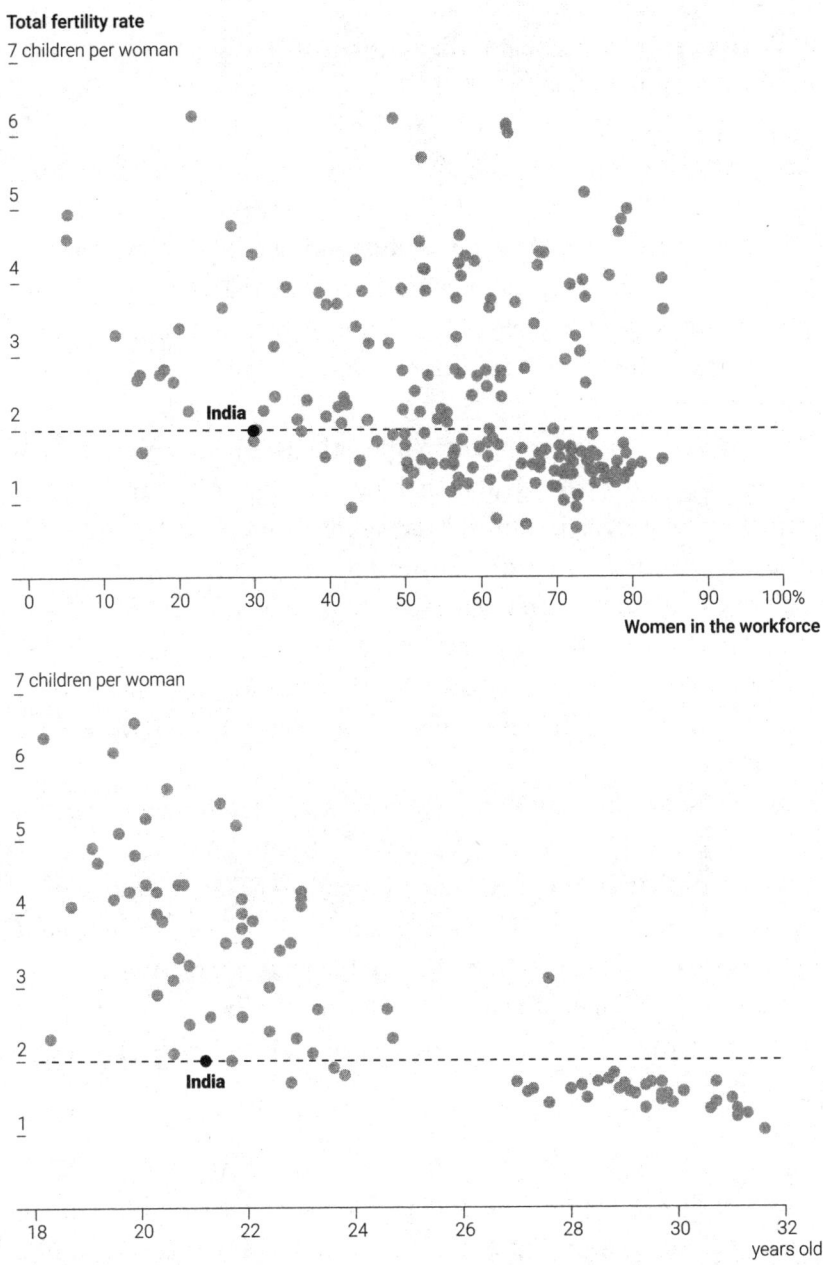

en's careers nor waiting to start having children could be a big factor that explains India's low birth rates.

What does it matter that India is different? For starters, India may be just one country, but one-sixth of people alive today live there. We can't just dismiss it. India is bigger in population than the United States, the European Union, Brazil, and Russia. Combined. Because India doesn't fit a simple story, the global decline in birth rates doesn't fit a simple story, either. Any theory that cannot fit these facts deserves skepticism. The big exception of India suggests that there are further opportunity costs of having another child—costs that could discourage having children even if somehow women's career trajectories could be held harmless.

In chapter 4, we saw another complication. There is no correlation between the gender pay gap and birth rates among rich countries. Differences among rich countries, between birth rates closer to 2.0 and birth rates closer to 1.5, aren't explained by women's treatment at work. The places where women's wages are higher, as a fraction of men's wages, don't tend to be the places where birth rates are lower. There's no relationship in the data, which tells us that the opportunity costs of choosing children include more than improvements to the work prospects of women.

Opportunity costs are rising for both women and men, across all domains of life. The opportunity cost of parenting would be greater in our times than in the past even if humans reproduced asexually—even if any person were able to create a baby all on their own. Even if we eliminated every dimension of social inequality and unfairness between women and men, the opportunity cost of having a child would still be greater in the richer, freer, better-entertained future than it was in the past.

•

Seema's life isn't part of the Indian puzzle of low fertility among women who don't work for pay. Her career trajectory looks less like the statistics for most Indian women and more like the statistics that

Claudia Goldin reported for U.S. women. And so Seema faces some big decisions over work, marriage, and childbearing.

We can't tell you yet how it all plays out. Her decision—to accept an arranged marriage or to push off her parents a little longer (or a lot longer)—hasn't happened yet. The KMC program managers have a speculative hope: There isn't a job of "head nurse" in the program yet, but if Seema stays for a few more years, they might see her growing into being the first one to create the role. Maybe someday. But if so, that would be a long way off. And it would mean stepping even farther away from the normal path for an Uttar Pradeshi woman. There are big opportunity costs of either choice. One day, Seema and her family will decide.

However Seema chooses, she is unlikely to have an above-replacement number of children. If she gets married, then she will probably have the one child she envisions, like many educated young women in India. If she stays unmarried, she would almost certainly not have any. We can envision many policies that might improve Seema's life. We can imagine marriages with widely different implications for Seema's wellbeing. But things would have to be radically different for Seema and her potential husband and in-laws to think that, say, three children would be right for them. The opportunity cost would be huge.

As alternatives improved, choosing children has become harder

Because so much is so much better, the trade-offs required to have a child cut deeper. It makes sense that a twenty-five-year-old, or a thirty-year-old, or a thirty-five-year-old would think about becoming a parent or having another child and despair that there's no way to fit it all in the budget—not merely the money budget, but the deeper budget of capabilities, constraints, resources, and relationships that we each manage as we build a life. It's in a bank balance, yes. But it's also at work and in the classroom. It's in the quiet moments with a romantic partner and in the wild times out with friends. It's wherever any other goal or dream or impulse competes with parenting.

The opportunity cost of a kid is growing around the world, not *despite* the fact that the world is becoming a better place to live, but *because of* it.

Understood this way, there is no puzzle anymore, no surprise. Having children is one way to have a good life, to build an identity, to choose a life story—but there are others. Those alternatives are better and more available today than they used to be.

In 2018, the *New York Times* reported a survey of U.S. adults about whether they wanted children and why. Most of the respondents who had no children said they did not want any or were not sure. Asked why not, 30 percent simply explained they had no desire for children. And the most common reason for that response was that they wanted more leisure time. A satirical headline in *The Onion* put a fine point on it: "Study Finds American Women Delaying Motherhood Because the Whole Thing Blows." We doubt parenting blows much more than it did decades or centuries ago. But in comparison, the other options blow considerably less.

One way of misunderstanding what we are saying would be to point to some short-lived, surprise bump in wages or in labor market options and ask: "Look, the opportunity cost of having a kid just changed, so next year we should see a lot more babies, right?" People's big life decisions don't work like that. Choosing a family and a life path isn't a twitch reaction. Having a kid, or another kid, shapes the course of (at least) your next few decades—where to live, who to live with, what you'll need, and what you'll be able to give. It wouldn't make sense to overreact to changes in the law or the job market that might soon change back. And nobody makes these choices fully alone. Families and friends, societies and cultures all influence what people choose—sometimes invisibly, sometimes with a heavy hand. Even if a potential mom's situation changes, her circle's circumstances might not, and that matters, too. How people understand their opportunity costs—and how their mothers and fathers understood their opportunity costs—shapes the culture and the concept of what a good life story would be. Those concepts do change, but only because of big, sustained causes.

Opportunity costs explain why cutting a check won't cut it

This chapter started with a question: If what matters is that children are so unaffordable, then why aren't birth rates in Denmark, Finland, Norway, and Sweden higher than in the United States? We wrote in the last chapter that governments can't redirect birth rates with the heavy hand of coercion. But what about doing a better job at normalish policy of the kind that liberal societies have tried?

Much of what such governments have tried boils down to giving money. Money for each child in a household, perhaps called a child tax credit, perhaps called a baby bonus. Money to take time away from work after a birth. Money to subsidize childcare. Maybe in the future there could be a universal basic income, or maybe a better social safety net, with fewer holes to fall through. Those wouldn't coerce anybody or take away their freedom not to parent. But they could give those who choose to parent a firmer freedom, less precarity. So what about turning up the dial on pro-family policy? A bigger day care subsidy? A few more thousands in the child tax credit? Even a thousand universal dollars every month?

Today there are large differences across countries in support for parents. So if there is a relationship between pro-parent policies and fertility, we should be able to see it in international data. UNICEF rates the world's rich countries according to "indicators to measure leave for parents as well as access, quality and affordability of childcare." We matched these with birth rates.

In no case is there evidence that more support for parents predicts more births. Not for parental leave, not for preschool enrollment, not for preschool or childcare affordability. Of nineteen countries where childcare is less costly than in the United States (after subsidies), fifteen have lower birth rates and the sixteenth, Sweden, matches the United States. *All* of the countries in this database have more paid, job-protected maternity leave than the United States, which offers no paid leave at all as a matter of national law. But of these twenty-two countries, each with better maternity leave, all but three have lower birth rates than the United States.

As we've said elsewhere, in researchers' hierarchies of data, cross-country comparisons like these don't supply very high-quality evidence. So, zooming in, what happened when Austria doubled paid maternity leave in 1990? Birth rates went up a little. Great, if that's what Austrians wanted. But one detail: The birth rate in Austria fell below 1.6 in 1983 and has never again risen to that level. In all the places where something like this has been tried, with various levels of actual investment and seriousness (California, Germany, Sweden . . .), paid maternity leave hasn't nudged birth rates up to two. In Spain, offering paternity leave to dads turned out to *reduce* men's desire for more children, according to one study by economists. In Canada, subsidizing public universities so tuition is much more affordable than in the United States hasn't brought birth rates up to the level of the United States. Free IVF in Israel didn't do the trick. Subsidizing assisted reproduction technologies in Australia didn't do the trick.

Other demographers agree that the types of policy changes that have been tried may have large *short-term* effects on the timing of births. But they fizzle out without making a difference to the total number of children born over a woman's *lifetime*, which is what matters for avoiding depopulation. Imagine that a new child tax credit policy offers a family $10,000 if they have a baby next year. So maybe they do. Instead of having her children when she is thirty-four and thirty-six, this mother has them when she is thirty-one and thirty-three. If the tax credit gave her the chance to have children at a time that was better for her, then good and perhaps worth the public expense. But if all a policy accomplishes is to accelerate motherhood to a younger age, with no change in lifetime fertility, then whatever valuable benefits it brings, avoiding depopulation is not one of them.

The problem with money is that it doesn't stack up high against the opportunity costs at stake. A few thousand dollars a year to parents is nice. It is a help. It is nowhere near to matching the stakes that parents have on the line. It does not change the fuzzy arithmetic of choices about career, family, friends, and other priorities.

Another problem with money is that it's a bit of a treadmill. In a richer society, it takes more to feel like you have enough. Part of why parenting feels unaffordable is that, in our ever-improving world, standards are rising everywhere. What it means to be a parent and what it takes to raise a child up to community standards increases whenever and wherever people become better off.

Take housing: In rich countries like the United States, there are still some children who sleep three to a bed, alternating head to toe, the way Mike's father slept with his two brothers. But fewer and fewer parents each generation find that sort of arrangement acceptable. Today people are more likely to want (and to get!) not only more beds per child but also more rooms in their home, compared with families in the mid-twentieth century when births were booming. The average U.S. child in 2020 lived in a home with 5.6 rooms; but the average was only 4.4 rooms in 1960, when the average child's home also held more children. The fact that a larger fraction of people today can afford a big house than in the poorer past speeds up the treadmill a bit more. We are all influenced by a culture that has been raising expectations for what counts as "good enough."

Expecting people to parent like it's 1999—never mind 1949—won't be a solution to anything. Whenever better becomes available, people come to expect better. That's good! Better childhoods are good! Social spending is a powerful tool against childhood hunger and illness, and that's reason enough to do it. But higher standards are one more reason why social spending, at the scale that anybody is used to, is not a powerful tool to increase birth rates. A $1,000 subsidy check goes ever less far, once humanity becomes accustomed to providing more for its children. We should be writing those checks to help lift children out of poverty, but we should not believe those checks will buy a solution to depopulation.

A difficult reality: Nobody fully understands low birth rates. Yet.

It would have been straightforward and tidy to say that women's expanding opportunities have pulled down birth rates in a clear line from cause to effect. But there is no clear line, the data showed us.

So what is the complete explanation?

We've heard people blame the free-market economy (or neoliberalism or capitalism). How can you make a lifelong commitment to raising a kid when you only have a paycheck until somebody decides to fire you? We especially hear this in the United States, where employees have fewer protections than elsewhere. But birth rates are even lower in countries with more regulated economies. The high-tax democratic socialist economies of northern Europe offer more public spending on the social safety net, and birth rates are low. And in China—where the economy has transitioned from communism a half century ago to something today that mixes state ownership and markets—birth rates are low.

We've heard people blame the decline of marriage. But the reason why birth rates in India are below replacement can't be that people there aren't getting married anymore, because people there *are* getting married. Marriage remains almost universal, happens early, and usually leads quickly to a birth. Divorce is unusual. And it's not only India: Birth rates are low in other places where marriage remains common. Among women aged fifteen to forty-nine (which is demographers' standard but outdated age range), three-fourths of women in Nepal are married and two-thirds of women in China are. So Nepal and China have a marriage rate similar to India's, and much greater than in Canada, Europe, and the United States, where about half of women in this age range are married. But fertility in Nepal is below two and in China is around one.

We've heard people blame feminism. We've heard people blame the evolution of cultures that has opened more options for women. But birth rates in South Korea are about the lowest in the world. And South Korea is no feminist paradise. Its gender wage gap is the largest in the OECD. In many ways it remains a traditional and conservative society.

We've heard people blame the individualism of the West, compared with the collectivism of the East. But low birth rates are worldwide. The region the UN calls "Eastern and South-Eastern Asia" has a fertility rate of 1.35, lower than "Europe, Northern America, Australia, and New Zealand" at 1.48.

We've heard people say it's contraception. Yes, contraception matters, so that when people want not to have children or not to have children right now, it's easier to hit that plan. But birth rates were falling long before modern contraception. Recall that birth rates in France began dropping before France aided the United States in its war for independence. And birth rates have continued falling in rich countries decades after contraception became widely available.

We've heard people blame modern liberalism itself. People aren't having as many babies because they don't have religion and tradition to guide them home to family life. But India contradicts this theory, too. Religion, of one faith or another, is almost universal there—not just on paper or in what someone calls themselves, but in the daily practice of people's lives.

Seema's hopes to make a difference in her job are different from Preeti's hopes to have a boy, which are different from what April, Mike, Diane, or Dean had on their mind when they thought about having a second child. That reality, and the facts we have seen, challenge any too-simple explanation of why *humanity-wide* birth rates are low and falling.

We'll have to do without a grand theory

Low birth rates are too big of a global change to be tidy. Depopulation is too big of a global change not to face that truth. There are still puzzles, still open questions for social science to answer. And if society applies itself to the task, we might start learning by trial and error how to give people the support they need to build a family that they want, even before a grand theory arrives. But nobody yet knows how, and nobody yet knows the One True Theory to guide us.

That is one way that responding to depopulation will be more challenging than responding to climate change. At every step along the way for decades, it has been clear what burning fossil fuels would cause: climate change. And it's also been clear *why* people burn fossil fuels. For our demographic future, we know what low birth rates will cause: depopulation. But nobody—no expert, no theory—fully understands why birth rates, everywhere, in different cultures and contexts, are lower than ever before.

Does this mean that whether to parent is not actually a decision about opportunity costs after all? No, every important decision is a decision about opportunity costs. For many of our ancestors on the path up the Spike, parenting might not have felt like much of a decision at all—it was part of a life. But it's a decision now.

Because it's a decision, people will be thinking about the benefits and thinking about the costs. They might not use those exact words, unless they happen to be economists. But they'll be weighing the consequences implicitly when they ask themselves: What do I want to achieve with my life? What do I want to be in my life? As long as options compete with and crowd out each other (which is to say, always), people will consider opportunity costs.

Social and cultural changes are happening everywhere. What do people think their lives and their families are for? What do you owe your parents? Your spouse? Your community, your religion, or your ancestors? Many would answer those questions differently now than in the past, and that matters, too. Whatever matters to someone—which includes values old and new—"having several children" now would cost a larger deduction from "having what matters to me" than ever before.

Even without a grand theory, we do know this: Because improvements everywhere for almost everyone probably won't suffer a sustained reversal (good!), they will continue to influence the opportunity costs of children and how future generations build their families. Social policy as usual does not pay those opportunity costs on parents' behalf. Governments' go-to tools, at any size that anyone has ever yet seen, will not work.

Can humanity choose to stabilize, instead of depopulate—assuming the first step, that many people agree on the goal? Not by coercion. Not by social policy or public spending as usual. Not with one change that will work for everyone. And not by any tried-and-tested strategy that anyone yet knows. So is there a solution?

Chapter 12

Aspire bigger

This chapter does not pretend to offer the Solution. There is no Solution with a capital *S*. Not yet. Not if a Solution means a foolproof plan that is both ambitious and detailed and that is capable of switching humanity from depopulation toward stabilization, while carefully balancing all the consequences for everyone. No one has such a Solution. The challenge is still too new.

That doesn't mean that there is no path forward, but we need to be clear-eyed. The strategies that humanity has tried so far to support parents have had at most small effects. Nobody knows how to fix all the headwinds against choosing parenting.

But now that you've reached the conclusion of this book, one more person is equipped with a better understanding of the stakes and of the facts. If you now think that finding solutions to depopulation should be added to humanity's to-do list, or if you now allow the possibility that stabilization might be better than unchecked depopulation—with the right caveats, at the right size, in the right time—then this book has done its work.

> **Our conclusion:** Humanity should choose to stabilize. Yes, avoiding depopulation would mean big changes in how we take care of one another—improvements that expand what feels possible to aspire to and achieve in life. But humanity has made big changes for the better before.

How can we be optimistic, if we aren't sure what to do? Because there is so much left to try! Paying forward the gift of parenting remains hard. Some policies have tweaked the edges of our societies and economies. But nobody has tried anything that would adequately challenge conventions, challenge social orders, and challenge what gets society's attention, power, and investment. No revolution has yet envisioned a future in which everyone who benefits from a healthy, joyful childhood looks forward to sharing in the work of giving one to the next generation.

This chapter is not an instruction manual. And this chapter is not merely a collection of facts and statistics about the past and present—though there is a bit of that, too. This chapter is an invitation to consider what kind of future we should build. We say that it's not time to give up on a big, abundant world—a future with many people thriving in it. It's time to aspire bigger.

•

It's a good thing Seema doesn't give up on vulnerable newborns. Her work for the KMC program is not only in the hospital ward. Some days it is her job to join the home-visit team that drives out to check on the discharged babies, scattered throughout villages across the district. And some days it is her turn to do *calls*. Seema is grateful for her good job. She eats cooked meals with the team every day, and she is proud to be making such good use of her education as a nurse. But, still. Phone calls are the worst assignment.

The nurse on phone duty sits with a laptop, dialing numbers from a spreadsheet, in a back room otherwise filled to the ceiling with baby scales and feeding cups and KMC wraps and thermometers. The goal is to hear how the mothers and babies are doing, to nudge the family toward better compliance with KMC practices and, if necessary for the baby's health, to persuade them to come back to the hospital.

The problem with calls is that many families don't want to be called. If the family is at home to get a phone call, then it means they left the hospital. Usually that is because the baby is doing well enough to move on. But sometimes it is because the family, typically the father, never wanted to keep their underweight baby (and its mother) in the KMC ward. And once a father has decided *that*, he will usually be grumpy when a nurse calls to try to change his mind. Those dads, Seema jokes, sound on the phone like they just woke up. So calls aren't fun.

Some families don't want to put the time and effort into KMC because they don't believe that their two-pound baby faces an especially serious risk of death, a risk greater than their village's average newborn. Other families say no despite the fact that they appreciate the threat, because they don't trust that the KMC program will help.

Seema's job, on the grumpy phone calls, is to balance communicating the seriousness of the situation with bringing optimism that improvement is possible. She is mysteriously good at it. "I don't know what she does," one of Seema's supervisors marveled at good-news text messages announcing the return of an underweight baby whose family Seema had called, and visited, and called again. "But if we send her, we get the baby back."

Seema is optimistic because she knows that, if they get the baby back, they can help. And many babies never need emergency trips back to the hospital in the first place. Most of the time, Seema gets to record "graduated" as the last entry in a baby's spreadsheet.

Preeti's baby is now a graduate. On the last home visit to Preeti and her baby, Seema collected the scale, feeding cup, thermometer, and cloth KMC wrap for the next mom to use. The file for each graduate has a photo: a finally chubby baby, on the scale for the last time or in a happy mother's arms. Some of the moms pose sternly when the nurse from the big-city hospital takes the picture, but Preeti smiled.

On a standard home visit, Seema is too professional to sing to the babies. But we won't say it never happens at these graduations. Confronting the challenges of underweight newborns in Uttar Pradesh needs both seriousness and optimism.

The first step on the long path ahead is to ask how things should be different

Confronting depopulation needs both seriousness and optimism, too. We believe that the facts and the arguments, the statistics and the ethics, will someday make stabilization a widely shared goal. We expect that this vision will emerge well before anybody has a good, detailed, evidence-based plan to achieve it. That's okay. Change often starts with just a vision and commitment.

At its beginning, the KMC ward in Uttar Pradesh was a messy vision toward a good goal: to staff up a new nursing program over just a few years within a long-standing state medical system. The founders had the ambition to implement high-quality, low-cost care in a place where many babies needed it, with professional management, philanthropic funding, and a detailed schedule for the nurses' work. Only later did the doctors and managers learn by trial and error what the detailed schedule should contain.

Before that? Kangaroo Mother Care itself started as a commitment to the idea that the lives of underweight babies can be saved even in places where intensive incubator care is unavailable. When that happened in 1978, there was no forty-seven-year plan, stretching to today. But there was that commitment.

The doctors in Colombia in 1978 never imagined the dynamically populated, phone-based spreadsheets that tell Seema which baby needs attention. They couldn't have. (Computers were too large to carry around when they invented KMC.) Thank goodness that nobody got distracted or disheartened because they lacked such detailed plans at the very beginning. Change needs vision and values and commitments before detailed plans can matter at all.

Change is possible. Change has happened. Change changes what people expect and demand.

Someday, a new parent could expect and believe in a bigger set of possibilities for their life. If enough changed, a new parent could expect parenting to fit alongside everything else they want to enjoy and accomplish. We're not just hoping: History has shown us that what people expect and demand can change, again and again.

Let's review some recent history for inspiration. If you've grown up in a world of universal primary schooling, flush toilets, and grandparents with healthcare, it's hard to imagine a good society without them. But these didn't always exist. And they are not taken for granted everywhere today. But in places where they are, they are so familiar that they hardly feel like examples of anything.

To be clear, these are not the changes that will rescue humanity from depopulation. They solved entirely different problems. We present them to show how radically society can improve when it chooses to. But more than that, we present them to illustrate how big changes can unlock entirely new possibilities for what people expect, demand, and aspire to.

In 1763, Frederick the Great issued the *Generallandschulreglement* (General Country School Regulations), establishing eight grades of primary education. Radically, local governments were required to pay for it. Every child was required to attend—boys and girls. The merits of free, universal, compulsory public elementary school are too obvious to spell out to a modern reader. But in the early 1700s, almost nobody, in any country, would have wanted or expected to send their children to eight years of school (or more!). Nobody thought of it as normal. School was for the privileged only. And it wasn't something a government would provide.

But this new idea caught on and spread. In the decades before the Civil War, states in New England became the first to offer a form of public education that you would recognize today. The Prussian education reformers succeeded by changing—over a bare handful of generations—what people expect in a good life. So now, people born into a society in which elementary school is free of charge, compulsory, and normal want and expect to send their children to school.

Sanitation infrastructure and sewer systems, too, have changed people's concept of the good life (or, really, the adequate life). Though Massachusetts adopted universal public schooling in the 1850s, it would be another two decades before Boston built a sewer system. That's not some peculiarity of Boston. Chicago and Brooklyn had the first U.S. sewers, but they, too, arrived after public education in Massachusetts. Across the Atlantic, London didn't build its sewers until later in the nineteenth century. And Paris, despite some progress dating back centuries earlier, hadn't connected most residences to the sewer system until the twentieth century.

Today, many of us take flush toilets, like elementary schools, for granted. But before the sewer came to town, city people would dispose of feces in pits, or empty their chamber pots into street gutters. In rural places, people might walk out into fields to do their business. Nothing much like what we would now consider toilets or sewers existed before the nineteenth century. At various points in history, some palaces or cities managed to build drainage systems, sometimes with fascinating ingenuity. But before the past hundred and fifty years or so, nobody *expected* to use a flush toilet that piped waste away from their home and to a treatment plant. Nobody considered that to be a minimum standard for a decent life, because nobody had ever used a flush toilet. Dean's dad, in 1940s rural Kansas, grew up using an outdoor pit latrine. In many parts of some developing countries, the switch to safe sanitation is still happening.

Chances are, your thinking about what to do with your waste is altogether different from what even rich people in the seventeenth century would have thought. And chances are, if you've raised a kid, you've taught them that your feelings about toilets are normal, so they expect to live a life with flush toilets, too. Perhaps the idea of using a toilet sounds too *normal* to be worth three paragraphs here. But that's the point. A big public investment can change what people expect to do, what people teach their children to do, and what people consider minimally acceptable.

Within living memory, public pensions and other social support in rich countries have revolutionized what people expect for older adulthood. In the United States, Social Security sends older Americans monthly money and Medicare pays for their healthcare. Would a drug that costs $4,000 per month ease the chronic pain and fatigue of your rheumatoid arthritis? Our society will help you get it. Do you have hepatitis C? Our social safety net will pay for the $30,000 course of treatment that over a few weeks will cure you of that disease.

These social innovations are even newer than Frederick the Great. The first Social Security check was paid in 1940 for $22.54. Before then, many more older Americans died in poverty. What is normal has changed radically in less than three generations.

Could radical change come to parenting or family life, too? Could we expect something wholly different from each other and from our communities and governments? In the most modest of possible improvements, could we expect, for example, a future in which the perpetual challenge for parents of what to do with kids in the summertime or on the days when school is off but work is on is just . . . solved? Not a scramble, not a stress, not a conflict. Solved? Of course we could. That would mean choosing it as societies, not as individuals. Individual choices did not create the system of Social Security. Universal primary education doesn't work as a classroom of one. And there is no sensible sewage treatment system only for one home.

Radical change is a group effort

Will radical changes that would make parenting easier, fairer, and better happen just because it would be best for the common good? For example, will most men—fathers and not—immediately step up their caregiving efforts for the good of the future, once they see and understand the Spike? Of course not. But in many places, over recent decades, some men have stepped up to do more. More men should make that choice, and we all can ask it of them. Most important, society can build something broader than individual, atomistic volunteer efforts.

Individual altruism toward the needy is good. A social safety net established and funded by law is better. Individual environmental responsibility is good. Developing technologies for a carbon-free energy system is better. Individual care for animals is good. A culture that promotes the humane treatment of animals is better.

Big challenges need policy, technical, and social change. Climate change and other big problems of collective action can't be solved by individual sacrifice and care alone, no matter what two consenting adults choose to do with solar panels in the privacy of their own home.

Improving parenting needs policy, technical, and social change. A dad jumping to be listed as the contact person at day care is good, as far as it goes. A new norm at the day care not to assume it's mom's job is better. Make that sort of change a thousand times—working through the whole list of gendered defaults about parenting—and maybe we're getting somewhere. That would be no small feat. But it isn't impossible, either.

> **Different societies choose differently.** How to divide the burdens and joys of caring for children across mom, dad, and others is a choice. We know because across times and places, different societies have chosen differently.

Families today don't divide household labor across gender lines in the exact same way that families did fifty, a hundred, or two hundred years ago. Even today, what men contribute to care work and housework is very different in, for example, Japan and Denmark. Nor do families divide household labor across generational lines as in the past. And societies don't divide the responsibility of caregiving across parents and nonparents as in the past, either.

So how to divide labor is a choice to make. And we can do even better than *dividing* a difficult burden over a wider set of shoulders. The shared responsibility, collective action, and social coordination that brought us elementary school, flush toilets, and happier grandmas really has been greater than the sum of its parts. Social Security and healthcare for the elderly don't merely bottle up an elderly person's financial misery and poor health and transfer that misery, undiminished, to some other person to feel. If each generation takes care of its elderly people, then society's misery is diminished. Things are better, overall. We don't know exactly what that coordination and sharing would mean in a better future of care for young people. But there's no reason to doubt that a society that was better for parents could be better for everyone.

Bigger change than pocket change

What if society blows wide open its support for parenting? Government spending would be part of that support, and it would have a price tag. What would be too much to spend?

We might start by pointing out that spending on children turns out to be an investment with clear returns. Many economic studies have shown that spending on helping children grow healthier, or on early-life education, produces a more productive, more innovative, healthier future population of adults. These adults go on to pay more in taxes and rely less on government support. And don't forget what we've learned about the benefits of other people for innovation, specialization, progress, and just generally having more good stuff—whether good to you means great television or cures for tropical diseases. In the long run, stabilizing the population may well pay for itself.

Even so, let's not be shy about this. Would radical support for parents cost society a lot of money, if only in an up-front down payment? For sure! Would paying care workers what that labor is worth be a radical realignment of our economies and societies? It would! Would there be serious economic harm done to some interests that are currently privileged? Yes!

Look. We're not saying we wouldn't get our hair mussed. But we do say:

> **What's the alternative?** If the choice is between either global depopulation or spending much more on families, then isn't there a price we should be willing to pay?

Is avoiding depopulation so much less affordable than the rest of what fits in societies' budgets? One of the best things humanity could do with its wealth and resources is to make it easier to choose children.

Making it better to choose better

Your two authors both take the bus to work. Mike gets off at 14th and I Streets and walks the last blocks to the White House. Dean gets off by the UT football stadium and walks the last block to the Population Research Center. Taking the bus is good for the climate and good for traffic and good for parking and good for other drivers. Isn't that virtuous of us?

Virtue has little to do with it. We each take the bus because it's a fast way to get from our homes to our offices. It's cheaper than a parking pass or an Uber. Our phones tell us when the bus is coming and they're generally right. It's *selfishly* a great option. The benefits of reduced carbon emissions, reduced local smog, reduced roadway congestion, fewer distracted drivers, and so on are a bonus. We do care about those things, but we might not take the bus if it wasn't also convenient, affordable, and basically comfortable. We're lucky that the choice that is better for us is also the choice that is better for our neighbors and for the planet.

Our good luck isn't just luck. It was earned by somebody's careful planning and somebody else's political organizing. We get to live in cities where citizens demanded, elected leaders approved, and urban planners and other civil servants worked hard to make public transit a good option. The bus routes from our homes to our offices are good *by purposeful design.* That design and effort by others made choosing the thing that is socially better for everybody also better for the person doing it.

Yes, parenting can be a selfless act. But should parenting have to be quite so selfless? To confront depopulation we should all be working to make parenting better for the people who volunteer for the work of raising children with care and love. We look forward to a future in which more people can choose to be parents to more children *because it would be a great life for those parents.* If *The Onion*'s satire is correct— "American Women Delaying Motherhood Because the Whole Thing Blows"—then, what if it didn't?

Every generation's experiences shape what they believe is possible and how they aspire

What will shape the long run is what future people aspire to. And that is something to be optimistic about because:

Future people don't aspire to anything yet. (That's it.)

Future people haven't been born yet. They don't hope for anything yet because they *can't* hope for anything yet. People's hopes are created by their experiences. People's aspirations are created by what they see other people enjoying, by what they see other people rejecting, by what looks like a flourishing life in the world they are born into. No generation can avoid setting an example for the next. The only question is what the message of that example will be.

It's no coincidence that Dean, raised in Oklahoma in a middle-class family in the 1980s and '90s, likes unpretentious (Mike may correct "cheap") Tex-Mex food. Decades later, on the two-day trip from Lucknow to Austin, Dean's preschooler anticipates getting to go to "the rice and beans restaurant" when he gets to Texas.

The number of kids we hoped for was shaped by our experiences, too. Not replicated one-for-one from our parents, but influenced by everything around us—from life stories to social and economic structures. We, your authors, spent years in master's degrees and PhDs and a postdoc and starting a nonprofit in Uttar Pradesh and . . . well, we started having children late and then struggled to achieve our desired family sizes. Dean was lucky enough to make it, on the last roll of the dice. Mike wasn't. What if we and our spouses had a different idea, earlier in our lives, of what was achievable in our careers and public service and families? What if we felt that way because it *was* achievable? We might have chosen differently.

The number of children people *want* has been falling. But why? No one is born with some exact family size imprinted into their soul. Your ideal number of children cannot be found in your DNA. People born in the past wanted more children because they lived in the past. They lived in a different environment, with different cultural influences, different institutions, different economies, and different expectations.

So what will future people want? They could want something different out of family life than many of us do today. They could, if they are born into a world where parenting receives all of the support that it deserves; where parenting can be combined with other paths to well-being and value; where parenting is fun, rewarding, and great more of the time; where parenting can fit with other goals—career, leisure, sleep!—more of the time; where they see men and women of all ages build care work into their good lives; where advances in medicine make carrying a pregnancy or breastfeeding less of a burden on a body and a mind. In that future, many people would want something different than they would if they were born into our present, like we today want something different than people in humanity's past.

How we structure education and work, where we invest our research efforts and budgets, what role we demand of governments in providing services to families, how we organize our households and communities around caring for the vulnerable in society—these all will make parenting more attractive or less attractive for present and future generations. They will shape what people perceive as possible for their lives.

Recognizing that attitudes are a product of the environment doesn't mean that what people want today or in the next decade is wide-open. Culture, economies, politics, and inequality don't change that fast. That sort of change is a generations-long project. But today some children will be born. And those of us who are adults today *could* change what parenting will be like for them. We could make it easier, better, fairer. We, here now, could bend over backward so a child born today could choose more when they grow up—more children if they wanted, more fun if they wanted, a more fulfilling career if they wanted, and maybe more of all of these—in a world where the trade-offs didn't bite so deep. Maybe by the time these children's children are born, that process of changing expectations might really be underway.

Your job: Join the conversation

We don't expect anyone to agree with every sentence of this book. We meant it when we wrote that this book is a call to join a big conversation about humanity's future. Now you're a part of that conversation, too.

There are many open questions that need attention and informed debate. Here's one that we struggled with, and still have no simple conclusion to offer you: Some people see a big problem and hope that governments will make it better. Some people see a big problem and worry that governments will make it worse. We understand this debate because our own experiences have pulled the two of us apart. Mike, in his work as an economist—first writing reports that he hoped would help the Congressional Budget Office score healthcare legislation or help the Centers for Medicare and Medicaid Services improve its programs, and now from the White House—knows government can be a solution. Dean, in his encounters with coercive and deceptive development programs in India, knows government can be a problem. We both respect and have learned from each other's experiences. The truth is, market failures are real and government failures are real. Externalities can be disasters and public policies to correct them can be inadequate, corrupt, or both. Or public policies to correct them can be fantastic successes.

So while some of us are designing and testing public policies and programs to support children and parents, others will be building social movements to deepen the culture of caretaking. That's good. Still others will be pushing the frontiers of what research can tell us. (That's what your two authors hope to do.) That's important because these issues need more investigation before we embark on any radical changes, however well-intentioned. There is more to learn about what depopulation will bring and how stabilizing our numbers might be possible.

But there's also plenty of reason for optimism. Scientific progress toward understanding population and families hasn't hit a wall. Most of the research in this book was created within only the last few decades— and some of it much more recently than that. When your authors were born, the Demographic and Health Surveys (where many statistics in this book come from) had never yet been collected. There was no macroeconomic theory of endogenous, non-rival technological progress. There were no integrated assessment models to connect economic and population changes to their climate consequences. Population ethics had barely started, and its major theorems were undiscovered. There were few ethnographies that detailed mothers' decision-making in communities where below-replacement fertility was common. While we were writing this book, we and our collaborators, and researchers at other universities, again and again discovered new facts. You have seen some of these discoveries, but many more could not fit. And there is plenty still to learn, understand, and decide.

Why care now?

We opened this book by cautioning that if we wait to confront depopulation, then the less inclusive, less kind, less calm voices in our societies will call depopulation a crisis and exploit it for their purposes. That's a reason to start engaging now. Another is that the political project of supporting children and their parents will grow more difficult as the average citizen gets older and demands that politics addresses *their* needs. And another is that we are far from knowing all we need to know to turn depopulation around. The search for good solutions could take decades. So if we want to start taking the right steps decades from now, we should start that search today.

Here's one more reason to care now: If humanity manages to mount a constructive response to depopulation, then *when* that happens will matter for *what* happens. On the downward edge of the Spike, every decade counts.

Figure 12.1 plots that what-if. And the when-if. It returns to the Spike and zooms in on the two centuries that will follow our own.

Figure 12.1. Even if fertility rates rebound to replacement in the 2100s, it makes a big difference when change starts

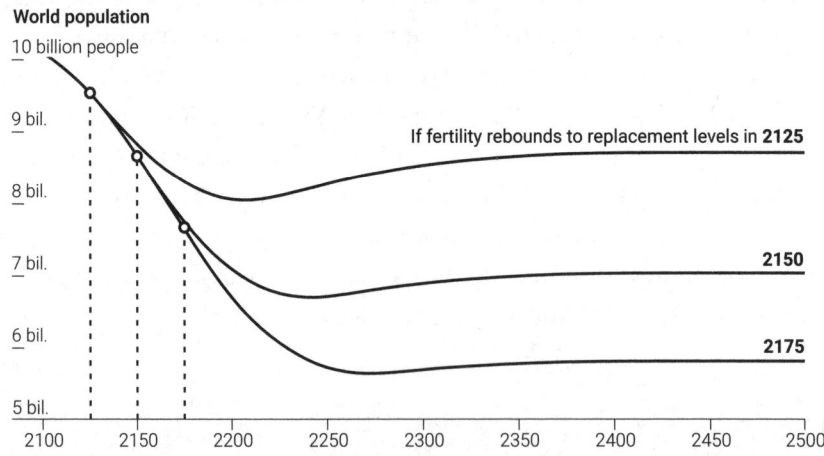

The three lines project three possible futures. In each of them, average global fertility eventually rebounds to the replacement fertility rate. The lines in the figure differ only according to whether the rebound starts in 2125 or 2150 or 2175.

Because the figure follows the methods of population science—tracing the lives of each birth cohort in each country over time as they are born, grow up, have children of their own, and eventually die—it cannot escape the facts of population momentum. So even if fertility rates begin climbing fast toward replacement in 2125, and even if all countries are modeled to converge at replacement, there still would be no leveling until long beyond 2200. Population levels change slowly even when birth rates change fast. Population changes accumulate over generations, not years.

What these hypotheticals teach us is that timing matters. That's because the later the rebound starts, the more depopulation precedes it. The calculations reveal that each year of delay in starting the rebound causes the final, stabilized population size to be almost a percent smaller, for as long as fertility holds at replacement levels. In our hypothetical, there would be a sustained population of 9.3 billion people if the fertility rebound starts in 2125. If it starts a mere fifty years later, then there will be only 6.8 billion people, each year, in perpetuity.

How large is a difference of 2.5 billion people—the 6.8 billion instead of 9.3 billion? How much does it matter if we pull up from depopulation's dive fifty years sooner? It is as large as the greatest number of humans who ever existed together before about 1950. Subtract 2.5 billion people from the number of us alive when Dean's and Mike's fathers were born, when the first Social Security checks were deposited, and you get a number smaller than zero. This book has left open the question of how many lives would be best in a stabilized future, but if somebody is considering this question in 2075, with the benefit of fifty more years of evidence, thinking, and debate, we doubt they'll consider the absence or presence of those 2.5 billion lives each year a matter of indifference.

We believe that so much wellbeing matters. But don't forget the inescapable math from chapter 1. For the population to stabilize at any size, even at a size much smaller than today's, the world would have to average two babies born per two adult lives, generation after generation. Everyone who wants to find a way—a good, free, and fair way—to make that happen at some population size or another is on the same team.

For the last time in this book, to say that something matters (in this case, timing) is not to say that it's the *only thing* that matters. And to say that timing matters is not to declare a crisis, because we're not declaring a crisis. Neither importance nor urgency means the same thing as crisis. Leaders declare a crisis when they want to discard the guardrails of caution. But this book is a call to be more thoughtful and careful, not less.

People matter. So let's get started.

People matter because of what we give to one another. People also matter for themselves. Because people matter, depopulation matters. Because people matter, depopulation deserves attention long before it comes. Humanity has a poor record of thinking constructively, factfully, and compassionately about distant challenges. But we've recently been building some useful experience.

Some of the best data documenting Earth's accumulation of carbon dioxide come from an observatory on Mauna Loa, a volcano in Hawaii. Two miles above sea level, a staff of eight measures the makeup of the troposphere. A plot of carbon dioxide concentrations cycles with the seasons around an unrelenting upward trend: to 425 parts per million in July 2024, from below 320 in 1958.

The data start in 1958 because scientists in the late 1950s had recognized the threat of climate change. They did not believe it was too early to get started. And they were right—even though it would be decades before leaders of the world's major economies would begin to so much as mouth promises to curb emissions; even though it would be more decades still before governments would do much about those promises through regulation, subsidies, and industrial policy.

We, writing six decades later about a depopulation looming perhaps six decades in our own future—or perhaps sooner—are realistic about the prospects for humanity rising to the occasion quickly. But we do not believe that it is too early to get started. Today there are reasons to hope for meaningful action on climate change—more than there would have been if some people had not started raising the call to action on climate sixty years ago, when the threat seemed distant and the tools for progress were few. We are in better shape now than we would have been without their decades of research and advocacy.

Climate scientists in the middle of the twentieth century could not have known the details of what we would someday need to do for climate progress. But they understood some big-picture facts. They understood the broad outlines of what would happen if humans continued to burn fossil fuels. We—us and now you—understand the broad outlines of what will happen if global birth rates stay below two. We, today, cannot know very much more than that.

Not yet. So let's learn. Let's talk. Let's think big. Waiting until after the Spike to learn how to respond to depopulation would be as imprudent as waiting until we burn the last ounce of coal to begin responding to climate change or waiting until a new disease emerges to develop the science of mRNA vaccines. Climate change taught us to accept that importance can come with uncertainty, and that uncertainty doesn't relieve us from a duty to hope, learn, and organize. Humanity is on a path to depopulation. That calls us to hope, learn, and organize again.

Acknowledgments

Part of the case for people is that we accomplish more when we support one another. The many people who helped us make this book give us one final chance to illustrate this fact.

April Geruso and Diane Coffey were essential editorial voices. Important parts of the book would have been much worse, and maybe awful, without each of them. Thank you for letting us share your stories. Thank you for supporting us in every way large and small during the years we wrote this book. Thank you for not settling for good enough. Thank you for everything.

Sara Chodosh collaborated with us to make the figures that present our data and tell our story. She and Jeremy Ashkenas first brought our Spike to wide attention on the pages of the *New York Times* in 2023. We're grateful to everyone who read that article and to the thousands who offered the comments with which we dialogue in this book.

We owe a special debt to Alba Ziegler-Bailey for accompanying us through the entire book writing process. Before we had a book proposal, an agent, or a publisher, we had Alba's wisdom and encouragement. We needed that—almost as much as we needed her later feedback on draft after draft after draft.

Several others deserve special mention for their editorial feedback. Hannah Groch-Begley's advice was invaluable. So, too, was input from Nathan Franz, Gardiner Harris, and Kevin Kuruc. Thank you.

Knowledge is the inexhaustibly cumulative resource that has propelled progress decade by decade and century by century. Thank you

Acknowledgments

to our collaborators on the research supporting this book for adding their share: Sam Arenberg, Gustaf Arrhenius, Kathleen Broussard, Mark Budolfson, Stuart Gietel-Basten, Prankur Gupta, Johan Gustafsson, Nicholas Lawson, Harvey Lederman, Melissa LoPalo, Narae Park, Melinda Roberts, Noah Scovronick, Orri Stefánsson, Christian Tarsney, Leela Visaria, and Stéphane Zuber. We are especially grateful to Sangita Vyas and Gage Weston for collaborating on the underlying population projections, and to Sangita for doing it again when the 2024 WPP came out.

We are grateful to our editors at Simon & Schuster, Robert Messenger and Johanna Li, for their excitement to bring this deep dive on population science, economics, and ethics to a general audience. Thanks to Carolyn Levin for her legal review. We thank Rob Sternitzky and Janet Byrne for excellent copyediting and fact checking, respectively.

We thank our literary agent, Don Fehr, and his team at Trident Media Group, including Miles Temel, for finding a home for the book at Simon & Schuster.

We are indebted to the staff at the UT Population Research Center who support our work, especially Meghan Tantum, Sylvia Celedon, and Stacy Brodie. Thank you to Kevin Carney in the economics department. Melissa Lopez of UT's Document Solutions came through for us again and again, even when we asked a lot. Gráinne O'Casey joined as our research assistant on the final leg and helped us get across the finish line.

We have many people to thank who read some or all of the book or talked with us about these ideas: Matthew Adler, Alícia Adserà, Abigail Aiken, Gustav Alexandrie, Cory Anderson, Ralf Bader, Calvin Baker, Radu Ban, David Beheshti, Julia Behrman, John Broome, Luzia Bruckamp, Allie Buckholts, Drew Burd, Kristen Burke, Krister Bykvist, Tim Campbell, Lucius Caviola, Richard Yetter Chappell, Shoumitro Chatterjee, Tyler Cowen, Rob Crosnoe, Michelle Eilers, James Feyrer, Zach Freitas-Groff, Subha Ganguly, Lauren Gaydosh, Liz Gershoff, Shagorika Ghosh, Jennifer Glass, Aashish Gupta, Jeff Hammer, Payal Hathi, Simon Hodson, Sambhav Jain, Tyler John, Chad Jones, Melissa Kearney, Avinash Kishore, Martin Kolk, Petra Kosonen, Jamie Law, Ester Lazzari, Amy Leff, Phil Levine, Will MacAskill, Eric Mann, Alex Mechanick, Yascha Mounk, Amanda Nagle, Ellu Nasser, Jake Nebel, Debbie Newmark, Toby Ord, Jason Orr, John Papp, Anna Pate, Michael Peters, Marcus Pivato, Marta Prato, Lant Pritchett, Chris Reina, Nicole Reina, Michelle Robert, Luisa Rodriguez, Sameer Sampat, Karen Schwartz, Jeff Sebo, Lizzie Shepelwich, Itai Sher, Beth Sully, Megan Sweeney, Anthony Swift, Ishaana Talesara, Nicole Tanzillo, Sam Trejo, Eshaan Vasanthakumar, Ashton Verdery, Eva Vivalt, Tom Vogl, Dietrich Vollrath, David Weil, Zach Weinersmith, Ben Weitz, Evan Wexler, Kenna Williams, and Kylie Jaeyun Yim. Many of you gave so much, in draft after draft, month after month, even year after year. Thank you, including for where you disagreed with us.

Chapter 8 (and perhaps the whole book) could not have happened if Mark Budolfson, Melinda Roberts, and Marc Fleurbaey had not welcomed Dean into population ethics in 2016, and been followed up by Gustaf Arrhenius, Krister Bykvist, Tim Campbell, Johan Gustafsson, and Stéphane Zuber. Thank you.

We thank the University of Texas at Austin, its College of Liberal Arts, and the UT Population Research Center for being our academic home, and we are grateful for the funding that supported the research referenced in this book: The Smith Richardson Foundation, the Eunice Kennedy Shriver National Institute of Child Health and Human Development, the National Institute on Aging, the Musk Foundation, and the Bill & Melinda Gates Foundation. This book does not necessarily reflect the views of any of the funders of our research, nor of any of the other people whom we thank, and no funder had the opportunity to review this book in advance. We also gratefully acknowledge the funders of the KMC program: GiveWell, Founders Pledge, and the donors to r.i.c.e. from the general public.

Mike thanks his colleagues at the Council of Economic Advisers for discussing some of the ideas in this book with him, especially Jacob Bastian, Jared Bernstein, Steven Braun, Amy Ganz, Kirabo Jackson,

Acknowledgments

Kyle Meng, Elena Patel, Asha Patt, Aastha Rajan, David Ratner, and Julia Turner.

Our work was improved time and again by presenting it to our colleagues and students and incorporating their feedback. We thank participants at the International Union for the Scientific Study of Population's International Population Conference in 2021; the Population Association of America annual meeting in 2022; the National Bureau of Economic Research's conferences on Fertility and Declining Population Growth in 2023 and 2024; the Global Priorities Institute Conference at Oxford University in 2022 and 2023; the 19th Annual De Jong Lecture in Social Demography in 2024; and several conferences we hosted at UT-Austin on the survey methodology of fertility preferences, macroeconomic growth and population, and social welfare evaluations. We learned from our students at UT, especially Dean's development and population students in fall 2022 and spring 2024 and Mike's public economics students in spring 2023.

Nikhil Srivastav routinely accomplishes astounding things. His leadership in the KMC program in Uttar Pradesh is only one of them. Thank you to Lovey Pant, to Dr. Assad Ali, to Kavita, to Reema, and especially to Seema. We are grateful to be a part of the r.i.c.e. team and its accomplishments.

As we were revising the book, Seema was promoted. The baby Dean and Diane saw in the Lucknow sonogram was born. Our friend Joe Potter died before he could read a draft. We are grateful that we got to talk with him about the ideas.

Finally, we are grateful for the joy we have found in working together over the past seventeen years. Of the hundred billion lives lived, wild chance flung us into healthy bodies and caring families in a rich country in the late twentieth century. Later it sent us into the same graduate student office on the third floor of Wallace Hall. Our unearned good luck was in part the gift of those who came before us. May we all give better still to humanity's future.

The Repugnant Appendix

What does it mean to build a better future, to make a better world? One thing it means is to make people's lives better. Nobody should dispute that the quality of life of everyone around the world matters. Back in chapter 8, we argued that quality of life is not the only thing that matters. The *quantity* of good lives also matters. There's value in an extra person getting to live a good life. More Good is Better, we said.

The idea that "More Good is Better" was all we needed there, because it's all this book needs. Stabilization would be better than depopulation both on average and in total—both for quality and for quantity—so there is no trade-off to weigh, no hard choice to make. More neighbors around—making, doing, wanting, contributing—means more good for each of us. Because both quantity and quality matter, depopulating when we could instead stabilize would be a huge missing-out.

Comparing depopulation against stabilization is difficult enough without being distracted by unrelated puzzles. So chapter 8 left open an unrelated puzzle: how, exactly, to trade off quality and quantity. But if you want to go further—to examine cases unlike stabilization, meaning cases that do trade off quality against quantity—then that's the question beyond the book's question that we address in this appendix. Imagine that, on some grand cosmic scale, 10 was the greatest life possible for a human, 5 was wonderful, and 3 was the average life today. If so, would we be better off hoping and working for 1 billion lives at 10 on the cosmic happiness meter, or 5 billion lives at 5? Or 10 billion at 3?

We mean the same thing by "better" here that we did in chapter 8.

We mean the general welfare, as in better to have exist, if one could stand over the universe and hope for one future or another after weighing the trade-offs: theirs versus ours, now versus later, quality versus quantity. And just like in chapter 8, nothing we have to say here assumes that the greater good is the only thing that matters. It could be joined by virtue, or rule following, or other notions of what else matters. We won't assume what matters to you. But we hope you agree that for humanity's biggest-picture social and policy questions, the greater good is, at least, one thing that matters and that we should take the time to ask which future would be better, overall.

So how should we think about the greatest good if we push the thought experiment about quality–quantity trade-offs to unrealistically hypothetical extremes? Imagine a quality of life that's positive and worth living, but only a little bit positive and worth living. Now imagine an enormous number of people, all of whom enjoy perfect equality without suffering, but only at that slightly positive quality of life. Here's the end point of the stress test: If quantity counts for anything, then couldn't any hypothetical universe with high-quality lives be outshined by some other hypothetical universe full of a much greater number of people each at the slightly positive quality of life?

Many experts in academic *population ethics* (although not all of them) report being troubled by the possibility that it ever could be better to have a large group that's worse off per person, instead of another smaller group that's better off per person. The claim that it could indeed be better to choose the bigger population is called the "Repugnant Conclusion."

> **Repugnant Conclusion:** A hypothetical set of lives with perfect equality at a slightly positive wellbeing would be better, if populous enough, than another hypothetical set of fewer lives with very high wellbeing, all else equal.

Why is that idea called the "Repugnant Conclusion"? It's a *conclusion* that one could draw from considering population ethics: the conclusion that a really big population could be better than a small one, even if the people in the big population, while happy enough, weren't *very* happy. And many philosophers of population find the idea *repugnant*—in that it feels somehow wrong or distasteful to them that quantity could ever trade off against quality in this way. So that name is branding, meant to nudge you to reject any principle that would endorse this conclusion.

The logic of this book does not require us to touch the Repugnant Conclusion. One can agree that stabilization would be better than de-population and can agree with our proposal in chapter 8 that More Good is Better without agreeing with—or even considering—the Repugnant Conclusion. That's why you're reading this in an appendix, not a chapter.

But we have found that many readers of this book—many readers who are interested in the future of the population—want to know about the Repugnant Conclusion. We couldn't ignore the Repugnant Conclusion in a book about population because most readers who have heard anything about population ethics, at all, have heard *something* about the Repugnant Conclusion. And what they have heard tends to leave a lingering bad taste.

Here's a sample of the attention the Repugnant Conclusion got during the months while we were writing this book. *The Economist* magazine wrote that "the fear of large populations of low quality lives has overshadowed the field of population ethics" in a long article about the Repugnant Conclusion in its end-of-year double issue. The statistician Nate Silver wrote about it in his book *On the Edge*. In a book calling for better treatment of animals, *Animal Liberation Now*, Peter Singer applied it to the context of animal lives. Matt Yglesias, author of *One Billion Americans*, wrote about it on his Substack. And so on.

So here, in the appendix, we address this issue and its implications. The question of what to make of the Repugnant Conclusion turns out to be what the scholarly study of population ethics has examined most closely and most enduringly for the past few decades. We'll explain why we don't find it so mysterious—and why we're optimistic that population ethicists can check it off the list of unresolved puzzles and turn their attention elsewhere.

The Repugnant Conclusion doesn't matter here. Sure, a larger group of equal, each-slightly-positive lives could be better, in the right hypothetical scenario. And no, that doesn't tell us that anything is wrong with the idea that More Good is Better. And it says nothing about whether we should stabilize or depopulate.

If you don't want to worry about the Repugnant Conclusion, don't (really!). We've just gone through a book's worth of evidence that tells us *not* to expect that bigger populations would lead to lower levels of wellbeing.

Even setting aside that important practical realization, we don't think the Repugnant Conclusion teaches us much nor poses a deep challenge—even in the abstract. But before we say why not, we need to explain the origin of this idea.

What the Repugnant Conclusion was supposed to be about

About four decades ago, under the leadership of the philosopher Derek Parfit, the scholars of population ethics had an arresting realization. The realization was that, in hypothetical principle, a large number of people enjoying "Muzak and potatoes" (that was Parfit's example, meant to evoke an okay-but-not-great life) could be preferable to some small number of people enjoying Mozart. In a world where there are worse things than Muzak and potatoes, this worry might feel elitist. But Parfit didn't like this realization, so he named this idea the "Repugnant Conclusion."

Parfit wrote about the Repugnant Conclusion in a genius book titled *Reasons and Persons*. In it, Parfit contrasted two theories for judging ethical trade-offs in what sorts of futures would be better or worse, in the sense of general welfare.

One of these theories we have already seen: the theory that better and worse are measured by average wellbeing. In the search for the right way to think about wellbeing in population ethics, average wellbeing is the core proposal and star candidate of the *only-quality-not-quantity* approach. We rejected it in chapter 8 for the same reason that Parfit did: Because this approach says that it would make matters worse to add a good life—even a life better than yours or ours—if it would pull down the average.

Parfit's other candidate theory was that better and worse is measured by total wellbeing. Total wellbeing is the simplest candidate that rejects the *only-quality-not-quantity* approach. And it also fits comfortably with how economists already evaluate which policies or futures would be better or worse.

Average wellbeing and total wellbeing aren't the only two theories for judging trade-offs. It's always possible to embellish a theory further, especially with the limitless options that math provides. Elsewhere, we and other professors have written for other experts in ways that worry over the many mathematical details of other theories. But that's not this appendix. These two straightforward options—total and average—will suffice here. They are the clearest way of accepting the *only-quality-not-quantity* approach (which average wellbeing does) and of rejecting it (which total wellbeing does). So it makes sense that the scholarly quest for the right theory of the greater good starts here.

And we've already made progress by rejecting average wellbeing back in chapter 8. But Parfit raised the alarm about total wellbeing, too. His concern was that if total wellbeing is the proper way to judge which future would be better, then we reach the Repugnant Conclusion. In this way, Parfit's *Reasons and Persons* raised a troubling question that has been dogging philosophers since. Does the Repugnant Conclusion compel us to abandon the total wellbeing approach? And if the total and average approaches both have problems, then what?

Putting aside the evaluation of whether anything is *repugnant* in the everyday sense of that word, the Repugnant Conclusion is indeed a mathematical implication of the total wellbeing approach.

The simplest way to see this is that "the total sum of wellbeing" is algebraically identical to "average wellbeing times the number of people." If you make trade-offs between quantity and quality that way, then the benefits of a larger number could outweigh the costs of a reduced average. That's just algebra. The question is what anyone concerned with overall welfare in society should make of it.

Why the Repugnant Conclusion offers no special argument against total wellbeing

The point of the Repugnant Conclusion was to guide and inform the search for the right approach to population ethics. To be useful in choosing the right theory, the Repugnant Conclusion must be implied by some plausible theories and not others. So let's see if it is.

In particular, let's see if the Repugnant Conclusion separates approaches that agree that More Good is Better from approaches that don't. It's time for a trial: Call forth the champions of both camps! For the principle that More Good is Better, total wellbeing will stand as the champion. For the *only-quality-not-quantity* faction that rejects that More Good is Better, average wellbeing will stand for trial.

Now we are ready to ask: The Repugnant Conclusion is supposed to be a special problem for total wellbeing, but not for average wellbeing. Is it?

No, it isn't.

Here is what we are going to argue: The Repugnant Conclusion should be understood to emerge from either approach, from average wellbeing and total wellbeing. The Repugnant Conclusion, we say, can be found somewhere within any plausible candidate for measuring overall goodness. That total wellbeing gets singled out as capital-R Repugnant may be a misunderstanding.

Consider the choice between Policy E and Policy F in figure A.1. Dean first made a version of figure A.1 with philosopher Mark Budolfson; it builds on earlier discoveries by Bill Anglin, a philosopher, and Tyler Cowen, an economist.

Figure A.1. An example where average wellbeing and total wellbeing both lead to the Repugnant Conclusion

POLICY E (QUALITY-FOCUSED)

	number of lives	per-person wellbeing
new very-high-quality lives	1 billion	20
new high-quality lives	0	-
unaffected population	100 billion	1

total wellbeing = 0.12 trillion
average wellbeing = 1.19

POLICY F (QUANTITY-FOCUSED)

	number of lives	per-person wellbeing
new very-high-quality lives	0	-
new high-quality lives	1 trillion	2
unaffected population	100 billion	1

total wellbeing = 2.10 trillion (highest option)
average wellbeing = 1.91 (highest option)

Figure A.1 is like the choice that the Repugnant Conclusion warns about. Policy could put the future on path F, the *quantity* path that creates a trillion future lives, each at a wellbeing of 2, which is a life worth living, but not a life we think of as great. Or policymakers could choose path E, the *quality* path of only a billion future lives, each at a great wellbeing of 20. The exact numbers don't matter. Just notice that 20 is ten times as good a life for a person as 2, but a trillion is one thousand times as many people as a billion.

What should happen? In this case, the numbers work out such that total wellbeing is greater with Policy F. What about average wellbeing? To answer, we need to know about the part of the population that is unaffected—the people who would be around under either policy, but whose lives and experiences don't change one bit according to whether Policy E or F is chosen. We shouldn't forget about them.

For the unaffected population, let's assume something inspired by the true, real-world case. The human species appeared at least one hundred thousand years ago. The Population Reference Bureau estimates that, since that time, about 120 billion people have ever lived. (We drew upon their estimates to make the Spike.) About 7 percent of those are alive today. Many past lives were lived without our modern conveniences (like adequate potato supply, sanitation, or healthcare at birth).

There is uncertainty about exactly how many human lives there have been and exactly how the wellbeing of each stacks up. But everyone should agree that there have been *many of them* and that on average they have been *not very good*. We specify that a lifetime wellbeing of 2, whatever it means, is better than this background average, which includes some good lives but also many that have been very, very bad. There is no alternative here, once we've decided to do these kinds of thought experiments, other than to choose some numbers, so figure A.1 sets the unaffected, preexisting population of 100 billion individuals at a wellbeing of 1.

Now we have the information to compute average wellbeing under Policy E and Policy F. Each person with a wellbeing of 2 pulls the background average up from 1. So does each person with a wellbeing of 20. In the end, a trillion 2s makes a bigger difference in terms of pulling up that average than a billion 20s, so the average is higher in the high-quantity case. Average wellbeing recommends Policy F, just like total wellbeing does. It recommends the Repugnant policy. The average and the total agree that adding a higher number of lower-quality lives is the best option.

The trial is a draw. If there is any stain of Repugnance here, both the average and the total bear it. And that means the Repugnant Conclusion offers no distinguishing argument against total wellbeing.

What is going on? The Repugnant Conclusion was supposed to be a unique, defining problem for total wellbeing, not a problem for average wellbeing. At least, that's how everyone talks about it.

When we made figure A.1, we tested the core idea: Could creating the many lives at low wellbeing ever be better than creating the fewer at higher wellbeing? But we departed from the particular example of the Repugnant Conclusion that Derek Parfit first offered. That's because we remembered to include the background, unaffected group of many lives that have actually existed in the real world. Parfit's classic example left those lives out. If we, too, ignored the 100 billion unaffected people, then average wellbeing would rank Policy E over Policy F merely because 20 is greater than 2.

But why ignore the background, unaffected lives that actually exist? Or, more to the point, why ignore the *possibility* of any unaffected group that might exist? We included *past* human lives in our average, but if that seems strange, one can construct the background population in other ways. Imagine instead that they existed contemporaneously, but on a different continent without communication, or are on a different planet too far away to affect, or are unaffected but in the future, or are unaffected nonhuman animals. The same logic applies.

The contingent introduction of the Repugnant Conclusion

We say that the instance of the Repugnant Conclusion in figure A.1 counts as an instance of the Repugnant Conclusion. The average and the total would point to different preferred policies only if we construct the example to rule out an unaffected, background population. We should not do that. Once we have agreed to learn from the very imaginary case that the Repugnant Conclusion presents, there is no reason to limit our imagination in this way, to just a subset of cases (where the background population is assumed to contain zero lives).

What if the history of the Repugnant Conclusion had been different? Over the years, various philosophers and economists—including leaders of the field—have never quite agreed with one another: They have used the name "Repugnant Conclusion" in subtly but importantly different ways. What if the version in figure A.1 was what came to be named the "Repugnant Conclusion"? Might the history of thought in population ethics have progressed differently?

Even given Parfit's formulation, the history of the Repugnant Conclusion could have been short, because it didn't take long for other researchers to answer Parfit's questions. In the late 1980s, the economist Yew-Kwang Ng proved a mathematical fact: The Repugnant Conclusion would arise from any complete theory that sorts every imaginable population into better or worse, if the theory followed a few rules that would be hard to criticize or do without. (The core two rules are that inequality isn't good and that adding valuable lives, all else equal, doesn't make the world worse.) A later philosopher, Gustaf Arrhenius, discovered other facts about the Repugnant Conclusion like Ng's. Arrhenius's logic uses other rules that are more complicated, so that they can be even less objectionable. Other researchers have carried this flag further, finding ever-less-objectionable arguments that lead to the Repugnant Conclusion, or closing off the holes left by earlier researchers' assumptions.

Decade by decade, journal article by journal article, this logic has built a wall of reasons to make our peace with the Repugnant Conclusion, whether or not anyone finds it "repugnant." Maybe suffering-free lives of Muzak and potatoes wouldn't be so bad. And if some scholar's devastating critique hinges on their favorite way of slicing, dicing, peeling, or mashing the concepts and definitions in their imaginary example, then maybe it isn't so devastating after all.

The average and the total don't agree about whether More Good is Better. But they do agree about the Repugnant Conclusion. Why? What average wellbeing and total wellbeing have in common as theories of the general welfare is that they both have a complete account of making trade-offs even-handedly, of weighing quality against quantity, of combining and weighing what's good and bad for different people in different futures, of aggregating. And it turns out that any way of evaluating the general welfare that has these properties will also imply some version of the Repugnant Conclusion.

We don't want to hide this possibility, so don't overlook that society has the nihilistic option of altogether rejecting "even-handedly weighing trade-offs to assess what's overall better for the greater good." But no sensible approach to governing or doing philanthropy or participating in public debate could do altogether without a way to evaluate trade-offs. Our operating assumption is still that the U.S. Constitution is right (along with the Indian Constitution and basically every practical modern theory of political philosophy) in saying that the general welfare *matters.*

And so, the Repugnant Conclusion isn't about whether More Good is Better. The Repugnant Conclusion is just an arithmetic way of pointing out that, however we aggregate overall goodness for everyone, advantages and disadvantages can balance one another out—including when one imaginary dimension or another gets hypothetically huge.

There are even more reasons to set aside the Repugnant Conclusion

There are other good reasons not to get hung up on the Repugnant Conclusion. For starters, the Repugnant Conclusion is only a problem because it *feels* like one. Maybe it feels like a problem to you, and if so, you've got company. But it does not feel like one to everybody. All along, there has been the option of being open to the possibility that some imaginary bigger population might indeed be better than some imaginary smaller population (if the numbers and the logic work out that way).

There is no feelings-based consensus about avoiding potato-and-Muzak lives. We find that our economist friends are less likely to be hung up on the issue than our philosopher friends. Yup, economists say, there are trade-offs. After all, most economists have already encountered similar math when they learned about computing statistical expectations of possible events (like in a health insurance contract, where a tiny probability of a huge consequence such as a rare cancer diagnosis can be more important than other considerations that feel more normal or likely).

Although the Repugnant Conclusion is sometimes discussed as a uniquely thorny issue for population ethics that should confound and arrest discussions of population size, difficult trade-offs really aren't particular to the questions of *changing* populations. One can restrict oneself to imagining only a fixed, unchanging assembly of 10 billion people, and still debate whether giving all 10 billion people a scoop of ice cream would justify making a randomly selected one of them suffer magic agony for four minutes, or whether it should be three minutes, and whether adding rainbow sprinkles to the ice cream makes a difference. It's great that theorists learn what they can from hypotheticals about billions of scoops of ice cream (truly!), and it's right that meanwhile the Environmental Protection Agency, the Council of Economic Advisers, and the Office of Information and Regulatory Affairs carries on evaluating the trade-offs in regulatory proposals.

Many philosophers shrug for other reasons, too. Some have pointed out that, whatever sort of puzzle the Repugnant Conclusion poses for philosophy, it's no worse than other paradoxes that captivate philosophers. Free will deserves further study, but its paradoxes haven't called courts or law schools to a halt. Other philosophers say that everybody has misunderstood how incomparably different a "life barely worth living" is from a great life. Their argument is that we shouldn't trade off between great lives for some people and just-okay lives for other people—"shouldn't" in such a deep way that it would block the logic of the Repugnant Conclusion and of most other policy analysis. That is not a view we share, but it would mean that the Repugnant Conclusion would simply never come up, even for total wellbeing.

And many other philosophers have argued that the intuition that the Conclusion is Repugnant is hardly a solid foundation for a theory. Why not? For one, a series of philosophers, including Johan Gustafsson, have offered a series of reasons why human minds might have trouble imagining the difference between trillions of lives that are barely good and trillions of lives that barely aren't. The Repugnant Conclusion is about hard trade-offs at the limits of imagination. So we can't draw any grand conclusions from the fact that humans' intuitions are boggled by that arithmetic.

We humans need conceptual tools and logic that can reach beyond what we feel about what we can imagine. Tools like that help humans to understand unintuitive but true things every day.

What does the Repugnant Conclusion tell us about whether to prefer stabilization or depopulation?

Now that we've seen what the Repugnant Conclusion is and what it implies, it's time to return to the question of this book. What does the Repugnant Conclusion tell us about whether to prefer stabilization or depopulation?

It tells us nothing. The Repugnant Conclusion asks whether a valuable increase in the quantity of positive-value lives can outweigh any decrease in the quality of positive-value lives—when that question is pushed to its most extreme numerical examples. And yet, not *every* decision requires hard trade-offs. Sometimes there really are win-wins. Sometimes one can choose more quality and more quantity. Win-wins tend to pop up in population economics because of scale effects and non-rival innovation.

In our vision for a stabilized future, relative to a depopulating future, people would have higher living standards; a bigger society would support more innovation and creativity; progress on decarbonization would make the added footprint of added people small; progress toward gender equity and reproductive freedom would come first; and a bigger future would be better prepared to resolve shared threats. And, finally, more people would get to live good lives, rather than not exist.

Our vision reaches a bigger future for all by becoming better for each. That's hardly the only future available for humanity to choose. But humanity *could* choose such a big, abundant future, and that wouldn't be a decision about hard trade-offs. So whether the Repugnant Conclusion is disturbing or, as we say, fine, it poses no big problem for a big future.

Notes

This book uses population projections published in the peer-reviewed article:

- Spears D, Vyas S, Weston G, Geruso M. 2024. Long-term population projections: Scenarios of low or rebounding fertility. *PLoS ONE*.

These projections use the cohort-component method of population science. That method makes deterministic projections based upon its inputs. In other words, they are *if-then* projections that answer the question: If birth rates and death rates follow this course, then how would population size change over time? Our core method is not to assume any particular future path for birth and death rates, but instead to demonstrate the robustness of our population projections by showing that a broad range of assumptions about birth rates and death rates yield similar results.

Complete census or vital registration records are often unavailable, especially outside of higher-income countries and for the past. Throughout the book, we use a hierarchy of authorities. These are the sources for demographic facts and quantities not otherwise attributed to other sources:

- First, where available, we follow the 2024 revision of the United Nations' World Population Prospects (WPP).
- Then, if a question cannot be settled with the WPP, we use the Human Fertility Database (HFD), which presents detailed estimates for certain advanced-economy populations where data are available. See Max Planck Institute for Demographic Research (Germany) and Vienna Institute of Demography (Austria). Available at www.humanfertility.org (data downloaded 2022–2024).
- Finally, if a question cannot be settled with the WPP or the HFD, we use the Demographic and Health Surveys (DHS), a globally comparable set of sample surveys. We especially often use India's DHS, called the National Family Health Survey. When we write about India in the present or in its most recent survey, we use the NFHS-5.

The Kangaroo Mother Care ward is a real place. Although the names are pseudonyms, Seema is a real person (whose story is told with permission) and the events in the book are based on Dean's collaboration with the project. It is officially the Project on Breastfeeding and Newborn Care, which is a collaboration between Bahraich Medical College and r.i.c.e. with the partnership of Population Health Insights and GiveWell and seed funding from Founders Pledge and the individual donors to r.i.c.e. We are grateful to Nikhil Srivastav, Dr. Asad Ali, and Diane Coffey for their leadership in this project and for allowing us to share its accomplishments. Read more about the KMC ward and donate to r.i.c.e., a 501(c)(3) nonprofit public charity, at riceinstitute.org/partnerships.

In some cases below we list research that informed our thinking, but that is not directly mentioned in the text. These are marked with †.

Prologue

- Dean Spears, graphics by Sara Chodosh. "The World's Population May Peak in Your Lifetime." *New York Times.* 2023 September 24. We thank everyone who commented on the *NYT* Spike article, especially those whose comments we respond to here: Chevy in South Hadley, Doug Muir, Ex-pat Steve in San Ramon, Grumpy Middle Aged Man, Mark in Montreal, Mark Caldwell in Tennessee, Mike in SC, S Lawrence in Nirvana, Tom in US, Uncle Albert in Snow Hill, Uofc English in Wilmette, whafrog in Winnipeg.
- **birth rates.** The total fertility rate is a weighted sum of age-specific fertility rates. For that reason it is more informative than the crude birth rate, but not as informative as cohort average parity after childbearing ages, if that is available. Although we distinguish among these when we teach population science classes or in our papers, here—before formalizing terms in chapter 2.0—we use "birth rate" for "total fertility rate" as we find that the term "fertility" sometimes confuses readers who interpret it as related to "infertility."

Chapter 1: The Spike

- **IIASA.** K.C. S, et al. 2024. Updating the Shared Socioeconomic Pathways (SSPs) Global Population and Human Capital Projections.
- **UW.** Vollset SE, et al. 2020. Fertility, mortality, migration, and population scenarios for 195 countries and territories from 2017 to 2100: A forecasting analysis for the Global Burden of Disease Study. *Lancet.*
- **Figure 1.1.** Authors' computations in Spears et al. 2024. 1950 to 2100 follows the WPP medium projection. Historical data before 1950 are based on Kaneda and Haub's article How Many People Have Ever Lived on Earth? Population Reference Bureau. Although Spears (2024) used the 2022 WPP, figure 1.1 and all figures based on the Spike were updated in July 2024 to use the 2024 WPP (thank you, Sangita Vyas).
- **U.S. Blacks, whites, or Hispanics.** Hamliton BE. 2021. Total fertility rates, by maternal educational attainment and race and Hispanic origin: United States, 2019. National Vital Statistics Reports.

- **per two adults.** A simplification; chapter 2.0 explains in full detail how formal demography defines replacement-level fertility.
- **Figure 1.2.** Authors' computations. These are hypothetical distributions that illustrate how an average completed cohort fertility of 1.62 and 2.0 could be reached.
- **teen births.** Buckles KS, Hungerman DM. 2013. Season of birth and later outcomes: Old questions, new answers. *Review of Economics and Statistics.*
- **Dalits.** DHS, as computed in NFHS-5 2019–2020 India report. Thanks to Srinivas Goli.
- **France's fertility fell.** Coale AJ, Watkins SC, eds. 1986. *The Decline of Fertility in Europe.* Princeton.
- **Figure 1.3.** Authors' computations based on Spears et al. 2024; see figure 1.1.
- **full childbearing lifetime.** This statistic uses completed cohort fertility from HFD. We specify the 1950 birth cohort because Estonia and Hungary both bounced around this range for women born in the 1940s before turning decisively down. The HFD data count East and West Germany as separate countries and count Scotland and the set England and Wales as separate countries. These fit the pattern, as do the unions, which are listed separately, which would make it 0-for-28 instead of 0-for-26.
- **climate change . . . facts have been known.** Jamieson D. 2014. *Reason in a Dark Time.* Oxford.
- † Basten S, Lutz W, Scherbov S. 2013. Very long range global population scenarios to 2300 and the implications of sustained low fertility. *Demographic Research.*
- † Bhattacharjee NV, Schumacher AE, et al. 2024. Global fertility in 204 countries and territories, 1950–2021, with forecasts to 2100. *Lancet.*
- † Gietel-Basten S, Sobotka T. 2021. Trends in population health and demography. *Lancet.*
- † Bricker D, Ibbitson J. 2019. *Empty Planet: The Shock of Global Population Decline.* Hachette.

Chapter two-point-zero: The dividing line between growth and decay

Something that matters more than the difference between 2.0 and 2.1, but that isn't highlighted in the chapter, is the difference between the *period* total fertility rate and the *cohort* total fertility rate. The period rate looks at fertility at a point in time (like a calendar year), during which twenty-five- to twenty-nine-year-olds are having babies at some rate, thirty- to thirty-four-year-olds are having babies at some other rate, and so on. The humans whose lives generate the data in each age group are different people, from different cohorts.

Period TFR aggregates across these cohorts and asks how many children a woman who survived from birth to age fifty would have if she experienced these age-specific birth rates as she aged through her life course. Cohort TFR (or, more properly, cohort parity at age fifty) is similar, but generates the age-specific rates in different calendar years, following the same people over time. It measures the twenty-five- to twenty-nine-year-olds, and then must wait five years to measure the same people at thirty to thirty-four. So we won't know the cohort TFR for babies born in 2020 until 2070. For this very practical reason, period TFR is the number you most often see presented here, and anywhere that someone uses the term "total fertility rate" without stipulating that it's a cohort measure.

- **Uttar Pradesh.** DHS.
- **Figure 2.1.** Authors' presentation of WPP.
- Gietel-Basten S, Scherbov S. 2019. Is half the world's population really below "replacement-rate"? *PLoS ONE*.
- **born this year in Texas.** Vital Statistics Data, Texas Health and Human Services. Example counts are 368,317 in 2020 and 377,710 in 2019.
- **average of seven times.** Hacker JD. 2003. Rethinking the "early" decline of marital fertility in the United States. *Demography*.
- **about six times.** Global TFR estimates for 1800 and 1900 from Gapminder Fertility Rates Dataset (v14 2024). These estimates are necessarily based on thinner evidence than the main data sources used throughout this book (UN WPP, HFD, DHS).
- **fallen near four births.** Haines MR. 1989. American fertility in transition: New estimates of birth rates in the United States, 1900–1910. *Demography*.
- **Figure 2.2.** Authors' computations. Crude rates are twenty-year moving averages, with annual data sourced from Our World in Data up to 1950 and the UN WPP thereafter. The bottom panel is the growth rate implied by the crude rate model, ignoring migration.
- Notestein FW. 1953. Economic problems of population change. *Proceedings of the Eighth International Conference of Agricultural Economics*. Oxford.
- **Figure 2.3.** Authors' presentation. Data before 1950 are from table 3.2 in Vallin J. 1991. Mortality in Europe from 1720 to 1914: Long-term trends and changes in patterns by age and sex, chapter in *The Decline of Mortality in Europe*. Data since 1950 are WPP, except Uttar Pradesh is DHS.
- Rostow WW. 1998. *The Great Population Spike and After*. Oxford. (Hat tip to David Weil.)
- DeLong JB. 2022. *Slouching Towards Utopia: An Economic History of the Twentieth Century*. Hachette.
- **Figure 2.4.** Authors' presentation of WPP.
- Raftery AE, Ševčíková H. 2023. Probabilistic population forecasting: Short to very long-term. *International Journal of Forecasting*.
- **after turning thirty.** Park N, et al. 2023. Near-universal marriage, early childbearing, and low fertility: India's alternative fertility transition. *Demographic Research*.
- **Figure 2.5.** Authors' computations in Spears et al. 2024 (updated for 2024 WPP).

† McKeown T. 1976. *The Modern Rise of Population*. Edward Arnold.

† Lutz W, et al. 2006. The low-fertility trap hypothesis: Forces that may lead to further postponement and fewer births in Europe. *Vienna Yearbook of Population Research*.

† Adserà A. 2017. The future fertility of highly educated women: The role of educational composition shifts and labor market barriers. *Vienna Yearbook of Population Research*. (Adserà makes the important point that the selectivity of education will continue to change as average education increases.)

† Thanks to Ashton Verdery for discussion on the history and accuracy of population projections and the future of kinship, and thanks especially for digging into the source files for our Spike projections.

Chapter 3: What people do to the planet

The modeling results at the core of this chapter are based upon our research in collaboration with Mark Budolfson, Kevin Kuruc, and Sangita Vyas: "Is Less Really More? Comparing the Climate and Productivity Impacts of a Shrinking Population." We are grateful for comments when we presented this paper at the National Bureau of Economic Research in 2023.

- **China faced a smog crisis:**
  - • Wong E. 2013. China lets media report on air pollution crisis. *New York Times*.
  - • Qiu C. 2023. $PM_{2.5}$ rebounds in China in 2023, after falling for 10 years straight. CREA.
  - † Kahn ME, Zheng S. 2016. *Blue Skies over Beijing: Economic Growth and the Environment in China*. Princeton.
- **no longer promote population reduction.** Bongaarts J, O'Neill BC. 2018. Global warming policy: Is population left out in the cold? *Science*.
- **Global average exposure.** World Bank World Development Indicators: $PM_{2.5}$ air pollution, mean annual exposure (micrograms per cubic meter).
- **Figure 3.1.** Authors' presentation of World Bank World Development Indicators: $PM_{2.5}$ air pollution, mean annual exposure (micrograms per cubic meter).
- Wallace-Wells D. 2021. Ten million a year. *London Review of Books*.
- **Dean wrote a 2019 book.** Spears D. 2019. *Air: Pollution, Climate Change, and India's Choice Between Policy and Pretence*. HarperCollins.
- Ehrlich PR. 1968. *The Population Bomb*. Ballantine Books. (Later editions would credit Anne Ehrlich as a coauthor, but she was not credited in the 1968 version. On sterilants in the water, Ehrlich wrote: "One plan often mentioned involves the addition of temporary sterilants to water supplies or staple food. Doses of the antidote would be carefully rationed by the government to produce the desired population size. Those of you who are appalled at such a suggestion can rest easy. The option isn't even open to us, since no such substance exists.")
- **Figure 3.2.** Authors' computations based on Spears et al. 2024.

Notes

- **NPR.** Kamenetz A. 2022. Why keeping girls in school is a good strategy to cope with climate change. *NPR.*
- **Figure 3.3.** Authors' computations in Budolfson et al. Our climate model research that we report in figures 3.3 and 3.4 uses a version of Nordhaus's global DICE model. Nordhaus WD. 2017. Revisiting the social cost of carbon. *PNAS.*
- **Figure 3.4.** Authors' computations in Budolfson et al.
- Ritchie H. 2024. *Not the End of the World.* Random House.
- **Figure 3.5.** Authors' computations based on Budolfson et al.
- McKibben B. 1998. *Maybe One: A Personal and Environmental Argument for Single-Child Families.* Simon & Schuster.
- † Bradshaw CJ, Brook BW. 2014. Human population reduction is not a quick fix for environmental problems. *PNAS.*
- † Ehrlich PR. 2023. *Life: A Journey Through Science and Politics.* Yale.

Our background research, often with Mark Budolfson, Noah Scovronick, and others from the Princeton Climate Futures Initiative, led by Marc Fleurbaey:
- † Scovronick N, et al. 2017. Impact of population growth and population ethics on climate change mitigation policy. *PNAS.*
- † Budolfson MB, et al. 2021. Utilitarian benchmarks for emissions and pledges promote equity, climate and development. *Nature Climate Change.*
- † Scovronick N, et al. 2019. The impact of human health co-benefits on evaluations of global climate policy. *Nature Communications.*
- † Lawson N, Spears D. 2018. Optimal population and exhaustible resource constraints. *Journal of Population Economics.*
- † Budolfson M, Spears D. 2021. Population ethics and the prospects for fertility policy as climate mitigation policy. *Journal of Development Studies.*

Chapter 4: Population starts in other people's bodies

- **Canada and Czechia.** HFD.
- **Figure 4.1.** Authors' computations to illustrate hypothetical distributions.
- **gender pay gap fell.** National Committee on Pay Equality analysis of U.S. Census Bureau data.
- **General Social Survey . . . CNN.** Coffey D, et al. 2018. Explicit prejudice: Evidence from a new survey. *Economic and Political Weekly.*
- Collins G. 2009. *When Everything Changed: The Amazing Journey of American Women from 1960 to the Present.* Little, Brown.
- **Figure 4.2.** Authors' presentation. The horizontal axis is the percent gender wage gap in median earnings, computed by the OECD for 2022. The vertical axis is period TFR in 2022 from the 2024 WPP. Observations are thirty-five OECD countries with TFR below 2, which excludes Israel, an outlier that, at

2.94, is not informative about low-birth-rate societies. The OECD does not report wage gap data for Ireland and Turkey.

- Kearney MS, Levine PB, Pardue L. 2022. The puzzle of falling US birth rates since the great recession. *Journal of Economic Perspectives.*
- **Bangladesh and India.** DHS.
- **EU's Gender Equality Index.** Barbieri D, et al. 2021. *Gender Equality Index 2021.* European Institute for Gender Equality (an autonomous body of the EU).
- **Jessica, a twenty-six-year-old from Peru** changes her name and substitutes a neighboring country for anonymity.
- Goldin C. 2021. *Career and Family: Women's Century-Long Journey Toward Equity.* Princeton.
- **Bureau of Labor Statistics.** American Time Use Survey. Time adults spent caring for household children as a primary activity by sex, age, and day of week, 2021 annual averages.
- **archive.** Thank you to McKibben in *Maybe One* for the imagery.
- **editorial in *Nature*.** 2023. Women's health: End the disparity in funding. *Nature.*
† Callahan A. 2023. Her doctor said her illness was all in her head. This scientist was determined to find the truth. *New York Times.*

Chapter 5: Adding new lives to an imperfect world

- **became this chapter.** Thank you, Naka, for getting us started here.
- Lam D. 2011. How the world survived the population bomb: Lessons from 50 years of extraordinary demographic history. *Demography.*
- **Figure 5.1.** Authors' presentation of "Daily supply of calories per person, 1274 to 2021" by Roser M, et al. Our World in Data based on FAO and other sources.
- **genetic difference in height potential.** WHO Multicentre Growth Reference Study. See also: Deaton A. 2013. *The Great Escape.* Princeton.
- **cognitive development.** Spears D. 2012. Height and cognitive achievement among Indian children. *Economics & Human Biology.*
- **moms are undernourished.** Coffey D. 2015. Prepregnancy body mass and weight gain during pregnancy in India and sub-Saharan Africa. *PNAS.*
- **Figure 5.2.** Authors' computations from Indian DHS.
- Wray B. 2022. *Generation Dread: Finding Purpose in an Age of Climate Crisis.* Knopf Canada.
- **Life expectancy.** CDC. Table LExpMort. Life expectancy at birth, age 65, and age 75, by sex, race, and Hispanic origin: United States, selected years 1900–2019.
- **global life expectancy at birth.** Riley JC. 2005. Estimates of regional and global life expectancy, 1800–2001. *Population and Development Review.* ("Global life expectancy at birth was about 28.5 years.")

Notes

- **Mike published.** Geruso M. 2012. Black-white disparities in life expectancy: How much can the standard SES variables explain? *Demography*.
- Rosling, H. 2018. *Factfulness*. Flatiron Books.
- **Figure 5.3.** Authors' presentation of life expectancy at birth from CDC/NCHS, National Vital Statistics System.
- † Spears D. 2020. Exposure to open defecation can account for the Indian enigma of child height. *Journal of Development Economics*.
- † Coffey D, Khera R, Spears D. 2022. Mothers' social status and children's health: Evidence from joint households in rural India. *Demography*.
- † Coffey D, Spears D. 2021. Neonatal death in India: Birth order in a context of maternal undernutrition. *Economic Journal*.
- † Vyas S, Hathi P, Gupta A. 2022. Social disadvantage, economic inequality, and life expectancy in nine Indian states. *PNAS*. (Congratulations on this prize-winning paper to our r.i.c.e. colleagues!)

Chapter 6: Progress comes from people

- **KMC is a technology.** World Health Organization. 2023. *Kangaroo mother care: A transformative innovation in health care.* Global position paper.
- WHO Immediate KMC Study Group. 2021. Immediate "Kangaroo Mother Care" and survival of infants with low birth weight. *NEJM*.
- **Romer was awarded.** Jones CI. 2019. Paul Romer: Ideas, nonrivalry, and endogenous growth. *Scandinavian Journal of Economics*.
- **A fact about facts.** Jones CI. 2022. The end of economic growth? Unintended consequences of a declining population. *American Economic Review*.
- **"Virtually all theories."** Peters M. 2022. Market size and spatial growth—evidence from Germany's post-war population expulsions. *Econometrica*.
- Kremer M. 1993. Population growth and technological change: One million BC to 1990. *Quarterly Journal of Economics*. Separate from his work we discuss, Kremer won the Nobel Prize in 2019 for his research in experimentation and evaluation.
- Galor O. 2022. *The Journey of Humanity*. Penguin.
- **before their grandchildren could know them.** We love and miss you.
- **Figure 6.1.** Authors' adaptation based on Nordhaus WD. 1994. Do real output and real wage measures capture reality? The history of lighting suggests not. Cowles Foundation for Research in Economics, Yale.
- **Edison.** Cep C. 2019. The real nature of Thomas Edison's genius. *New Yorker*.
- † Marçal K. 2016. *Who Cooked Adam Smith's Dinner?* Simon & Schuster.

Chapter 7: Dodging the asteroid. And other benefits of other people

- **Median home prices.** Kiplinger personal finance. 2020. Home prices in the 100 largest metro areas.
- **Figure 7.1.** Authors' presentation of World Bank World Development Indicators: "Urban population (% of total population)," compiled from UN World Urbanization Prospects 2018.
- *very inexpensive* **compared to the other lifesaving strategies.** GiveWell details their reasoning around funding this KMC program in "r.i.c.e.—Newborn Care Program Focused on Kangaroo Mother Care (November 2022)" at givewell.org.
- **hospital in Texas.** Newman E. 2021. Hospital breaks record with "baby boom" of over 100 babies born in 91 hours. *GMA*.
- **things you do care about.** Comment by Doug Muir in response to "What if there were far fewer people?" at crookedtimber.org. 2024 January 8.
- **mRNA.** Dolgin E. 2021. The tangled history of mRNA vaccines. *Nature*.
- **parts per million.** NOAA Global Monitoring Laboratory. Monthly Average Mauna Loa CO_2. 2024 July.
- **removing that carbon.** We first understood the implications of cleaning up past carbon emissions as a fixed cost when our economist collaborator Kevin Kuruc discovered it serendipitously in a climate-economy model: Our larger-population scenario (meaning, stabilization) caused lower distant-future temperatures than if we assumed the depopulation future. We present this in our research paper Budolfson et al. This negative emissions mechanism is not responsible for the result in chapter 3 because (to focus on that chapter's mechanism) we turn off negative emissions in the model runs we show.
- † Glaeser E. 2012. *Triumph of the City*. Penguin.
- † Yglesias M. 2020. *One Billion Americans: The Case for Thinking Bigger*. Penguin.

Chapter 8: More good is better

We intend More Good is Better to be a basic principle of population ethics that many can agree with. More Good is Better doesn't specify a full approach to population ethics. In particular, it says nothing about what to do when all else isn't equal. It is consistent with many views in population ethics.

To agree that More Good is Better, one need not accept the particular arguments that we presented for it in chapter 8. But these arguments touch on some of the cornerstones of the population ethics literature. Here are those cornerstones:

- *Impartiality*. We assume that the general welfare is impartial, treating everybody evenhandedly.
- *Pareto*. We assume that it makes things better, overall, to make anybody's life better, if nobody else is harmed.

Notes

- *Completeness.* Between any two possible futures, one would be better than the other, unless they are both exactly as good. This is what we mean when we say that it makes sense to compare two futures, even if they don't have the exact same set of people in them. Philosophers debate this one, but economists almost always accept it. The real world has never been one unchanging set of people. If a changing population means that you can't say what's better or worse, then you couldn't say that climate change or casteism is bad and girls' education in India is good. Our argument here builds upon the *Depletion* argument of Derek Parfit and the *Greedy Neutrality* argument of John Broome.
- *Independence.* This is the principle of Loren Eiseley's starfish rescuer: In asking which of two possible futures would be better, you only need to consider the people who are affected. The people for whom it doesn't make a difference don't influence which outcome would be better. There are two important arguments in favor of Independence.

  Our discussion of Independence builds upon one of the most powerful arguments in population ethics: Jefferson McMahan's Stone Age argument, which Derek Parfit writes about as the Egyptology objection and economists know as Independence of the Utilities of the Dead. Whether it would be better to add a life cannot depend upon unknown facts about long-dead people in the Stone Age (or in the distant future, outside of our ability to control, or otherwise somewhere unaffected). That's enough for Independence, once you've accepted Impartiality.

  The other powerful argument for Independence emerges from considering risk and uncertainty. All important policy and social decisions indeed involve risk and uncertainty. A long tradition of research in decision-making shows that the only plausible way to say which risky prospects are better ends up to be by taking *expectations*, which sharply narrows the theoretical possibilities toward Independence. In research with Johan Gustafsson and Stéphane Zuber, Dean has shown how variable-population Independence emerges from John Harsanyi's framework for social decision-making under risk (building upon Broome and Marc Fleurbaey).
- *Continuity.* We didn't actually argue for this in chapter 8. It's a technical principle that says that tiny enough differences in people's wellbeing can't make large differences in our overall evaluations of which futures would be better or worse. A tiny enough consequence for one person is not more important than countervailing consequences for many, many people.

This is an important list: Impartiality, Pareto, Completeness, Independence, and Continuity. Together, they imply that welfare economics or axiology has to have an additive form, meaning that the way to assess whether one future would be better than another is to add up some transformed value for each person's wellbeing. In symbols, $\Sigma_i f(w_i)$, where w_i is the wellbeing of person number i and f is some increasing transformation that turns wellbeing levels into numbers that can be added.

Blackorby, Bossert, and Donaldson proved, in a formal theorem, that these principles imply this formula. The logic of the theorem is that Independence says that unaffected people cancel out; terms that cancel, in a formula, are a short step from addition. If somebody wants to reject the impartial adding-up approach, they will have to reject one of these five principles.

The theorem specifies that the general welfare is additive, but it does not say what form the "some transformed value" (that is, f) takes. The transformation could oppose inequality in a way known as "prioritarianism," although that is controversial. Separately, it could take a different controversial stance with what is known as a "critical level." So there are details left to fill in, even if one accepts these five principles. But, however these details are settled, this impartial adding-up approach fits readily with economists' familiar practices in evaluating programs and policies. And it coheres with our claim that More Good is Better.

- Broome J. 2004. *Weighing Lives.* Oxford. (**Figure 8.1** and **Figure 8.2** are the authors' illustrations, inspired by Broome.)
- Thomson JJ. 1971. A defense of abortion. *Philosophy and Public Affairs.* (Hat tip to Mark Budolfson and Richard Chappell. Tyler Cowen makes a similar point in *Stubborn Attachments.*)
- Roth AE, et al. 2007. Efficient kidney exchange: Coincidence of wants in markets with compatibility-based preferences. *American Economic Review.*
- † Blackorby C, et al. 2005. *Population Issues in Social Choice Theory, Welfare Economics, and Ethics.* Cambridge. (The adding-up formula is characterized in Theorem 6.10, assuming an ordering of populations as finite-length vectors of interpersonally comparable lifetime wellbeings that can be represented with the order and topology of the real numbers.)
- † McMahan J. 1981. Problems of population theory. *Ethics.*
- † Parfit D. 1984. *Reasons and Persons.* Oxford. (Depletion §123, Egyptology §143.)
- † Broome J. 2005. Should we value population? *Journal of Political Philosophy.*
- † Gorman WM. 1968. Conditions for additive separability. *Econometrica.*
- † Adhami M, et al. 2024. Population and welfare: The greatest good for the greatest number. NBER.
- † Gustafsson J. 2024. The need for merely possible people. *JESP.* (Gustafsson shows the self-defeating logical trouble one runs into by trying to maintain that the interests of future people matter, but the interests of possible yet non-actual future people do not.)
- † Relevant to Future B adding only top-quality lives, see the inequality-sensitive criterion in: Asheim GB, Zuber S. 2014. Escaping the repugnant conclusion: Rank-discounted utilitarianism with variable population. *Theoretical Economics.*

More diffusely, this chapter and note is based on Dean's background research in collaboration with Mark Budolfson, Stéphane Zuber, Johan Gustafsson, Orri Stefánsson,

Christian Tarsney, and Harvey Lederman, most of which amounts to commentary on Theorem 6.10, and on:

- † Tarsney C, Geruso M, Spears D. 2023. Egyptians, Aliens, and Okies: Against the sum of averages. *Utilitas*.
- † Spears D. 2020. Matt Yglesias has a plan for one billion Americans. His prescriptions may not be radical enough. thewire.in.

Chapter 9: Depopulation won't fix itself

A core idea in this chapter is from our coauthored research on intergenerational correlations in fertility in *Demography*: Arenberg S, Kuruc K, Franz N, Vyas S, Lawson N, LoPalo M, Budolfson M, Geruso M, Spears D. 2022. Research note: Intergenerational transmission is not sufficient for positive long-term population growth. *Demography*.

- Stone L. 2018. How long until we're all Amish? *In a state of migration* on Medium.
- **Amish growth rate.** The Young Center for Anabaptist and Pietist Studies at Elizabethtown College reports an increase of 116 percent from 2000 to 2023. $\ln(2.16) \div 23 = 3.3$ percent. A population of 350,000 Amish growing at 4 percent per year for two hundred years reaches about 1 billion.
- Juniewicz I. 2022. Global decline in fertility rates. Presentation at Oxford University.
- **Indian Muslims.** DHS.
- **Catholics of Canada.** Long LH. 1970. Fertility patterns among religious groups in Canada. *Demography*; Westoff CF, Jones EF. 1979. The end of "Catholic" fertility. *Demography*.
- **Figure 9.1.** Thanks to Jeannie.
- Gershoni N, Low C. 2021. Older yet fairer: How extended reproductive time horizons reshaped marriage patterns in Israel. *American Economic Journal: Applied Economics*.
- **lamb.** Partridge EA, et al. 2017. An extra-uterine system to physiologically support the extreme premature lamb. *Nature Communications*.
- **self-reported by women in surveys.** From 2017 to 2019, the National Survey on Family Growth asked women in the United States: "Looking to the future, do you, yourself, want to have a baby at some time?" Less than a third of those age thirty-five to thirty-nine said yes.
- † Weil D. 2023. Replacement fertility is neither natural nor optimal nor likely. Presentation at NBER.
- † Johnsen S, Sweeney MM. 2022. Female sterilization in the life course: Understanding trends and differentials. *Demographic Research*. (Thanks to Megan Sweeney for discussion on unintended pregnancy and sterilization regret.)

† Bruckamp L, Lazzari E. 2024. Shifting the reproductive window: A research note on the contribution of art and egg donation to fertility rates in the UK.

Chapter 10: Government control cannot force stabilization

This chapter builds upon Dean's research with Nicholas Lawson: Lawson N, Spears D. 2024. Equilibrium effects of abortion restrictions on cohort fertility: Why restricting abortion access can reduce human capital, social welfare, and lifetime fertility rates.

- **tends to be close.** Pritchett LH. 1994. Desired fertility and the impact of population policies. *Population and Development Review.* See also: Gietel-Basten S, LoPalo M, Spears D, Vyas S. 2024. Do fertility preferences in early adulthood predict later average fertility outcomes of the same cohort?: Pritchett (1994) revisited with cohort data. *Economics Letters.*
- **newspaper explainers.** Mashal M, Travelli A. 2023. India is passing China in population. Can its economy ever do the same? *New York Times.*
- Feng W, Cai Y, Gu B. 2013. Population, policy, and politics: How will history judge China's one-child policy? *Population and Development Review.*
- **Figure 10.1.** Authors' computation of moving averages from WPP, averaged over three-year spans to smooth out noise and jumps. We draw a starting line at 1980, but see Greenhalgh: "Some accounts date its birth to January 1979, others date it to September 1980, while still others fudge the issue by using 1979–1980. Some observers place the key decision on the policy in the summer of 1978, others maintain it occurred in February 1980, while yet others believe it happened in June 1980. Given the importance of this policy, the lack of agreement about something so fundamental as when it came into being is truly surprising" (p. 30). Altering the date that appears in the figure would not change our interpretation of these statistics.
- Greenhalgh S. 2008. *Just One Child: Science and Policy in Deng's China.* University of California.
- **"what it was like."** Le Guin UK. 2016. What it was like. *Words Are My Matter.* Small Beer Press.
- **Figure 10.2.** Adapted from Lawson and Spears. Vertical axis is tempo-adjusted TFR from HFD. Horizontal axis is from Singh S, et al. 2017. *Abortion Worldwide 2017: Uneven Progress and Unequal Access.* Guttmacher Institute.
- Aiken AR, et al. 2024. Provision of medications for self-managed abortion before and after the *Dobbs v Jackson Women's Health Organization* decision. *JAMA.*
- **more contraceptive options for women.** Duster C. 2024. Biden administration proposes a rule to make over-the-counter birth control free. *NPR.* (Within the Biden-Harris administration, Mike was part of a wide effort to expand access to contraceptives for American women under the proposed rule "Enhancing

Coverage of Preventive Services Under the Affordable Care Act," 89 Fed. Reg. 85750; proposed October 28, 2024.)

† Connelly M. 2010. *Fatal Misconception: The Struggle to Control World Population*. Belknap.

† Hartmann B. 1987 (3rd ed., 2016). *Reproductive Rights and Wrongs*. Haymarket.

† Merchant E. 2021. *Building the Population Bomb*. Oxford. ("For most Americans, the idea that population growth is the primary culprit for the world's problems and the belief that population control offers a solution seems obvious or commonsensical. As I have shown in this book, these ideas did not simply follow from the realization that the world's population was growing; they originated in specific political programs aimed at controlling that growth" [p. 204].)

† Foster, DG. 2021. *The Turnaway Study: Ten Years, a Thousand Women, and the Consequences of Having—or Being Denied—an Abortion*. Simon & Schuster.

† Gemmill A, et al. 2024. Infant deaths after Texas' 2021 ban on abortion in early pregnancy. *JAMA Pediatrics*.

† Farin SM, et al. 2024. The impact of legal abortion on maternal mortality. *American Economic Journal: Economic Policy*.

† Kligman G. 1998. *The Politics of Duplicity: Controlling Reproduction in Ceausescu's Romania*. University of California.

† Scott JC. 1998. *Seeing Like a State: How Certain Schemes to Improve the Human Condition Have Failed*. Yale.

Chapter 11: Is cash the answer?

- **using contraception.** DHS for Uttar Pradesh. National Survey of Family Growth for U.S.
- **Figure 11.1.** Author's presentation based on WPP TFR and World Bank ICP GDP per capita, 1990–2021.
- Kearney MS, et al. 2022. The puzzle of falling US birth rates since the great recession. *Journal of Economic Perspectives*.
- Oster E. 2000. *Cribsheet: A Data-Driven Guide to Better, More Relaxed Parenting, from Birth to Preschool*. Penguin.
- Goldin C. 2014. A grand gender convergence: Its last chapter. *American Economic Review*.
- **Figure 11.2.** The figure and finding about female labor force participation is based on Dean's collaborative research with Stuart Gietel-Basten and Leela Visaria, presented at IPC in 2021 and PAA in 2022. The figure and finding about age at first birth is based on Dean's collaborative research with Narae Park, Sangita Vyas, and Kathleen Broussard, published in *Demographic Research* in 2023. Not every country has data available for age at *first* birth, so we combine two sources: OECD data are for 2019, to match India's NFHS-5, and

DHS data are from various years (the most recent for each country, updated since Park et al).

- *New York Times* **reported a survey.** Miller CC. 2018. Americans are having fewer babies. They told us why. *New York Times.*
- **UNICEF rates the world's rich countries.** Gromada A, Richardson D. 2021. *Where do rich countries stand on childcare?* UNICEF. We use HFD numbers for average birth rates, tempo-adjusted for changes in the age of childbearing.
- **Austria.** Lalive R, Zweimüller J. 2009. How does parental leave affect fertility and return to work? Evidence from two natural experiments. *Quarterly Journal of Economics.*
- **Spain . . . paternity leave.** Farré L, González L. 2019. Does paternity leave reduce fertility? *Journal of Public Economics.*
- **Australia.** We learned this from Ester Lazzari, in conversation and across several papers, including Australia. Lazzari E. 2022. Assisted reproduction, late fertility, and childlessness in Australia. PhD ANU.
- **rooms.** 1960 data from decennial U.S. Census; 2020 data from American Community Survey (thank you, Sam Arenberg).
- **marriage remains common.** WPP.
- † Gauthier AH. 2007. The impact of family policies on fertility in industrialized countries: A review of the literature. *Population Research and Policy Review.*
- † Brainerd E. 2014. Can government policies reverse undesirable declines in fertility? IZA World of Labor.
- † Sobotka T, et al. 2019. Policy responses to low fertility: How effective are they? United Nations Population Fund.
- † Gietel-Basten S. 2019. *The "Population Problem" in Pacific Asia.* Oxford.

Chapter 12: Aspire bigger

- **Sanitation infrastructure.** Before the KMC ward, Dean's passion was latrines and sanitation in low-income countries. So we have to clarify that infrastructure like flush toilets coupled with sewers and treatment plants is neither necessary nor sufficient for safely managing human excreta. Not sufficient because people have to use and maintain the infrastructure. Not necessary because, for example, septic tanks emptied with vacuum trucks can be great options.
- **Japan and Denmark.** OECD. Employment: Time spent in paid and unpaid work, by sex.
- **may well pay for itself.** Many economic studies have shown how investments in children pay for themselves:
  - † Lawson N, Spears D. 2016. What doesn't kill you makes you poorer: Adult wages and early-life mortality in India. *Economics & Human Biology.*
  - † Hendren N, Sprung-Keyser B. 2020. A unified welfare analysis of government policies. *Quarterly Journal of Economics.*

Notes

† Arenberg S, Neller S, Stripling S. 2024. The impact of youth Medicaid eligibility on adult incarceration. *American Economic Journal: Applied Economics*.
- **Figure 12.1.** Authors' computations in Spears et al. 2024 (updated for 2024 WPP).
- **parts per million.** NOAA Global Monitoring Laboratory. Monthly Average Mauna Loa CO_2. July 2024.

Repugnant Appendix

Parfit introduces the Repugnant Conclusion in section 131 of *Reasons and Persons*. The core of this appendix is Dean's research with Mark Budolfson, with predecessors in the observations of Bill Anglin and Tyler Cowen:

- Spears D, Budolfson M. 2021. Repugnant conclusions. *Social Choice and Welfare*.
- Budolfson M, Spears D. 2022. Does the Repugnant Conclusion have important implications for axiology or for public policy? *Oxford Handbook of Population Ethics*.
- Anglin B. 1977. The Repugnant Conclusion. *Canadian Journal of Philosophy*.
- Cowen T. 1996. What do we learn from the Repugnant Conclusion? *Ethics*.

Other notes on the Repugnant Conclusion:

- *The Economist*. 2022. Should we care about people who need never exist?
- **many mathematical details of other theories.** What about critical-level versions of the total view with a positive critical level? Our view is that these approaches are not plausible candidates because the positive critical level (or boundaries of a set of critical levels) are indefensibly arbitrary. But on the Repugnant Conclusion, we agree with Broome in *Weighing Lives* (§14.4, "the standardized total principle is really the total principle") that critical-level approaches should be understood to yield yet another instance of the Repugnant Conclusion, where many lives that are barely good enough to not make matters worse can always add up to be better than any other population.
- Ng YK. 1989. What should we do about future generations? Impossibility of Parfit's Theory X. *Economics & Philosophy*. The two principles that we discuss are Mere Addition and Non-Antiegalitarianism, in the context of a complete order of populations as finite vectors of real-valued lifetime wellbeings.
- Arrhenius G. 2000. An impossibility theorem for welfarist axiologies. *Economics & Philosophy*. Arrhenius builds upon the theorems in this paper in *Population Ethics: The Challenge of Future Generations*. The Strong Quality Addition Principle is related to the approach of Budolfson and Spears.
- **Free will.** Moberger V. 2024. Impossible ethics: Do population ethical impossibility results support moral skepticism and/or anti-realism? *Pacific Philosophical Quarterly*.

- **never come up.** Nebel JM. 2022. Totalism without repugnance. *Ethics and Existence: The Legacy of Derek Parfit.*
- **fixed, unchanging assembly.** Some population ethicists have the view that it's no worse to have the large, lower-quality population than to have the small, higher-quality population, so long as all of the people in the two populations have different identities. On an archetypal person-affecting view, an outcome can only be worse than another because it is worse for some specific someone, and you don't count as someone if you don't exist in the outcome that happens. We don't find the person-affecting approach plausible, because it would have a hard time making sense of many big, long-term policies that change who lives. Parfit rejects it in §135. But it's notable here as an instance of some philosophical experts being okay with an instance of the Repugnant Conclusion.
  † Narveson J. 1973. Moral problems of population. *The Monist.*
  † Golosov M, Jones LE, Tertilt M. 2007. Efficiency with endogenous population growth. *Econometrica.*
  † Roberts MA. 2024. *The Existence Puzzles.* Oxford.
  † Adler MD. 2019. *Measuring Social Welfare.* Oxford. §7.1.3.
- † Masny, M. 2020. On Parfit's wide dual person-affecting principle. *Philosophical Quarterly.*
- † Zuber S, et al. 2021. What should we agree on about the Repugnant Conclusion? *Utilitas.* Dean led this unusual twenty-nine-author collaboration, alongside Budolfson, Gustafsson, and Zuber.
- **intuitions are boggled.** Gustafsson JE. 2022. Our intuitive grasp of the repugnant conclusion. *Oxford Handbook of Population Ethics.*

Our background research:

- † Arrhenius G, Budolfson M, Spears D. 2021. Does climate change policy depend importantly on population ethics? *Philosophy and Climate Change.*
- † Franz N, Spears D. 2020. Mere addition is equivalent to avoiding the Sadistic Conclusion in all plausible variable-population social orderings. *Economics Letters.*
- † Spears D. 2021. The Repugnant Conclusion is a puzzle that has occupied philosophers and economists for decades. Medium.
- † Spears D, Stefánsson HO. 2024. What calibrating variable-value population ethics suggests. *Economics & Philosophy.*

Index

Page numbers of illustrations appear in italics.

Index

Index

Index

Index

About the Authors

Dean Spears and Michael Geruso are Associate Professors at the University of Texas, in the Department of Economics and Population Research Center. In addition, Geruso served as Senior Economist at the White House Council of Economic Advisers from 2023 to 2024, and Spears is Executive Director of r.i.c.e., a research and advocacy non-profit focused on child health and wellbeing in India.